THE GERMAN EXAMPLE

Also available from Continuum

Citizenship Education in Japan, edited by Norio Ikeno

Comparative and International Education: An Introduction to Theory, Method and Practice, David Phillips and Michele Schweisfurth

Education as a Global Concern, Colin Brock

The German Example

*English Interest in Educational Provision
in Germany Since 1800*

David Phillips

continuum

Continuum International Publishing Group

The Tower Building	80 Maiden Lane
11 York Road	Suite 704
London	New York
SE1 7NX	NY 10038

www.continuumbooks.com

© David Phillips 2011

British Library Cataloguing-in-Publication Data
A catalogue record for this book is available from the British Library.

ISBN: 978-1-4411-4130-9 (hardcover)

Library of Congress Cataloging-in-Publication Data
A catalog record for this book is available from the Library of Congress.

Typeset by Pindar NZ
Printed and bound in Great Britain

Contents

For Becky and Janet

Illustrations

Figures

Tables

Acknowledgements

The European Parliamentary Labour Party has kindly granted permission to use the illustration included as Figure 6 in Chapter 8, and I am grateful to Professor Peter Sloane of the University of Paderborn for the diagram of the German dual system of vocational education and training used in the same chapter (Figure 10).

In Chapter 8 I draw on text from a paper given at the 1991 Annual Conference of the Comparative and International Education Society in Annapolis, Maryland.

Over the past few decades I have written extensively on education in Germany and its attraction to British policy makers. This present book reproduces some text previously published in various journals, and especially that of a long paper published in pamphlet form in Lisbon in 2002: *Reflections on British Interest in Education in Germany in the Nineteenth Century (A Progress Report)*. I am grateful for permission to use such texts in the present study. In every case the original source is indicated.

As ever I am grateful to the staff of the library of the Oxford Department of Education and of the former Institute Library of the Department of Comparative Education of the Humboldt University, Berlin (now incorporated into the new University Library and sadly no longer situated in the 'Kommode'.)

I am especially grateful to Janet Howarth and Harry Judge, who kindly read the manuscript and made many helpful suggestions for correction and improvement.

A Note on the Text

I have for the most part retained all the idiosyncracies of nineteenth-century texts. Spelling and punctuation sometimes appear strange, but I have kept faithfully to the originals, even to the extent in most cases of reproducing inaccurate German and variants like Wurtemberg/Würtemberg/Wirtemberg (for Württemberg). I have where necessary corrected the spelling of *Volksschule*, since it is so often misspelt in English texts. I have retained the initial capitalisation of words in cases where it would not nowadays be used.

One peculiarity in the use of German terms should be mentioned. There is a choice for English speakers of writing, for example, either 'the *humanistische Gymnasium*' (on the grounds that the term in German is '*das humanistische Gymnasium*' and that 'the' replaces *das*) or 'the *humanistisches Gymnasium*' (on the grounds that without the German definite article, the term 'humanistic secondary school' would be '*humanistisches Gymnasium*'.) I have preferred the latter usage, even though the former might seem more logical.

David Phillips

Chapter 1

Policy 'Borrowing' in Education and the German Example: Historical and Theoretical Perspectives

I hope with time to convince people that I do not care the least for importing this or that foreign machinery, whether it be French or German, but only for getting certain English deficiencies supplied.

Matthew Arnold, 1868[1]

The true greatness of a people does not consist in borrowing nothing from others, but in borrowing from all whatever is good, and perfecting whatever it appropriates.

Victor Cousin, 1834[2]

Comparative inquiry in education and the attractiveness of the German example

Throughout the long history of comparative inquiry in education one of the constant aims has been to identify what lessons might be learnt from the example of educational provision 'elsewhere'. Often the result of such lesson learning is termed 'policy borrowing', though – as we shall discuss below – purposive borrowing is only part of a spectrum of processes that constitute the transfer of ideas between nations.

This study is concerned with ways in which the example of education in Germany (at all levels) has been used by those concerned with policy making and by other interested observers in England over the past two hundred years or so. There has been a consistent tendency over that long period to refer to the German example[3] in education at one extreme to promote ideas for change and development ('do this and we shall be as good as the Prussians') and at the other extreme to warn against innovation and reform ('do that and you will end up as bad as the Prussians'), with various shades of attraction and repulsion in between. This is not to say that policy makers have failed to find provision in countries other than Germany attractive: at various times France and the United States, for example, have received much attention as 'referent' nations; so too have Sweden, in the 1960s, and Japan, especially during the 1970s and 1980s. More recently, following that country's successes in the PISA[4] surveys of the Organisation for Economic Cooperation and Development (OECD), considerable attention has focused on Finland. But Germany has attracted the interest of policy makers in a concentrated way that is unmatched by any other country that might be used as a viable comparitor with England.

The two countries of course have had a long and complex relationship which has veered between degrees of friendship, rivalry, and mutual suspicion in peace and disastrous enmity in war. But whatever the political background, there has been a consistent popular British fascination with Germany and the Germans and a determined intellectual endeavour to understand and come to terms with what Ashton calls 'the German idea'.[5] The early popularisers of German culture – among them Samuel Taylor Coleridge, Thomas Carlyle, George Henry Lewes, and George Eliot, together with lesser-known but well-informed commentators like Henry Crabb Robinson or William Howitt – made an educated public conscious of developments in German literature and philosophy. Nineteenth-century periodicals such as the *Westminster Review*, the *Edinburgh Review*, and the *Quarterly Review* frequently reported on German themes. Queen Victoria's marriage to Albert of Saxe-Coburg brought a close association with things German to the court and those surrounding it, Albert engaging enthusiastically with 'modern' themes, not least in connection with education and technology and through his active promotion of the Great Exhibition of 1851 and the development of the institutions in South Kensington which became possible as a result of the Exhibition's success.[6]

We see the German example in education being used in parliamentary debates, in the deliberations of select committees of the House of Commons, in the great Royal Commissions on education in the nineteenth century and beyond, in the work of scholars and administrators in Britain and elsewhere like Victor Cousin, Horace Mann, and Matthew Arnold and in the huge output of Michael Sadler throughout his life, in serious commentary in the press, in the commissioned reports of the Inspectorate and of the Board of Education and its successive central institutions, in the reception of the results of large-scale international surveys of pupil attainment, in the published work of experts in comparative education, and in a vast range of popular accounts in the form of 'travellers' tales' and journalism. The potential sources are immense. The impact of such consistent reference to education in Germany remains tantalisingly difficult to assess in terms of any direct cause and effect relationship, but there have been rather more pleas to emulate or learn from the German example than urgings to dismiss it. As we shall see, rather than finding evidence of direct 'importation' of German practice in education, there has been a tendency to focus on principles of policy and provision and to interpret them in ways that have suited the home context. The German example has clearly served to stimulate debate and to encourage – especially in the context of competition between the two nations – fresh thinking about the possibilities for reform.

A traveller to Germany in the late eighteenth century describes a problem familiar to comparativists who struggle with the concept of 'national character':

It is true, different persons see the same things in different lights, and consequently may form different or opposite ideas of them. This leaves considerable space for diversity; but it reduces the history of *travels* to the history of *opinions*; and descriptions given of the most striking objects, become mere transcripts of the author's *conceptions* and *feelings* concerning them. The customs, manners, and scenes that are the most *opposite* to those with which the traveller has been the most familiar, must be to _him_, the most striking, and thus, while he imagines that he is drawing a personal likeness, his pencil, being under the guidance of his particular feelings, will produce a _caricature._[7]

The 'national character' problem is specifically addressed:

> Superficial observance must be erroneous in ten thousand instances. No one is qualified to delineate national character who has not enjoyed frequent opportunities of conversing familiarly with different classes, and of viewing them in various circumstances and situations:- who is not able to discriminate the dispositions, passions and prejudices that are common to man, and are to be found in the individuals of every country from the peculiarities belonging to the one he would investigate:- who does not examine the good and the bad with strict impartiality, that he may mark both the nature and the preponderancy of both virtues and vices, excellencies and defects. If he directs his sole attention to their _best_ qualities, and conceals their _worst_, he will compose a _panegyric._ If he selects all the _bad_ with malicious eagerness, and connects them together in some idle narrative, he will make every country in its turn, from _Lapland_ to _Malta, Les Sauvages de l'Europe._[8]

There are many examples of the extremities described here, and they often demonstrate the facility with which authors succumb to exaggeration or caricature, usually through an emphasis on the exotic or exceptional features of what has been observed or reported on. Almut Sprigade quotes a remarkable piece published in _The Times_ of 1833:

> According to the German _Pedagogic Magazine_ there dies lately in Swabia a schoolmaster who for 51 years had superintended an institution with old fashioned severity. From an average inferred by means of recorded observations, one of the ushers has calculated, that in the course of his exertions he had given 211,500 canings, 124,000 floggings, 109,000 custodes, 136,000 tips with the ruler, 10,200 boxes on the ear, and 22,700 tasks to get by heart. It was further calculated that he had made 700 boys stand on peas, 600 kneel on a sharp edge of wood, 5,000 wear the fool's cap, and 1,708 hold the rod.[9]

The popular press was ever prone to emphasising the exotic in this way, and there are many instances of exaggeration of all aspects of educational provision in Germany throughout the period with which we are concerned.

* * * * *

In his study _The Ends of Life_, Keith Thomas discusses the methodological issues involved in using a large number of quotations, citing Walter Benjamin as intimating that his 'ideal work' would consist only of quotations, 'put together so skilfully that it could dispense with any accompanying text'; and indeed in the case of this present study there is so much quotable material on the German example in education in English sources over the last 200 years and more that it is difficult to resist a dense concatenation of quoted text. Thomas goes on to consider context and the problems of the representativeness of opinions expressed in 'very different social and intellectual milieux and different periods of time'.[10] I have tried to locate the opinions of the many observers, commentators, and policy makers quoted in the context of educational development both in England and in Germany, and though the treatment is largely chronological, some retrospection and anticipation of events and opinions has been necessary at times. The task throughout has been to identify instances of both positive and negative use of the German example in education that are indicative of trends over the longer period. The principal focus is on the official or influential voice, on policy making and influence at the national level, but a wide range of other instances of investigations and use of the German example in education will also be drawn upon. The approach is for the most part deliberately episodic, concentrating on the main preoccupations in policy making and educational debate at particular key moments since 1800. Quotations are used to bring to the fore the voices of those concerned with contributing to or formulating or commenting upon educational policy with reference to German models. The concern throughout is not to write the history of education in the two countries but to focus on particular periods when observers in England were attracted to educational development in Germany (for a variety of reasons) and to situate that attraction in the context of policy and developments in both nations at those particular times.

The transfer of ideas and policies

To gain an idea of whether any 'borrowing' has taken place on the basis of knowledge of the nature of educational provision in Germany we need to consider the processes of educational transfer. In what might 'borrowing' consist? The transfer of educational ideas between nations can take many forms. Figure 1 below postulates a spectrum of transfer, ranging from the imposition of policy and practice (in the case of post-conflict occupation of or political domination of one country by another) to purposive borrowing of particular aspects of policy or practice observed elsewhere and general influence (as with, for example, the ideas of Dewey or Piaget in the twentieth century, or Pestalozzi and Froebel in the nineteenth.)

Spectrum of Educational Transfer

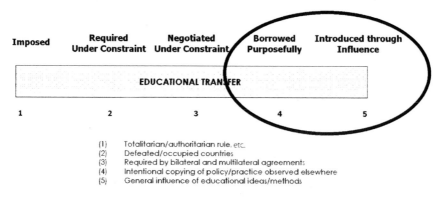

Imposed	Required Under Constraint	Negotiated Under Constraint	Borrowed Purposefully	Introduced through Influence
		EDUCATIONAL TRANSFER		
1	2	3	4	5

(1)   Totalitarian/authoritarian rule, etc.
(2)   Defeated/occupied countries
(3)   Required by bilateral and multilateral agreements
(4)   Intentional copying of policy/practice observed elsewhere
(5)   General influence of educational ideas/methods

FIGURE 1   (Source: Phillips & Ochs (eds), *Educational Policy Borrowing: Historical Perspectives*, p. 9)

The instances of policy attraction with which I am concerned are contained within the circled domain of the spectrum. Attraction can be seen as originating in a variety of impulses for change and concentrating on various policy features. These are illustrated in Figure 2 below.

This diagram attempts to identify the policy ambitions that can spark an interest in learning from examples 'elsewhere'. They range from general guiding philosophies or ideologies (democracy, equality . . .) and goals (universal elementary education, equal provision for boys and girls . . .) through the strategies employed to achieve such philosophies and aims (persuasion, compulsion . . .), 'enabling structures' (shape of the school system, employment of teachers . . .), to processes (examinations and qualifications, inspection . . .), and techniques (teaching and learning styles, classroom arrangements . . .). These ambitions are the result of impulses emerging from a variety of problems identified in the 'home' system, and they have to be seen in context.

The impulses which mark the starting point for attraction to foreign approaches can take various forms. An obvious factor would be internal dissatisfaction with the *status quo*: this might arise in the time leading up to and immediately following political change. Political change itself might in some circumstances (in Eastern Europe in 1989, for example) result in systemic collapse and something of a fresh starting point when the influence of approaches observed elsewhere might be likely. Or an education system might be subject to various types of negative external evaluation (through PISA, for example). Such public evaluation will result in a rethinking of provision of the kind seen in Germany following the first round of PISA in 2001). Another impetus to look elsewhere for models might emerge as the result of novel configurations following a country's membership of a regional or economic group (as with the European Union) or a willingness

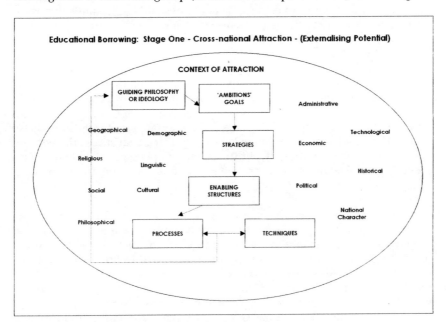

FIGURE 2   (Source: Ochs & Phillips: *Towards a Structural Typology of Cross-National Attraction in Education*, p. 11)

to accept agreements such as those reached in the Bologna Process. Various technological advances and economic needs might also result in a necessity for change on the basis of observed successful practice in other countries.

Definitions and periods

A problem in a study of this kind is one of definition.[11] If from time to time there is talk of 'British' interest, this is deliberate in order to avoid the limitations of referring only to 'English' documents, though it is inevitable, given the main sources used, that the English voice will predominate. It would be an interesting exercise to focus specifically on, say, the Scottish voice, and to associate it with developments in Scotland, but that is beyond my intention.

At least in the British and specifically English context it should at any historical point be straightforward to define geographical parameters. With Germany of course we face a number of problems. In the early years of the nineteenth century 'Germany' for British observers constituted an often imprecise geographical entity whose parameters depended in many cases on the personal interpretation of individual writers and commentators, and so 'education in Germany' should properly be defined in terms of what has been understood by 'Germany' at any particular point of time. As Madame de Staël put it early in the century, 'The whole German nation can be made to agree in some principal features only; for the diversities of the country are such, that it is difficult to bring together under one point of view, religions, governments, climates, and even people so different'.[12] Another commentator on education in Germany took a rather different view in 1840:

> We must bear in mind that the German States, although under different governments, are not nations as distinct from, and independent of each other, as France and Spain, or as Russia and Great Britain. Each of the German States is influenced more or less by every other: the whole lying in close juxtaposition, and being linked together by the bond of a common language and literature. The boundary line that separates Prussia from Hesse on one side, or from Saxony on another, is not more defined than that of a county or parish in England. A stone in a field, or a post painted with stripes, in a public road, informs the traveller that he is passing from one State into another, but these territorial divisions make no change in the great characteristics of the people; whatever the name of the State, or the colour of the stripes, the people, with merely provincial differences, are the same: from the Baltic to the Adriatic they are still Germans.[13]

There are also difficulties with periodisation. In common with others I have rehearsed in previous papers the problems associated with any comparative periodisation of the history of education in Germany and England,[14] and so the vexed question as to what constitutes a 'period' and how its parameters might be delineated in terms of the 'events' – political or otherwise – which signal some kind of change and therefore mark the beginnings and ends of periods, need not delay us here. But it will be helpful to define some periods in the development of educational policy in Germany and England which have structured what follows.

According to Friedrich Paulsen[15] we might identify three broad periods in the growth of the German education system in the nineteenth century. They are: 1800–40; 1840–70; and 1870–1900. Michael Sadler[16] agrees, and his descriptions may be paraphrased as follows:

> *reconstruction*, inspired by patriotic enthusiasm and belief in the political value of intellectual achievement;
> *consolidation* with some reaction to the ideals of the earlier period;
> an era of *further advance* 'brilliant in its administrative achievement and its systematic readjustment of educational arrangements to modern needs'[17]

These periods may be associated with different stages in the increasing fascination Germany held for British observers in the nineteenth century.

For England, Sadler also identifies three periods: (1) 1800–39 (when the Committee of Council on Education was established): this was 'in the main an era of philanthropic and religious effort in popular education helped by small State subsidy from 1833'; (2) 1839–70: 'an era of parliamentary investigation, of rapid increase in the number of elementary schools, and of internal reform in secondary and higher education'; (3) 1870 to the mid-1920s: a period of 'rapid increase of educational opportunity throughout the kingdom and a marked growth in the administrative authority of the State in educational affairs'. He summarises:

> The chief characteristic of the first period was associated philanthropy; that of the second, educational self-government under the supervision of the State; that of the third, the slow construction of an educational system more closely articulated in all its parts and more systematically aided out of public funds.[18]

I have also chosen to divide the century into three periods as far as England is concerned:

1. 1800–33: This was a period which marked the beginnings of British interest in education in Germany. Its end point is the first vote of government money for education in 1833.
2. 1833–70: During this period there was steady progression towards greater state involvement in educational provision, building up to legislation that required compulsory school attendance.
3. 1870–1902: A period of consolidation, developing from the Forster Act of 1870 and culminating in the 1902 Balfour Act.
   (These periods coincide roughly with those proposed by Paulsen and Sadler for Germany.)
4. 1902–18: For the twentieth century, with regard to England, I take the period 1902 to 1918, sandwiched between the Balfour and Fisher Acts, to be a time when local control in education was being firmly established and a modern system was taking shape.
5. 1918–33: From the end of the First World War to the 1930s, let us say for the sake of simplicity until the beginning of National Socialist power in Germany in 1933, is seen as a period of educational experiment and reform proposals against a background in Germany of heightened artistic experiment and increasing political turbulence.

6. The period of the Second World War and that of post-war reconstruction in Germany (1939–49) can be taken together. In England the 1944 Education Act marked the beginning of a new era of greater opportunity; in Germany the end of the Second World War brought massive disruption and uncertainty and a period of occupation during which the Allies were in control.

7. The long period 1949–88 takes us from post-war reconstruction to radical reform. With the founding of the Federal Republic in 1949 there began a period of consolidation and stability, characterised by Konrad Adenauer's catchphrase *keine Experimente!* (no experiments!) and by a desire to move 'on from Weimar'. Gradually, with the economic success of Germany encapsulated in the term *Wirtschaftswunder* (economic miracle), there was an increasing desire in England to learn from whatever it was in the education system that had contributed to it, the German vocational education model being a principal source of attraction. By the end of the period England had embarked on the far-reaching reforms of the 1988 Education Act, in the lead-up to which there was much discussion of education in Germany.

8. 1988 onwards: The final period can be characterised as one of performance-led anxiety about policy. With the growing significance attaching to studies of pupil attainment such as those undertaken by the International Association for the Evaluation of Educational Achievement (IEA) and the OECD, there was the possibility of measuring outcomes to a degree previously unheard of. The resulting performance tables provided the chance to analyse what features of systems elsewhere might result in high performance levels.

For the sake of concision and exemplification I shall concentrate in what follows principally on references to education in Prussia as far as the earlier periods are concerned. And I shall use the device of a number of snapshots illustrating the focus of interest at particular moments. These snapshots might be in the form of a Royal Commission's report, a new piece of legislation, an influential non-governmental publication, new theories of education, or published results following performance-measuring surveys.

The literature is vast. I hope that the comprehensive references alone will provide a useful source for others pursuing particular aspects of the discussion of German education in Britain. In using published and unpublished sources I have made use of the groundwork undertaken by Armytage in *The German Influence on English Education* (1969), by Haines in his two studies of German influence on education and science in England, 1800–66 and 1867–87, by Walz in *German Influence in American Education and Culture* (1936), and by Geitz et al. in their collection *German Influences on Education in the United States to 1917* (1995). Gougher's 1969 bibliography of English and American views of the German University is a useful source. Of particular importance for the early period is Almut Sprigade's ground-breaking study of 2005 – not limited to the German example – *Where there is Reform there is Comparison: English Interest in Education Abroad, 1800–1839*.[19] Sprigade demonstrates through detailed analysis of wide-ranging contemporary sources that what has often been characterised as the 'travellers' tales' period of educational comparison was in fact informed by serious attempts at sophisticated analysis and use of the foreign example. Other important studies include Friedrich Schneider's *Geltung und Einfluss der Deutschen Pädagogik im Ausland* of 1943, Bernd Zymek's seminal account *Das Ausland als Argument in der Pädagogischen Reformdiskussion* (1975), and Philipp Gonon's *Das*

Internationale Argument in der Bildungsreform (1998). Stuart Marriott's study of English-German relations in adult education is a helpful source on aspects of continuing education in the two countries.[20]

Michael Sadler's work on education in Germany – not concentrated in one major study but to be found throughout his voluminous writings – is particularly valuable: he was always able to capture the moment in education, and to relate it to historical development.[21] He knew Germany well and he followed progress in education at all levels in the country throughout his long life, engaging too with policy making in England in a number of significant ways. In this study, as in many others, his perceptive views on the strengths and weaknesses of educational provision in Germany will play a significant part. Among the early mainstream academic comparativists Issac Kandel stands out since he devoted much attention to education in Germany, from his 1910 study *The Training of Elementary School Teachers in Germany* to his *History of Secondary Education* published in 1930.[22]

While this book was with the publisher, Peter Watson's study *The German Genius* was published. In this important new book there is comprehensive coverage of historical advances in German research and scholarship which will be of great value to future attempts to evaluate the German example in a variety of contexts.

Chapter 2

Testing the Ground: The Beginnings of British Interest in Education in Germany

This system, already so prolific of the happiest results, has attracted the attention of all Europe; and England, among the rest, is said to be taking a lesson on this most important branch of government, from the benignant absolutism of Prussia.

Frances Trollope, 1834[1]

Provision in education: England 1800–33

At the beginning of the nineteenth century most children in England were not receiving a formal education for any appreciable length of time. Educational opportunities were sparse and haphazard, provided for the most part by various charitable institutions and the churches. Education had been left – as Matthew Arnold was later to put it – 'to the chapter of accidents';[2] what eventually emerged during the last quarter of the century as something approaching proper public provision was the result of 'a long course of experiments, compromises, traditions, successes, failures and religious controversies', effected by 'philanthropy, by private enterprise, by religious zeal, by ancient universities and endowed foundations, by municipal and local effort, and only to a small extent by legislation'.[3]

Elementary education in the early 1800s was provided by many kinds of charitable and philanthropic institutions. There were the charity schools: those under the aegis of the Society for Promoting Christian Knowledge (SPCK, founded in 1698) which had steadily increased in number throughout the eighteenth century; and those run by the Dissenters. There were the Sunday schools, which had grown considerably since about 1780 (when the Sunday school movement began in earnest) and which experienced further impetus for growth following the founding of the Society for the Establishment and Support of Sunday Schools in 1785; they have in fact been seen as marking the beginnings of popular education in England.[4] And there were the notorious privately run 'dame' schools and similar institutions, familiar through the caricature of Dotheboys Hall in Dickens's *Nicholas Nickleby* (1838–9) and elsewhere.[5] Providing an education beyond elementary level there were the endowed grammar schools, and the famous (predominantly boarding) public schools, many of which of course – like the grammar schools from which they had emerged – had long, if not always distinguished, histories.[6]

For the period before reliable statistical information started to be systematically collected it is difficult to make an accurate assessment of how many children were actually attending schools of whatever kind for any length of time. It has been estimated, however, that the school attendance rate in England and Wales was about four per cent of the total population in the middle years of the eighteenth century. In Scotland the number was rather more than double that. By 1818 the estimated figure for England had risen to 6.6 per cent; for Wales it was 4.8 and for Scotland 10.9 per cent.[7] These figures have to be approached with caution, since they do not reflect the age ranges of children attending school, the types of school attended (many of which would simply have been Sunday schools), the periods of attendance, or social class and regional differences. Henry Brougham (1778–1868), a very significant figure in early attempts to legislate for educational provision, estimated in 1820 that one in fifteen of the whole population of England was attending school; in terms of children of school age this meant, he argued, that one in five was receiving no education at all. For 1803 the attendance figure was reckoned to have been one in twenty-one of the whole population.[8] What is clear, despite the vagueness of these statistics, is that the attendance rate over a long period was low and that it was especially low for the poor.

It is clear too that there was much opposition to the notion of expansion of this meagre provision, particularly in the form of compulsory school attendance. Employers of children were against it, and so too were parents of the labouring classes, who depended on the income their children might generate: one of the recurrent themes in the British analysis of educational policy in Germany was to be how compulsory attendance could be enforced, given such resistance. But there was also a widespread disinclination on the part of those higher up the social order to promote the cause of popular education, and this contributed to the failure of various attempts at legislation in the first three decades of the century. The opposition was rooted in fear of the ambitions of an educated proletariat (the consequences of whose potential disquiet having been all too apparent in the events in France following the revolution of 1789), as well as in the interests of the landowners and factory proprietors needing to retain a young workforce. Even William Cobbett (1763–1835) – the 'poor man's friend', the 'spokesman of the common people' – was not convinced that education was the means by which social ills could be addressed, arguing towards the end of his life that 'a smattering of education gave the labourer the idea that he was not born to work'.[9] As we shall see, he argued against the first grant of government money to education in August 1833.

The initiatives of the Anglican Andrew Bell (1753–1832) and the Quaker Joseph Lancaster (1778–1838), however, did much in the early years of the century to establish the feasibility of providing a basic education for large numbers of children. Bell had introduced a 'monitorial' system of education, involving pupils (monitors) teaching other pupils, during a period in the 1790s as superintendent of the East India Company's Madras Male Orphan Society, and had described his system in *An Experiment in Education*, published in 1797. Lancaster first established a school in Southwark in 1798 and later (1801) founded his renowned school in the Borough Road; he published details of his version of the monitorial system in *Improvements in Education* in 1803, and received royal patronage after being summoned to visit King George III in 1805. The King, who was a generous benefactor of many charities, had also taken an interest in the Sunday school movement, and he famously expressed his desire at their meeting that every poor child in his dominions should be taught to read the Bible.[10]

The monitorial system involved strict discipline and highly organised rote learning (drills and exercises) orchestrated by the monitors under the supervision of a master. In this way large numbers of children could be taught simultaneously: Lancaster's Borough Road school came to have more than a thousand pupils. The American defender of popular education Horace Mann (1796–1859) indeed reported in the 1840s that in Lancasterian schools he had seen 'a thousand children in a single room'.[11] The monitorial approach developed to the extent that by 1820 there were over 1,500 schools using the system to provide an elementary education for some 200,000 children;[12] in 1826 there were 2,200 National Schools, educating 330,000 poor children.[13] Bell had boasted, 'Give me twenty-four pupils today, and I will give you back twenty-four teachers tomorrow'.

Lancaster's non-sectarian 'Royal Lancasterian Institution' was set up in 1808 and became known later as the 'British and Foreign School Society'. In 1811 the Church of England's 'National Society for Promoting the Education of the Poor in the Principles of the Established Church' was founded, with the aim of providing a school in every parish. There was considerable rivalry between the two bodies, centering largely on the question of religion. On Lancaster's behalf it was said in 1811 that though he had supervised the education of more than 7,000 children none had become a Quaker,[14] his aim being to provide a Christian but decidedly non-sectarian education. The National Society, on the other hand, wished to reinforce the authority of the Church of England. In these early years the 'vehemence of the struggle' between the two societies has been seen as serving to stimulate them to do more: by the 1830s there were 3,500 parish schools associated with the National Society.[15] Religious controversy was of course to remain a principal stumbling block in the debate about national provision in education throughout the century and beyond.

The monitorial system attracted much attention in other countries, including Germany.[16] A report in *The Times* in 1819 indicated, however, that there was no enthusiasm for the system in Bavaria:

> The Second Chamber of the State-General of Bavaria, in rejecting a proposition for introducing the Lancasterian system of education, assign a reason which is not a little surprising. They say that 'it is adopted, at the best, only for communicating elementary ideas to a people destitute of education, such as that of France, England, and the United States; but is much too mechanical in itself, and too little favourable to the development of mind, and besides completely useless in a country such as Germany, where every village has its primary school'.[17]

And by the mid-1840s Horace Mann could report only 'mere vestiges' of the system in the poor schools of Prussia, and this was in his view clearly no bad thing:

> [A]t least nine tenths of all the monitorial schools I have seen, would suggest to

me that the name, 'monitorial', had been given them by way of admonishing the world to avoid their adoption.[18]

By the time the first school inspections were undertaken (from 1839) the monitorial system was seriously damned, a verdict strongly reinforced in the Newcastle Commission's report of 1861, which used evidence from inspections in the period 1839–46 to demonstrate the system's inadequacy:

> The unanimous testimony of the inspectors was that the teachers were bad, and that the monitors, from their extreme youth, were of little use. They were fit only for the discharge of routine duties, and even these they discharged without interest, without weight, and without authority. They were frequently untrustworthy, and almost always ignorant. The consequence of this was that the schools were generally in a deplorable state in every part of England.[19]

The utilitarian view of the monitorial school saw it as 'a piece of labour-saving machinery on a par with the mechanical inventions of the early Industrial Revolution'.[20] Lancaster was criticised for his emphasis on discipline, Bell for his unbending dogmatism. Both had been instrumental in starting a system that was unflaggingly dull and factory-like but which was in its own terms efficient and 'attractive to a society looking for easy, cheap solutions'.[21]

Louis Simond (1767–1831), an expatriate Frenchman resident in the United States, gives a lively and in the end not wholly critical account of a visit to Lancaster's Borough Road school:

> We found ourselves under a spacious shed, lighted by a sky-light, about 20 or 35 feet wide, and 100 feet long. There was at one end of the extremities a platform, two or three feet above the general level; the rest of the room was paved, and benches arranged one behind the other, fronting the platform, the back of each bench having a shelf serving for a desk for the boy behind; a narrow passage led along the wall, all around the room. Seven or eight hundred boys, from six to twelve years old, filled these benches. They were all talking together and making a great noise. They seemed divided into classes or sections, distinguished by small flags; some of the classes writing on sand, others on slates, that is to say had written, or might have written, for none were doing any thing but playing. Out of compliment to us, for the good of his scholars, or to show his authority, one of the monitors made a sign, and at the instant the eight hundred little heads bowed down, showing instead of a field of white faces, one of dark crops. We asked what the object of this evaluation was, and were answered that it was *light and shade* – but what for? Before we could receive a reply, another signal had been given, and all the styles or pencils were brandished in the air – those who had none pointed their finger – at another sign they all came down again. Several other evolutions took place of as little obvious use – a great buz and talking all over the room, and the monitors vociferating. Two boys were lying under a sort of hamper or hen-coop, placed upon the platform; they were there, we were told, for *playing chicken*, that is to say for leaving their places, or playing during the lesson – they did not seem to mind the punishment. [. . .] There is a separate school for girls, less numerous [. . .]. It struck twelve – the monitor gave the order to clear the school – the boys

rose and filed off by benches, making as much noise, and as much dust with their feet as they could.

This is an account of what we saw faithfully reported. I regret it, for it lowers (not much, however) the very favourable opinion I had formed of the good order, the economy of time, the general application, and prodigious utility of a mode of teaching, by which a single master may direct 1000 scholars, better and more effectually than he could have done by any former method. It is obvious that this was not intended as a day to receive visits.[22]

* * * * *

The time span from 1800 to 1833 in England has been described as 'the philanthropic period';[23] and it has been characterised politically as a 'generation of hesitation and controversy'[24] and as a time of 'legislative quiescence'.[25] There were some attempts to introduce national legislation for educational provision, but they came to nothing.

It can be argued that the 'Health and Morals of Apprentices Act' of 1802 is the earliest of the Education Acts inasmuch as it restricted the working hours of apprentices in the cotton and woollen industries and provided for some basic instruction – but it remained essentially ineffective. Its importance, however, is seen in the fact that despite the lack of government involvement in its drafting, it helped to establish the principle that the state could step in to put right certain deficiencies in areas in which it would not normally interfere.[26]

The attempt in 1807 by the reform-minded Whig politician Samuel Whitbread (1758–1815) at a bill to help pauper children met with great indifference in Parliament, and though it passed a second reading in the House of Commons it was rejected by the Lords. Henry Brougham, one of the earliest supporters of popular education and a frequent contributor to the *Edinburgh Review* on educational topics, introduced no fewer than five education bills between 1820 and 1839, all of which failed. In 1816 he had initiated the appointment of a Select Committee to look into the education of the 'lower orders of the Metropolis', an inquiry expanded to cover the whole country: it 'sat for two years, gathered together a wealth of valuable information, and raised a storm of criticism and abuse'.[27] And he was successful in 1818 in securing the appointment of a Royal Commission to investigate educational charities. In 1820 the first of his bills, 'for the better education of the poor in England and Wales', was introduced, but in the face of fierce criticism it was eventually withdrawn. Halévy doubts – probably unfairly – whether Brougham had any more serious aim than making a sensational speech,[28] but the very fact that a proper plan for state involvement in the provision of elementary education had been introduced at all was of itself significant.

And so the period 1800–33 in England was one of dispute, controversy, and uncertainty, with the state remaining for the most part aloof and indifferent. While there were some very concrete measures taken to provide for the education of the poor (in which the state had acquiesced), they still depended on individuals and voluntary bodies for their implementation; accessibility to schooling remained a matter of chance and depended in any case on the willingness of parents to take advantage of such opportunities as existed. The provision of elementary schooling was often motivated largely by the need for poor relief and the desire to reduce crime. But at the same time this was the age of reform, peaking in the Great Reform Act of 1832 which expanded the franchise.

The situation in Germany was quite different.

Provision in education, Germany 1800–40

Locating Germany historically creates a number of problems. Early in the nineteenth century 'Germany' could, technically speaking, be taken to embrace the sixteen states of the *Rheinbund*, the Confederation of the Rhine (1806). Later, from 1815 until 1866, we can talk of the thirty-nine states of the German Confederation (*Deutscher Bund*, which included Bohemia and parts of Austria); from 1834, of the states constituting the *Zollverein*, the Customs Union; and from 1871, of the unified Germany of Bismarck's *Deutsches Reich*. And so any discussion of 'education in Germany' should properly be situated in terms of what has been understood by 'Germany' at any particular point of time. It will be expedient, if contestable, for the most part to take Prussia as a proxy for 'Germany': to do so, however, is to ignore the differences between that powerful state and, for example, Bavaria or Württemberg, and so at times it will be necessary to consider the Germany beyond the borders of Prussia. 'La Prusse n'est pas l'Allemagne,' as Claude Diebolt has put it, 'mais elle a fait l'Allemagne. Elle en est le moteur principal et le régulateur'.[29]

As far as the situation in education in Prussia during the first decade of the nineteenth century is concerned, this was a time of reform, a period which created favourable conditions for the shaping of the schools and universities of Prussia that Wilhelm von Humboldt (1767–1835) would initiate during his rather brief period as head of the Prussian Section for Education and Instruction in 1809–10.

Prussia had first introduced the notion of compulsory school attendance under Frederick William I in rescripts of 1716 and 1717, but they were not enforced and remained essentially 'an exercise in wishful thinking'.[30] These early attempts to legislate for children to attend school were at least indicative of a general will to put schooling on a firm footing, even if it would be wrong to assert – as many commentators have done – that Prussia introduced universal compulsory elementary education at this early point in the eighteenth century.

Frederick William I's intention in his *Principia Regulativa* for East Prussia of 1736 was to make school provision more of a reality. This edict contained clauses allowing the free provision of wood for the construction of school buildings and for fuel, with the parishes maintaining them as they would houses for the clergy and church officials. The churches would be responsible for the remuneration of teachers, who would be given a cow and a calf, two pigs and some hens and – by the King – a small portion of land.

Additional payment would be made on the basis of the number of local children aged five to twelve, whether they attended school or not. These early regulations, as was the case with legislation under Frederick the Great, envisaged the active engagement of the clergy in school provision, not as representatives of the church but as instruments of the state with a duty to fulfil its wishes with regard to educational provision. On the King's death in 1740 there were said to be some 1,700 *Volks- und Landschulen* in East Prussia.[31]

Frederick the Great's *General-Landschul-Reglement* of 1763, however, was far more significant; it required that children attend school from their fifth to their thirteenth or fourteenth year; fines were imposed for non-attendance; and provision was made for the fees of the very poor to be paid from parish funds. The *Reglement* applied throughout Prussia (unlike earlier edicts) and initiated the 'uniform system of compulsory schooling' for which Prussia was to attract so much attention from foreign observers,[32] though it did not have a huge immediate effect:

> The Prussian School Regulations of 1763 provided a model and impetus for reform in other states as well, although it is clear that even in Prussia these early reform proposals remained pretty much a dead letter. Still, these early laws set an important precedent for central direction of schools.[33]

Frederick cannot be credited with a wholly enlightened perspective on the need to provide universal elementary education; in an order of 1779 to his minister for Ecclesiastical Affairs, Karl Abraham von Zedlitz (1731–93), he expressed the view that for the peasantry a little reading and writing would be sufficient, otherwise they might leave for the cities and become clerks.[34] For all that education was seen to be in the general interest of the state, there was no question of upsetting the social order; rather, the people were to be educated to support and defend the state, to be aware of their part in its progress and stability. Both military and economic – rather than altruistic – motives have been suggested to explain Frederick's interest in education; as a recent historian puts it, 'Peasants might well have to be taught to be – and to stay – peasants';[35] Paulsen concluded that among the things which Frederick really cared for popular education was not exactly high on the list.[36]

Following the *General-Landschul-Reglement* there were various other legislative measures affecting education, but it was the *Allgemeines Landrecht* of 1794 that affirmed the principle of state control in education and that of compulsory school attendance, with responsibility for the maintenance of schools falling to the communities:

> (Section 1) Schools and universities are state institutions charged with the instruction of the youth in useful information and scientific knowledge.
> (Section 2) Such institutions may be founded only with the knowledge and consent of the state.
> (Section 9) All public schools and educational institutions are under the supervision of the state and are at all times subject to its examination and inspection.
> (Section 10) No one shall be denied entrance into the public schools on account of difference of religious belief.
> (Section 11) Children who are to be educated in another religious faith than that of the school which they attend, cannot be compelled to take the religious instruction in that school.
> (Section 34) The maintenance of school buildings and teachers' dwellings must be borne by all the patrons of the school.
> (Section 43) Every inhabitant who cannot, or will not, furnish the necessary instruction for his children at home, is compelled to send them to school after they have completed their fifth year.
> (Section 44) Only with the consent of the civil and religious authorities is a child allowed to postpone attendance at school.

(Section 46) Instruction in school must be continued until, in the opinion of the pastor, the child has acquired that knowledge necessary for every reasonable man in his walk of life.

(Section 48) It is [the duty of the school inspectors], with the aid of the civil authority, to see that all children of compulsory school age are kept in school, if necessary by force and by punishment of negligent parents.[37]

This enlightened legislation provided the basis for the development of the Prussian education system in the nineteenth century, when, as Paulsen puts it, 'Germany took the lead in the educational movement among the nations of Europe'.[38]

There followed the Napoleonic Wars, which disrupted continental Europe for a generation and caused the humiliation of Prussia at the Battle of Jena in 1806 and the fall of Berlin. In the aftermath of that disaster for Prussia, it was a philosopher who was to raise the spirits of the Prussians and to reinvigorate the efforts to improve educational provision.

In 1807–8 Johann Gottlieb Fichte (1762–1814), later to become the first Professor of Philosophy at the new University of Berlin and its first elected rector, gave his famous lecture series, the *Reden an die deutsche Nation*. It was these lectures which firmly established the necessity to look towards education as a crucial factor in achieving the long-sought aim of German national unity. The *Reden*, delivered during the French occupation of Berlin, represent the crystallisation of Fichte's practical views on education, which he saw as the only reliable basis for the future prosperity of the nation. He strongly affirmed the state's duty with regard to the education of its people, and he did much to establish the principle of state control, as well as introducing the educational ideas of his friend Johann Heinrich Pestalozzi (1746–1827) to Germany. In a later series of lectures on the 'Theory of the State' given at the University of Berlin in 1813 he was to make the point that

> *compulsion* itself is education – i.e., education to understanding of moral destiny . . . The principle is now quite easy that the State, with all its compulsory measures, must regard itself as an educational institution for making compulsion unnecessary.[39]

This principle, formulated so early in the nineteenth century, demonstrates the beginnings of a fundamental difference in approach between the German and English systems; as Michael Sadler describes it:

> Without serious misgiving, Germany adopted the principle that the control of national education is a function of the central State. England . . . hesitated between two opposing theories, namely, the theory of State control and the theory of group autonomy under the general supervision of the State. Germany came to a decisive conclusion on this fundamental question of procedure. Great Britain (and particularly England) remained divided in conviction about it and therefore irresolute in policy. Germany standardised her education upon a system. Britain, distrustful of State control, compromised. Hence, Britain was dilatory while Germany was prompt. Britain temporised because she was feeling her way by instinct to some new adjustment of the claims of the State and of the various social groups of which the State consists.

Germany cast in her lot with a consistent theory and acted vigorously in accordance with it.[40]

Fichte's *Reden* represent the climax of his fervent nationalism. A national system of education would be the cure for all the ills of Germany: a better generation would be created, a better society, free of poverty and criminal elements; such passionate defenders of the state would be produced that the army itself would become redundant – indeed, Fichte believed that undreamt-of economic prosperity would result from a national system:

> All branches of economy will, in a short time and without much trouble, attain to such a flourishing state as has never been witnessed yet, and the State, if it must needs calculate, will gain interest a thousandfold on this its first investment.[41]

The *Reden* had a clear influence on the reforming Prussian Minister Baron vom Stein (1757–1831), whose draft *Proclamation* following his (forced) retirement mentions specifically the need for educational change in the direction of the 'long-prepared uniform system of national culture based upon a new and solid foundation', a theme taken up in his *Political Testament*.[42] Gordon and White see Fichte as having a direct and indirect impact on reform in England in terms of: (i) his influence on Humboldt, who redesigned educational provision in Prussia to the extent that it would attract the attention of Matthew Arnold in the 1850s and 60s; (ii) his influence on Thomas Carlyle, the great transmitter of German ideas in England; and (iii) the work of his pupil Johann Friedrich Herbart (1776–1841), whose writings were to become widely known in England towards the end of the century.[43]

In Germany it was left to the principal progenitor of the nineteenth-century Prussian education system, Wilhelm von Humboldt, to take up Fichte's challenge and to fulfil Stein's expectations. Very reluctantly – he wished to stay in Rome as Prussia's envoy to the Holy See – Humboldt became head of the Prussian Section for Education and Instruction in 1809, and although he resigned this post in 1810, his work was sufficiently advanced to enable his assistants to put many of his plans into action in the following years. Nineteenth-century Germany was to become, in Nipperdey's words, 'a country of schools' – *ein Land der Schulen*.[44]

Fichte had visited Pestalozzi as early as 1793; Humboldt had started as a critic – he had expressed scepticism about Pestalozzi's method in correspondence with Goethe in August 1804, finding a review of it too lenient – but he became, perhaps initially for political reasons, an overt enthusiast against the background of a developing vogue for Pestalozzi's work. As Humboldt's biographer puts it: 'In the Prussian reform party a Pestalozzian consensus had come into being'.[45]

Humboldt established the principle that the ordinary worker should have the same foundation in education as the most sophisticatedly educated person.[46] And his belief that *Bildung* should be at the heart of all educational endeavour, that the individual should count, is essentially Pestalozzian and was to inform a new approach to elementary education. Twelve young teachers were sent to Switzerland to be trained by Pestalozzi and to train others on their return; and experimental schools were established, employing the new methods. There were even – *pace* Bell and Lancaster – attempts by Karl August Zeller (1774–1840), a follower of Pestalozzi brought to Königsberg to set up a 'normal' teacher training institute, to develop the practice of older pupils teaching younger children, though informed by a rather different philosophy from that of the monitorial system in England.

Humboldt believed in an all-round humanistic education of the whole person, and he argued that beyond elementary provision the best basis for formal education was the study of ancient Greek. He effectively established the concept of *Bildung* as the cornerstone of post-elementary education in Germany. All pupils at this level should be taught ancient languages; next in importance for him came mathematics and history. His enthusiasm for Greek culture inspired a new emphasis in the *Gymnasium* curriculum, but there were unfortunate side-effects which endured in the *humanistisches Gymnasium* well into the twentieth century. First, as one critic has expressed it:

> Our classical ideal of education could hardly have made its appearance at a more unfavourable moment than when the social world began one of its most powerful transformations.[47]

And second, as others have put it:

> What to [Humboldt] was a philosophy of language inevitably ended up in the schools as soul-destroying grammar teaching. Knowledge of the rules of Greek grammar does not by any means necessarily guarantee an understanding of classical humanism. Hence his demand that 'everyone, even the poorest, should receive a complete education as a person' remains well-meaning but unrealistic theory.[48]

Humboldt is also especially remembered for his founding of the University of Berlin in 1810 and as the father of the modern concept of the university, rooted in academic freedom and in the unity of research and teaching. The Friedrich-Wilhelms-Universität (renamed the Humboldt University by the authorities of the German Democratic Republic in 1949), was to become a focal attraction for many British observers and the object of much praise. Matthew Arnold famously declared in 1868 that the 'French university has no liberty, and the English universities have no science; the German universities have both', so firmly was the Humboldtian philosophy of university education established by then.[49]

Humboldt's contribution generally to the establishment of a *system* of education in Prussia was outstanding. What he achieved has been summarised as:

> The state's sanctioning of the formal universality of education at all levels of teaching: at the elementary level in the spirit of Pestalozzi, in the senior school in the spirit of the new humanism, and at the university in the spirit of the philosophical concept of organic scholarship.[50]

We shall return to Humboldt and his influence in Chapter 5.

The nationalistic spirit in Prussia – strengthened both by the military defeat at Jena and the victory at Leipzig in 1813 – eventually demanded that some priority in education be given to training in skills potentially useful to the state. Humboldt's concept for general education (*Allgemeinbildung*), though still a strong force in German education, had eventually to give way in part to the more practical consideration of training people to work in the emerging industrial society. Humboldt had warned against the dehumanising processes of 'technocracy and bureaucracy',[51] and had refused to see the virtues of more utilitarian considerations. For him the school should first and foremost equip the child with the necessary foundations of knowledge and intellectual skill to be able to go on to acquire further knowledge and develop particular expertise. But the needs of those not destined to be among the intellectual elite were not to be neglected, and it was especially in technology and the practical application of well-taught skills that Germany was to excel as the century progressed.

Paulsen describes the period from 1815 to 1840 in Germany as one of 'quiet and fruitful work'.[52] It was left to Johann Wilhelm Süvern (1775–1829) and Karl, Freiherr von Altenstein (1770–1840) to see through the reforms set in motion by Humboldt. There were many advances in teacher training, with Pestalozzi's methods dominating.[53] And there seems to have been a general and genuine desire to promote elementary education in the spirit of the new philosophy, notwithstanding the cold water poured upon the notion of educating the masses by Friedrich Wilhelm III. Altenstein reported in a rescript of 1822 that the King

> could not but but approve of the zealous endeavours for the cause of primary education, but, at the same time, wished to point out that a line must be drawn somewhere, as otherwise the masses might be turned into half-educated sciolists ['superficial pretenders to knowledge'], quite unfit for their future vocation.[54]

Despite the progress, the number of children attending school in Prussia and elsewhere in Germany was, however, surprisingly low in the first decades of the century, given the ambitions of the school legislation. In 1816, of about 2.2 million children of school age in Prussia, only about 1.3 million (around 60 per cent) were attending school; the percentage for the Province of Prussia was 54.1 per cent; for Saxony it was above 80 per cent, for the Rheinland 50 per cent, for Western Prussia 40 per cent, for Posen not even 20 per cent.[55] But, as with the statistics for England in the early decades of the century, there are few reliable figures until the beginnings of the official collection of statistics after 1820.

Süvern's proposed reforms of 1819, which were to be much referred to as a result of their coverage in Victor Cousin's work of 1833 (to which we shall return in Chapter 3) include in a preamble an unequivocal statement on the educational role of the state. Every state, says Süvern, has an educative influence on its citizens by means of its constitution and its legislative and administrative measures: it is itself to some extent an educational institution on a large scale, providing intellectual and ethical direction.

Early British interest in German provision in education

To what extent was knowledge of what was happening in Germany available to British observers at the beginning of the century? Ability in the German language was not widespread – even by as late as the 1820s it was reckoned, for example, that only two or three senior members of Oxford University knew German.[56] There was much despair among those who tried throughout the century to learn the language. 'German is at once monotonous and vulgar', said one traveller in 1818, 'its elevation is a painful effort; there is no nobleness in its passion; its force is rough, coarse, and unmanageable'.[57]

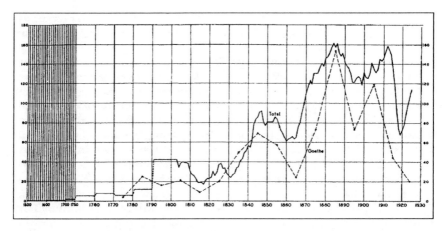

Figure 3 Translations of German Books into English, 1500–1927 (Source: Morgan, Critical Bibliography, p. 8)

Throughout the nineteenth century, however, information on German life and literature became increasingly more accessible to the non-German-speaking British reading public through translations of German works. Morgan's *Critical Bibliography of German Literature in English Translation* charts the number of translated works and demonstrates an increase in such publications from 1800 to the peak decade of 1880–90 of the order of some 300 per cent (Figure 3). Morgan accounts for the peak at the close of the eighteenth century in terms of the growing interest in German literature of the period, particularly in the works of Schiller and Goethe, and a curious vogue for the dramatist August von Kotzebue. The following two-decade slump he interprets as reflecting economic depression after the Napoleonic Wars and a distrust of the perceived 'revolutionary' nature of German literature. The peaks of the forties and fifties are seen as reflecting economic recovery and industrial expansion, as well as the promotional work of Carlyle and others in Britain and the United States. The spectacular rise of the eighties is attributed to Germany's development to world power status, and the trough of the nineties to growing political tension.[58]

Some informed observers of the German scene

Travel was limited. Despite the general hardships of long and hazardous journeys in the days before the railways, the Napoleonic Wars – and the embargoes introduced by Napoleon's 'Continental System' (1805–13) – effectively closed the Continent to British travellers for the first fifteen years of the new century, and it was only with the Peace of 1815 that a new tide of travel to the Continent began. The influx of tourists was then of such proportion that it could be joked about as the 'British invasion of Europe'.[59] English-speaking travellers' accounts of Germany are relatively scarce between 1800 and 1815; thereafter the amount of travel literature increases significantly, though it contains few detailed accounts of education before the 1830s.[60] Most travellers headed for the Rhine. In 1827 some 18,000 passengers were taking steam trips up the river; by mid-century the numbers had risen to one million tourists and locals.[61] The huge growth in railway travel made it easier than ever to visit Germany, even if only on a Sunday-to-Wednesday short break for the small sum of 12s 6d in second class.[62]

A significant exception to the relative lack of accounts of Germany in the early years of the century is that written by John Quincy Adams describing his travels in Silesia in 1800 and 1801, published in London in 1804.[63] Adams (1767–1848) was at the time the US Minister Plenipotentiary in Berlin; the son of an American president, he was to hold among other offices the post of Ambassador to Great Britain, and to be elected to the Senate. He became the sixth US president in 1825. Adams's description of progress in elementary education in Prussia was known in Britain and was later to be quoted in the 1839 report of the Committee of Council, *Recent Measures for the Promotion of Education in England*, to which we shall turn in Chapter 3.[64]

In a letter from Berlin dated 7 March 1801 Adams writes appreciatively of the educational reforms of Frederick the Great; it was due to 'the zeal with which he pursued the purpose of spreading useful knowledge among all classes of his subjects' that, compared to the United States,

> Probably, no country in Europe could so strongly contest our pre-eminence in [elementary education] as Germany.[65]

Adams mentions in particular the training of teachers and the seminary established by Johann Ignaz von Felbiger (1724–88) in Sagan, leading to similar establishments elsewhere in Prussia:

> The teachers are directed to give plain instruction, and upon objects applicable to the ordinary concerns of life; not merely to load the memory of their scholars with words, but to make things intelligible to their understanding; to habituate them to the use of their own reason, by explaining every object of the lesson, so that the children themselves may be able to explain it, upon examination. The candidates for school-keeping must give specimens of their ability, by teaching at one of the schools connected with the seminary, in the presence of the professors at the seminary, that they may remark and correct any thing defective in the candidate's method.[66]

And he cites too the regulations in place for compulsory attendance and for inspection:

> The school-tax must be paid by the lord and the tenants, without distinction of religions. In the towns, the school must be kept the whole year round. It is expected that one month shall suffice to make a child know the letters of the alphabet; that in two it shall be able to join them; and in three, to read. The boys must all be sent to school, from their sixth to their thirteenth year, whether the parents are able to pay the school-tax or not. For the poor, the school-money must be raised by collections. Every parent or guardian who neglects to send his child or pupil to school, without sufficient cause, is obliged to pay a double school-tax, for which the guardians shall have no allowance. Every curate must examine, weekly, the children of the school in his parish. A general examination must be held annually, by the deans of the districts, of the schools within their respective precincts; and a report of the condition of

the schools, the talents and attention of the school masters, the state of the buildings, and of attendance by the children, made to the office of the vicar-general, who must transmit all these reports to the royal domain offices. From these, orders are issued to the respective landraths, to correct the abuses and supply the deficiencies indicated in the reports.[67]

The important study by Madame de Staël (1766–1817),[68] *De l'Allemagne*, first appeared in English translation in 1813, predating the banned original version in French. This work dated from 1810, before Humboldt's reforms had been felt, and it should be remembered that its author has been shown to be unreliable in reporting her personal views with full honesty.[69] There is much on the nature of university education in Germany ('Intellectual education is perfect in Germany, but every thing there passes into a theory') and on the importance of the study of ancient and modern languages; and there is praise for the work of the (Swiss) educationists Pestalozzi and Fellenberg, but nothing in terms of comment on actual school provision in Prussia (despite a chapter headed *Of particular Institutions for Education, and Charitable Establishments*). But a contemporary English reader of de Staël's substantial work would have gained an impression of considerable advances in educational thought in 'Germany' and would have been clearly reminded of Fichte's expectation that the regeneration of the German nation could be achieved on the basis of Pestalozzi's approach to education.[70]

One of the earliest significant British commentators on German education was the self-taught radical economist, political commentator and journalist Thomas Hodgskin (1787–1869). Hodgskin reported on his observations – especially on what he saw in Hanover – in a two-volume work, *Travels in the North of Germany*, published in 1820, in which he developed what has been termed a 'minimalist conception' of the state.[71] In order to conduct his inquiries into the 'social and political institutions, the agriculture, manufactures, commerce, education, arts and manners' of Germany he used a questionnaire put together by Jeremy Bentham.[72] And the result was a study of some sophistication for its time, despite his taking Hanover 'as a criterion for judging of the whole':

> When the number of children instructed can be calculated, – when the population of the town is known, – when what is taught, and the manner of teaching, are described, – then a tolerable correct judgment may be formed of the general state of education in the whole country.[73]

All of this he attempts in two full chapters which combine attention to the detail of numbers and prices with analysis and observations of an often polemical nature.

He was generally impressed by what he observed. 'There may be even said to be a sort of mania for schools,' he writes.[74] He covers compulsory school attendance, payments to teachers, and fines levied on parents who do not send their children to school: 'Fortunately, however, parents are becoming sensible of the value of instruction, for there is now much less necessity to enforce this law than formerly'.[75] He deals with the training of teachers, the education of girls, and the subjects taught in the various schools he visited. He judged the overall situation in Hanover to be good:

The institutions for education in the town of Hannover, independent of boarding-schools, provide means of instruction to at least 2100 children, the great mass of which are between the ages of six and fourteen years, and belong to the middling and poorer classes of people. The whole population of the town does not exceed 21,000, and certainly, therefore, the means of instruction are abundant and cheap. In fact, there are very few children who do not go to school, and hardly any grown-up person who is unable to read and write. I have heard it remarked by a clergyman who had been catechizing all the children of his parish, that he was surprised to have found a very few who hardly knew how to read. This was for him a singular circumstance, and proves the extent of instruction. Girls share in all the advantages of these schools, and they are by no means behind boys in their acquirements.[76]

On the style of teaching he has much to say that resonates with practices still observable in German schools today, especially the notion of 'learning the lesson' and being tested on it:

When what is to be taught is any thing which can be learned alone, such as the rules of grammar, a portion of the catechism, or the facts of geography, the teacher selects a portion of it, which he reads to the class; and they often write it down after his dictation, and this they are obliged to learn when they are out of school. On the following day the instructor examines the whole class to know if they have learned the lesson. The examination is promiscuous, or made in such a manner that no one is sure he will not be questioned, although but few are. The probability of being questioned, and the reproof which the children receive if they are not capable of answering, obliges them all to learn; and the frequent repetition which even those who are not asked hear made by others; even the mistakes of the inattentive, when rectified by the master, serve to inform the whole class, and fix all that has been taught in the memory of all.[77]

He expresses scepticism about the controlling function of the state, arguing that a national education is only a good thing if it reflects the 'whole community'. He observes that while there was no need in Bavaria 'to disturb the existing establishments to introduce the improvements of Lancaster and Bell'[78] – as we have noted above – there was evident in the teaching he observed in the schools of Hanover something of the principles espoused by the two British innovators:

Neither of these methods was copied from the other, but in both countries a want of something better was felt, and in both countries improvements were the consequence. Their simultaneous origin proves that they were the natural consequences of the state of society, and that something of the same kind would have taken place even if the illustrious individuals whose names they bear had never existed. It is consolatory thus to see the improvements of the species depending on general laws, and that they are not subject to the accidents of time, nor submitted to the control of any individual.[79]

Hodgskin deals too with university study, covering the nature of the courses, the habits and customs of the students, and the costs involved, digressing at length on student disturbances in Göttingen in 1818.

Hodgskin's work is significant as an early attempt at a social analysis of education in Germany, using some of the analytical tools which were then in their infancy (and which owed much to Jeremy Bentham, who left '70,000 pieces of un-indexed paper' on his death in 1832, such was his data-gathering zeal.[80]) But beyond the reporting of facts and figures he has much to say that is of interest with regard to what was actually being taught and how. This latter aspect of his work is his main strength. His study would have served to provide much valuable information to the readership of his day.

Pestalozzi and other thinkers

Pestalozzi was of course Swiss, but so closely was he associated with developments in education in Germany that his nationality was largely irrelevant and he is regarded as playing a very significant part in the early shaping of educational thinking in Prussia in particular. Pestalozzi's work was to receive considerable attention in England, though (as can be the case with new theory) it was often misreported. By 1831 a substantial work by Eduard Biber (1801–74) had appeared in English that attempted an accurate interpretation of Pestalozzi for an English-speaking audience:

> It would be an endless task to recount, and an hopeless one to refute, all the erroneous and absurd notions which are afloat [. . .]; nor can the public be held responsible for the mistakes and prejudices into which they have fallen, since the only sources of information accessible to them, were a few meager accounts, most of them drawn up by persons but superficially acquainted with Pestalozzi's views.[81]

Biber, who had fiercely criticised Pestalozzi in a polemic of 1827[82] which caused the latter considerable anguish shortly before his death in that same year, covers all aspects of Pestalozzi's writings, interspersed with an account of his life and the work of his associates, with much space devoted to practical teaching method. It would be followed by many other studies that helped to popularise Pestalozzi's theories. Here is an account of Pestalozzi's importance by William Hickson, written in 1840:

> Pestalozzi . . . may almost be considered as the father of popular instruction, and as the greatest benefactor to the cause that has yet appeared. [. . .] The scene of his labours was Switzerland, but by his example and writings he diffused a new spirit among the schools of primary instruction all over the continent, and materially changed their character. His influence has been felt, where his name has not been heard. His leading principle was that the mind should be governed by love rather than by fear; that the schoolmaster should become the affectionate parent instead of the dreaded tyrant; that he should mould the will, rather than coerce it. He contended that whoever was incompetent to gain the affection of a child was unfit to teach even the elementary principles of religion to a child; for without love to man there could be no love to God.
>
> The basis of his plan of instruction was not so much teaching, as first setting about to create in the mind of the child the disposition to learn, and then, instead of at once satisfying its curiosity, putting it in the way of finding out for itself what it wanted to know.[83]

The eighteenth century was dubbed by Joachim Heinrich Campe (1746–1818) *das pädagogische Jahrhundert* ('the century of education') and it produced a number of significant thinkers on education whose work has lasted. Pestalozzi, born in 1746, was the elder statesman of a generation of philosophers who were to influence the shape of educational provision in Germany and whose work would become known in England.

Among them we must mention two who were very important. Johann Friedrich Herbart had a lasting effect on teaching style well into the twentieth century. His famous 'five steps' consisting of preparation, presentation, association, exemplification, and testing became a bedrock of teacher training, spreading far beyond his own work in Germany.

Friedrich Froebel (1782–1852), a thinker in the neo-humanist tradition, brought to the world the word *Kindergarten* in 1840 (a term which was adopted in English usage by the 1850s) and developed a method based on play and natural exploration, still kept alive in England in institutions devoted to his approach and through the National Froebel Foundation. As a result of the Prussian government ordering the closing of every Kindergarten in 1851, adherents of the Froebel method took his ideas abroad, and the first Kindergarten was started in London in the same year. The Revised Code of 1882 gave a degree of official recognition to the Kindergarten, as did the London School Board in 1888.

The work of these prominent thinkers – and of others less well known in England, like Friedrich Diesterweg (1790–1866) – was in contrast to the standard approach to teaching and learning in most German schools of their day, but it created a climate of different thinking about approaches to education which had an obvious and lasting international impact.[84]

Some travellers and their accounts of education in Germany

Some early English travellers to Germany could not disguise an innate superiority and arrogant (if elegantly formulated) condescension when reporting on education. Charles Edward Dodd, author of *An Autumn Near the Rhine* (1818), is such a one:

> The ordinary plan of education of German boys, from the higher down to all but the lowest classes, is at the Public Gymnasium, a free school, to be found in every considerable town. They a good deal resemble the grammar-schools in our large towns, except that the ranks of the boys are even more mixed – and the system of education and discipline by no means comparable. [. . .] Latin and Greek, of course, form a principal part of their instruction – but it is a proof of the defectiveness of the system, that in spite of drilling at the Gymnasium, and a residence, at least of two years, at the University, you seldom find a man, in the higher ranks, who possesses more than the merest smattering of classical attainments.[85]

Dodd goes on to warn against the liberality of the German princes in supporting the provision of educational opportunities in their realms, reflecting the view that too much education was a dangerous thing:

The more shrewd well-wishers to despotism see clearly that the rising generation are educating at the Gymnasium and the University with ideas of independence, ill-suited to the capitals of the little monarchies. But the Princes' easy apathy, in this and other instances, lets things take their course and unintentionally favours the progress of liberal ideas, which must in the end, either bend or break the governments with which, in their present state, they can never go hand in hand.[86]

On the German university and its students Dodd is no less enthusiastic than he is about the *Gymnasium*:

Nothing can be imagined more striking than the contrast between an English and a German University. In the former, the Gothic buildings, the magnificent colleges, the noble libraries, the chapels, the retired walks, the scholastic grace of the costume, are all so many interesting indications of the antiquity, the munificence, and the dignity of the institution. The University of Heidelberg is one of the most distinguished in Germany – but the constitution of a German University has necessarily no monument of architecture, no appendage of dignity, scarcely any decent building connected with it. The . . . public build-ing, containing the library and the lecture rooms of the Professors, barely comes under this last description. An Englishman might pass the town a dozen times without remarking any traces of its institutions, unless he happened to encounter a string of swaggering mustachioed youths, their hair flowing on their shoulders, without cravats, with pipes in their mouths, parading the streets with a rude impudence.[87]

John Russell, in a much cited book on a tour in Germany in 1820, 1821, and 1822, devotes considerable space to a discussion of the character of German universities, with an interesting disquisition on the founding of the University of Berlin, 'after Göttingen, the most flourishing and reputable in Germany'. He recounts in detail the arguments between Friedrich August Wolff (1759–1824), the university's 'brightest ornament' and Stein, the minister who had opposed the idea of having a university in Berlin.[88] But most space in his account is given over to Jena.

Here we see the kind of description which would become familiar later in the century from the writings of William Howitt and Henry Mayhew. 'Nowhere', says Russell, 'do all [the] elements of the *beau ideal* [sic] of a modern university concur in greater perfection than in Jena'.[89] He covers the constitution of the university and the appointment of professors and of the *doctores privatim docentes*, the *Privatdozenten* ('in the eyes of great part of the students, this appendix, like the postscript of a lady's letter, is the most important member of the Alma Mater'.[90]) He deals with fees and lecture courses and their style of delivery, remarking on the traditional lack of close supervision of the students which has characterised universities in Germany:

There is no other superintendence of their studies, than that of the Professor in his pulpit, telling them what he himself knows; there are no arrangements to secure, in any degree, either attendance or application. The received maxim is, that it is right to tell them what they ought to do; but that it would be neither proper nor useful to take care that they do it, or prevent them from being as idle and ignorant as they choose.[91]

There is much coverage of smoking and drinking and singing among the *Burschen*, and of the *Landsmannschaften* and of duelling, and the reader is left with a vivid and somewhat disapproving account of the exotic features of student life which is in contrast to the positive verdict on the academic standing of the university, though even that is cast into doubt at times. On the appointment of a professor from a list of three candidates Russell reports:

> I was assured by members of the university that the senate has been known, from mere envy of superior talent, to pass by a man of acknowledged genius, and give in a list of three acknowledged blockheads.[92]

The soldier and writer Moyle Sherer (1789–1869), in an account published in 1826, strays into a comparison of English and German students much in the style of Russell:

> Of German students I can only speak pictorially . . . Their costume, when clean, I am far from disliking, and their sins of smoking and singing appear to me venial offences; even the drinking of beer where they cannot get wine I forgive.
> [. . .]
> Of the students in German universities the great majority are poor.
> In their universities there is none of that wholesome discipline so honourably distinguishing those of our native country.
> [. . .]
> I mean not to institute an unfair and impossible comparison between the comparatively wealthy gownsmen at our universities and the poor burschen of Germany, but I want more allowance for the latter than is generally made.
> No man can pass an hour in a room with German students without discovering that they are worshippers of knowledge, and lovers of their father-land.[93]

The translator and man of letters John Strang (1795–1863) wrote a detailed account of his travels in Germany in 1833 in which he showed much enthusiasm for educational provision in Prussia:

> In the progress of improvement, Prussia has . . . made prodigious advances by means of her educational system. [. . .] [N]owhere is the education of the people better attended to, or better understood. The National Schools of Prussia have long been her chief boast. [. . .] Indeed, during the last ten years, the system of national education may be said to have reached perfection, and its effects are delightful to the philanthropist; so well, too, are these understood and appreciated in Prussia, that they have created a spirit of emulation over all the various districts of the country . . .[94]

Strang's comparative figures for school attendance are: for France, one pupil per seventeen inhabitants; for England, one out of fifteen (cf. Brougham's estimate); for Prussia, one in seven. His description of how the whole system operates encapsulates the detail:

> This admirable system of education may be thus shortly explained. Its leading principles prescribe – first, that every individual within the confines of the monarchy, shall be bound to undergo a regular course of elementary study; and secondly, that each district, town, or parish, shall provide funds for defraying the expenses. The law of Prussia requires, that every town and commune should, by a local tax leviable on individuals possessing a certain income, annually raise sufficient funds to provide for the salaries of schoolmasters and schoolmistresses, and for the building and repairing of school-houses, and that this provision shall be made in accordance with the number of the inhabitants of the town or parish.* The whole schools are under the surveillance of the Minister of Education. But the immediate superintendence of the schools are vested in the magistracy of towns, and in the clergyman and a committee of the principal payers of parishes. Over the local boards there is an inspector, who watches over each circle or county, who reports to the Council of the District in which the particular circle is situated, and this council keeps up a regular correspondence with the head of the whole educational department in the capital. You will thus perceive, that while each parish-school is under the immediate superintendence of the local authorities, the whole are placed under the direct control of the Central Board, producing at once an energetic and a uniform system over the kingdom. While the law demands that every Prussian shall send his child of either sex to the public elementary school, from the age of seven to fourteen years, it also permits of the hours of study being so arranged as to allow the children of the poorer class a certain time for labour. The course of study is admirably adapted to its ends, and far outstrips the much-talked of parochial system of Scotland. In the town schools, for instance, besides teaching the language of the country, writing, arithmetic, geography, geometry, the history of Prussia, music, and gymnastics, the pupils are taught the rudiments of the Latin tongue, and the elements of the physical sciences. It is perhaps worthy of remark, that every pupil must go through the regular prescribed curriculum of study. Tuition here is strictly national, for no individual is allowed to open a private seminary in any parish or town, without permission of the local authorities. [*For every 1500 inhabitants residing in towns, there must be at least *one* school][95]

This concise and enthusiastic account reflects the attractiveness of the Prussian model for a certain type of informed observer in the period just before the first government grant for education in England.

Brief popular accounts of education in Germany

Those wishing quick access to information on education in Germany might turn to various popular compendia: a range of handbooks, gazetteers, and guides was available to the curious reader. Typical of very minimal coverage in such sources is an account of a tour in Germany over the period 1816–18 which appeared in 1827. In Prussia, the author reports,

There are eighteen schools of different descriptions; the principal one is the Gymnasium, and the others are all attached either to the churches or charitable institutions*. The latter consist of five general hospitals, besides a poor-house, orphan asylum, lazaretto, almshouse, benevolent society, Bible society, and amicable society. The nature of the last mentioned is to educate free of expense, boys of low condition, whose abilities in any of the sciences are found to be very superior.

[* In each town in Prussia there is a school supported by the state. In the *whole* of Germany, it is calculated there are 22 universities (chiefly similar to our "Public Schools,") in which at present there are 15,746 students, and 1045 professors.][96]

What his readers made of the likening of the universities of Germany (Berlin? Jena? Halle? Göttingen? Leipzig?) to English public schools (Eton? Winchester? Harrow? Rugby?) can only be conjectured.

There were many types of popular source providing basic information, among them publications like *Chambers's Encyclopaedia*, which contained brief information on education in Prussia. The prolific American author Charles A. Goodrich (1790–1862), in his *Universal Traveller* of 1836, acknowledged the lofty status of the *Gymnasien* but situated the German universities at a rather higher and more appropriate level:

The gymnasia of the north of Germany are celebrated; they are schools preparatory to the universities; but the studies pursued in them are equal to those of the universities in some countries. [. . .] The universities of Germany are the best in the world.[97]

Later the *Cabinet Gazetteer* reported briefly but very positively:

Public instruction under the gov[ernment] is greatly developed in Prussia. [. . .] The system of education is of a thoroughly practical nature, and is considered the most complete and efficient in Europe. The different classes of schools are – 1. the elementary, at which the great majority of the people receive their education; 2. the city school, which is always attached to a gymnasium; 3. the gymnasium, in which Latin and Greek are taught. In most of the small towns are normal schools for the training of teachers. Attendance at school is compulsory.[98]

Such encapsulated perceptions played a role in the creation of an image in the public mind of what the Germans were achieving in education. They were clearly not as developed or accurate as the accounts in the thorough studies of later observers, but they helped to prepare the ground for use of the German example in education in the debates of the middle decades of the century.[99]

* * * * *

During the first three decades of the century the debate in England dwelt on the basic questions of what sort of education might be provided for the people and by whom. While there was acceptance that local provision of various kinds was acceptable, there was little agreement about any involvement of the state, either in a general controlling function or through financial support. The example of Germany provided an indication of what might be possible, though it worked both to support and to object to intervention on the part of the state. The 1830s saw the first major steps towards state involvement in educational provision, and this is the main focus of the next chapter.

Chapter 3

Establishing State Involvement in Education: The German Example in England, 1833–70

The [English] schools for the instruction of the people during week days are still miserably deficient, both in number and kind, and as yet there appears no prospect of concert of effort to bring about a better state of general education.

Alexander Dallas Bache, 1839[1]

The spirit of the whole of Germany has always been intellectual.

William Edward Hickson, 1840[2]

In the early 1830s school attendance in England was still low. The situation in Manchester was indicative of the scale of the problem:

Out of every ten children of school age, four went to no school at all, three went to Sunday schools only, two attended the very unsatisfactory dame and common day schools and one only received an [acceptable] education.[3]

Statistical information for the period continues to be highly problematic, however, with some contemporary interpretation presenting a more optimistic evaluation of the wider scene:

A far greater proportion of the English population are now [1833] sent to school than is usually supposed, and currently stated. [. . .] [A current] statistical work . . . declares the proportion to be only one in 17 for England, one in 20 for Wales. What is the fact? Why, that our population for England and Wales amounts nearly to 14 millions, and that the number of children receiving elementary education in 1828 are, by the returns, 1,500,000. An additional 500,000 being supposed, not without reason, to be educated at independent schools, not calculated in the return. Thus, out of a population of 14 millions, we have no less than two millions of children receiving elementary education at schools.[4]

There could be more confident description of the situation in Germany:

In Germany elementary education is a monopoly of the state, and in reality we find in that country that education is without question widespread among the mass of the people; the school system of Prussia is especially renowned. Already in 1826 there were in Prussia 21,633 elementary schools, attended by 1,664,278 children. If we calculate the number of children of school age at that time to be 1,923,000, it appears that of 15 children of school age 13 were actually attending public schools. In the districts of Magdeburg, Merseburg, Erfurt, Liegnitz, Breslau, Arensburg, and Münster this was the case for all children. [Present author's translation.][5]

The *Edinburgh Review* reported in October 1833 on returns for school attendance in Prussia for 1831:

The population of the Prussian Monarchy, by the last census, was 12,726,823
Which is somewhat more than a million short of the
last census for England and Wales.
Of these twelve millions and a half, there are,
between the ages of seven and fourteen, which is
the period allotted for attending schools, 2,043,030
And the return of children actually in attendance
in 1831, was 2,021,421

—————
Difference, 21,609

The difference could be accounted for in part by those educated at home and privately; the *Edinburgh Review* enthused: 'From this statement, so glorious for Prussia, it follows, that every human being in it not only has the means, but actually enjoys the advantage, of a good education'.[6]

In 1833 it was calculated that about 9 per cent of the population (one in eleven) were receiving an education at day schools in England and Wales.[7] The National School Society, in reports for 1832 and 1833 had lamented that 'England is yet uneducated'.[8]

Around the middle of the century there was still much discussion about precisely how many children were being educated in England and Prussia. A problem relating to the nature of the comparative statistics on educational provision was raised in the House of Commons debate on the second reading of the 1850 ('Secularist') Education Bill:

[Lord Ashley] would take only one case, because, as the same fallacy ran through the whole argument, one would sufficiently answer his purpose. He would take the case of Prussia. [It was] stated, that in Prussia there were one in six receiving education, while in England there were, according to some, only 1 in 8½; but, according to his own estimate, only 1 in 13. Now, supposing this statement to be correct, the comparison was not a fair one, and for this reason, that the Prussian statistics included every person, from the highest student to the lowest street-sweeper, who was undergoing a course of education, while the English statistics included only those who received inferior degrees of education at eleemosynary establishments. Now, this difference was very great, because, if they wished to make a fair comparison they must add to the estimate of those who were receiving education in England all those who were educated at our universities and great schools, as well as all the establishments maintained for private profit, or by private benevolence. What would be the result? That those who were educated at private expense, and were not to be reckoned as receiving State education, and who were not much more than one-twenty-sixth of the whole number educated in Prussia, in England were at least one-third; and, therefore, in order to institute a fair comparison, the one-third must be added to the number of England. This fallacy ran through all the comparisons with foreign countries, it being a known fact, that in no country of the World did people make such efforts as in England for the independent education of their children. Besides, the accuracy of the statement that one in six of the people in Prussia was receiving education was very questionable, for according to the returns for ten great towns in Prussia, the proportion was nowhere one in six, and averaged about one in nine — a fair estimate for the whole population.[9]

But there was clearly general concern that in contrast to Germany England was educating only a small proportion of its school-age population to anything like an acceptable level.

Public perceptions of the contrast with Prussia were informed by the work of several prominent commentators. First among them was Victor Cousin, whose *Rapport sur l'état de l'Instruction Publique dans quelques pays de l'Allemagne* of 1833 was to become widely known and hugely influential in England and elsewhere. In 1838 the American Alexander Dallas Bache (1806–67), great grandson of Benjamin Franklin, published his *Report on Education in Europe*, which devoted a lot of space to orphanages and to elementary and secondary instruction in Prussia, as well as covering Britain, France, Holland, and Switzerland. This substantial report was followed in 1837 by the *Report on Elementary Public Instruction* of Calvin E. Stowe (1802–86), recounting a visit to Europe in 1836, and by a *Report of an Educational Tour* (1844) by Horace Mann (1796–1859), covering Germany and parts of Great Britain and Ireland, which was published in London in 1846. These three reports emanating from the United States provided significant detail and so formed an important part of the foundations of knowledge in the English-speaking world about educational provision in Germany. In addition there were the various publications on Germany from the pen of the educationist Henry Barnard (1811–1900), who acknowledges a debt to the work of Bache, Stowe, and Mann, and to that of the British observer, to whom we shall return below, Joseph Kay (1821–78). Barnard, the founder of the *American Journal of Education* and a prolific writer on education, toured Europe in 1835–6 and produced among other publications *National Education in Europe* and *German Pedagogy*. But it was Victor Cousin's account of 1833 that was to have the most profound impact on British observers of the German educational scene.

Victor Cousin and Sarah Austin

In 1833 Sarah Austin (1793–1867), a very active translator of works from German and other languages and today recognised as a significant figure in the early history of comparative education,[10] published in the *Foreign Quarterly Review* a lengthy account of Victor Cousin's important report on Germany.[11] Cousin's book was also widely reviewed elsewhere, and it became very influential in the debate in England about the desirability of a national system of education. Cousin (1792–1867), called by Bulwer Lytton 'one of the profoundest and most eminent men in France',[12] was a philosopher and administrator, one-time director of the École Normale and Minister of Public Instruction. He had undertaken his study of education in Germany on behalf of the French Minister of Public Instruction.

Sarah Austin, who moved in circles which included Mill and Carlyle and who corresponded with Gladstone,[13] was to translate Cousin's work into English in 1834 and to contribute a preface on national education (in which, incidentally, she quotes cheekily from her own anonymously published and, as she describes it, 'excellent article' in the *Foreign Quarterly Review*).[14] She had lived in Germany and was well informed about German culture and society, her best-known book being an account of German life from 1760 to 1814.[15] Carlyle referred to her as 'a true Germanized spiritual *screamikin*'[16] and Mill called her *Mütterlein* ('little mother').[17]

Austin was a strong believer in the need to create a national system and she asks in her review of Cousin's work what lesson the Prussian system teaches and what light it throws on the issue of national education:

> In the first place we may remark, that it proves incontestably, by the solid and substantial argument of complete practical success, that a system of national education is not a mere chimera; that it is not a phantom of the brain, imagined by dreaming philosophers; but a mode of insuring the elementary instruction of all children, which may be established and maintained not less than an army or navy. There is no doubt that the institution of such a system is encompassed with many difficulties and impediments [. . .]; but that by wisdom, zeal and perseverance these difficulties and impediments may be overcome, the conduct of the Prussian government has irrefragably demonstrated.[18]

Cousin's comprehensive report had a profound influence on thinking about educational provision both in France (where its publication coincided with and influenced the reforms introduced by François Guizot (1787–1874), which established a primary education system) and in Britain, where it was to be widely quoted. The *London and Westminster Review*, for example, published an extraordinarily lengthy (54-page) account of 'Dutch and German Schools' which covered five publications, including Cousin's reports on Germany and Holland.[19] The reviewer attempts to identify aspects of the continental experience in education that might have implications for the 'improvement and extension of popular education' in England. Such factors are grouped under several headings: administrative organisation; government-dependent organisation of schools and instruction; compulsory education; and 'interference' of the state in secular instruction 'prescribing either its extent or the methods that should be employed'.

Cousin spent the period 5 June to 20 July 1831 in Berlin. He knew the Minister, Baron von Altenstein, and was able to interview him; and he was assisted and accompanied by the Privy Councillor Johannes Schulze (1784–1860) of the Prussian education ministry. His report demonstrates a remarkable mastery of detail, including statistical tables, examples of timetables and curricula, and plans of school buildings. Cousin begins with a general account of the organisation of public instruction in Prussia and then focuses on primary education, covering six main areas:

> The duty of parents to send their children to school;
> The duty of the parishes to maintain primary schools at their own expense;

The 'general objects and different gradations of primary instruction';
The training, placement, promotion, and disciplining of primary
teachers;
The government of primary instruction;
Private schools.

The renowned German educationist Adolf Diesterweg noted inaccuracies in
Cousin's report and felt that he 'perceived only the brighter side of the German
system'.[20] And it is clear that the adulatory style did much to promote interest
in education in Prussia among those looking for a model system. But there
was a curious anomaly in the report that went largely overlooked. Cousin had
based much of his account on the 1819 draft (*Entwurf*) education bill of Johann
Wilhelm Süvern, which was not in fact enacted. This curious feature of Cousin's
report was noticed much later by Mark Pattison in his report on education in
Germany for the Newcastle Commission:

> Nearly half of M. Cousin's report is occupied with Prussia. It is sufficient to say,
> that the whole of M. Cousin's account of primary education in that country
> is taken from a scheme of Von Altenstein, Minister of Education in Prussia at
> the time of M. Cousin's visit. This scheme (*Entwurf*) was never attempted to
> be put into execution, – was never enacted, or even published, – but remains
> still in the secret archives of the Ministry of Education at Berlin. M. Cousin,
> however, treating it as the existing Prussian system, says in one place "that
> it has the force of law." Though once or twice naming it "projet de loi;" he
> prefers generally to call it "the law of 1819." And says of it, "that it is the most
> comprehensive law on primary instruction with which he is acquainted." This
> extraordinary mis-statement has never been fully exposed. Its nature is only
> understood when we become aware of the fact that Prussia has never had a
> general law on education. Her administration in this, as in other branches, is
> provincial, and her existing system the growth of time, varying locally accord-
> ing to the circumstances of the different populations of which the monarchy
> is composed.[21]

There was therefore a significant shortcoming in Cousin's report, published as it
was some fourteen years after Süvern's draft bill, but perception in this case was
as effective as reality. Cousin had established a notion of educational provision
in Prussia which was to resonate powerfully.

Cousin writes at the end of his report that he intended to move on to consider
secondary and higher instruction in Prussia, and he did so in a number of short
documents between 1834 and 1841,[22] but it is his original report that made the
greatest impact on his British readership.

Victor Cousin came to be cited very frequently as the debate about educational
provision in England quickened pace. In the same year (1833), for example, the
Whig Radical MP and popular novelist Edward Bulwer-Lytton (1803–73) devoted
considerable space in his *England and the English* to the question of education,
referring in detail (and with much use of exclamation marks) to Prussia and
relying on Victor Cousin for his information. He argues for a national education,
'as Prussia and Holland already enjoy – as France is about to possess'[23]; he praises
the textbooks of Saxe-Weimar, quoting from Cousin's favourable opinion of
them, and he turns to Prussia ('There, universal education is made a necessary,

pervading, paramount, principle of the state'[24]) and the proposed law of 1819, describing the curriculum of elementary and advanced schools. The programme of the elementary schools is seen as 'an education that exercises the reason, enlightens the morals, fortifies the body, and founds the disposition to labour and independence'.[25] In an appendix he elaborates his thoughts on education, arguing that it should be a 'state affair' (as in Prussia), rather than 'left to the mercy of individuals', as in England; for the appointment of a minister of public instruction as head of an appropriate department, with a council to assist him; and – interestingly – in favour of 'moral [rather] than legislative compulsion' as far as school attendance is concerned:

> We cannot transfer to this country the wholesale education of Prussia; in the latter it is compulsory on parents to send their children to school, or to prove that they educate them at home. A compulsory obligation of that nature would, at this time, be too stern for England'[26]

This caveat on compulsion was not unusual and proved remarkably persistent, up to and beyond the Newcastle Commission's recommendations of 1861 and the 1870 Education Act.

First vote of funds for education

Again in the same year, on 17 August 1833, the House of Commons voted (for: 50; against: 26) the sum of £20,000 for the building of schools under the aegis of the two societies. This sum was in the region of one-twentieth of the Prussian government's annual grant to education[27] and was reckoned to be equivalent to half the yearly cost of maintaining the King's stables.[28] But the grant marked the beginning of the state's commitment to educational provision, and despite the opposition to the measure, there was to be no going back. 'That the vote would lead to some all-pervading national system was never in doubt', as one historian has put it.[29] (By 1839 the sum had been raised to £30,000.)

The sum was to be disbursed through both the National Society and the British and Foreign Schools Society. An attempt in Parliament on 30 July 1833 by the Radical John Arthur Roebuck (1801–79) to gain approval for measures to promote 'the universal and national education of the whole people'[30] had failed to attract support. His important speech on that occasion is, however, remarkably prescient of what eventually was to be the shape of the education system in England; he 'offered proposals which stand out from the hesitant and limited conceptions of the time'.[31]

Roebuck sought to define education as extending far beyond simply learning to read and write and perhaps to manage a little arithmetic:

> Education means not merely the conferring [of the] necessary means or instruments for the acquiring of knowledge, but it means also the so training or fashioning the intellectual and moral qualities of the individual, that he may be able and willing to acquire knowledge, and to turn it to its right use. It means the so framing the mind of the individual, that he may become a useful and virtuous member of society in the various relations of life. It means making him a good child, a good parent, a good neighbour, a good citizen, in short, a good man. All these he cannot be without knowledge, but neither will

the mere acquisition of knowledge confer on him these qualities; his moral, as well as his intellectual powers, must contribute to this great end, and the true fashioning of these to this purpose is right education.[32]

He dismissed the assertion that 'men will wish to leave their actual station, and be unfitted for the common duties of life, by being taught to long for a higher and more luxurious condition'[33] on the grounds that if all were educated all would be alike and therefore no distinction would be apparent that would cause a desire for particular privilege.

Early in the speech Roebuck mentions Victor Cousin's report and the Prussian example:

In Prussia and in Saxony a more complete system of public instruction is now in operation than has ever yet had place in any nation of the world.[34]

It was remarkable that the French government had looked to Prussia when considering its own reforms:

Speaking of these two nations, with respect to their systems of education. Professor Cousin pointedly observes — "I consider France and Prussia the two most enlightened countries in Europe — the most advanced in letters and in science — the two most truly civilized, without excepting England herself — all bristling with prejudices, Gothic institutions, and semi-barbarous customs over which there is awkwardly thrown the mantle d'une civilisation toute matérielle." I cannot pass this work of Professor Cousin, without pointing out, as an example to our own Government, the circumstances which produced this admirable work. The French Government, desirous of framing a law on this all-important subject, and not being too proud to learn from the experience of others, sent one of its most renowned philosophers to make inquiries on the subject. It sent him, too, into a State to which the people of France are peculiarly hostile — namely, Prussia; thus showing that idle prejudices could not divert them from the path which wisdom pointed out.

Roebuck covers the content of education, the means by which it should be delivered, and the regulatory authority necessary. Provision in Prussia is mentioned with regard to compulsory school attendance, Roebuck quoting the Prussian code as 'express[ing] pretty distinctly what I intend', and in connection with religious tolerance in education, mentioning Prussian law on the subject as providing 'a useful lesson to all people': 'Any people or Government pretending to the character of being civilized, would strictly adhere to these admirable instructions'.[35]

The £20,000 grant was made not without dissent. Among others, William Cobbett spoke in the Commons debate against the proposal. Cobbett argued that he

could not consent to take from the people one single farthing in the way of taxes, directly or indirectly, in order to teach the working classes reading and writing. He was sure he should not be accused of a wish to degrade them, or to deprive them of any advantages, but he thought the word education was much mistaken. Education was the knowledge necessary for the situation of life in which a man was placed. Take two men for instance — suppose one of them to be able to plough, and the other able to plough and make hurdles and be a good shepherd. If the first man knew how to read as well as to plough, and the other man did not know how to read, even then he should say, that the latter was the better man. Let hon. Members go into the agricultural districts and take father and son, what would they find? Why, that in almost every instance the father was the better man — he was the better labourer — he knew better how to do his work, and he was more able and more willing to do it. The Reports that were from time to time laid on the Table of the House, said that men became more and more immoral every year: those Reports must be taken to be true. Then what became of the benefits of education? for education had been more and more spread, but what did it all tend to? Nothing but to increase the number of schoolmasters and school-mistresses — that new race of idlers. Crime, too, went on increasing. If so, what reason was there to tax the people for the increase of education? It was nothing but an attempt to force education — it was a French Doctrinaire-plan, and he should always be opposed to it.[36]

These are also sentiments that proved to be persistent throughout the century, despite the many advances towards some kind of national system. They are echoed, for example, in Lord Salisbury's pronouncements in 1860 in the *Quarterly Review* and much later, when he was prime minister, in a letter to Balfour:

Though [the working man's] neighbour's child has learned the heights of all the mountains, and the length of all the rivers, and the breadth of the straits in the world, these acquirements have not helped the boy much, for he is now above his work and objects to scaring crows. (1860)[37]

Where the three Rs were enough twenty years ago, now you must have French, pianoforte playing and trigonometry; and no doubt German and astronomy will come next. Where £150 a year was sufficient for a teacher he must have £300 now: and that will not be the limit of his rewards. The educationist is one of the daughters of the horse leech: and if you let him suck according to his will, he will soon have swallowed the slender increase of sustenance you are now tendering to the Voluntary schools . . . You had much better give no grant at all, and let the money go to build an ironclad. (1896)[38]

Such fears about the dangers of educating the people would have to be overcome on the long road to the 1870 Education Act, though they clearly persisted long after.

Mrs Trollope on education in Germany

At a popular level, Frances Trollope, that prolific and controversial commentator on other countries, had visited Germany in 1833 and like others had only praise for what she discovered about education in Prussia:

In this little village, as in every other part of the kingdom of Prussia, the education of the people is the business of the state. So deeply are the benevolent and philosophical lawgivers of this enlightened country impressed with the belief that the only sure method of rendering a people pre-eminently great and happy, is to spread the light of true knowledge among them, that the government leaves not the duty of providing instruction for the children of the land to the unthinking caprice of their ignorant parents; but provides for them teachers and books; selected with a degree of vigilant circumspection which would do honour to the affection and judgment of the tenderest father. Nor is this all:- not only are the means of instruction thus amply and admirably provided, but the children of the people are not permitted to absent themselves from school on any plea except that of sickness, which must be authenticated by the certificate of a physician.[39]

The contrast Trollope makes with the situation in England highlights the shortcomings of provision:

And how is this all-important business transacted with us? In some places, a teacher is appointed by the clergyman, who would regulate his parish school with the same anxious care which he exercises in the government of his own family. In others, some vain and canting Lady Bountiful has the power of nomination, – and selects a person who shall look sharply after the uniform, and take care that the children show themselves off well, upon all public occasions.

In one village, a stanch constitutional Tory shall exert his utmost influence that the little people about him may be brought up to fear God and honour the king. He may watchfully see them led to the venerated church of their fathers, and teach them to look up, with equal love and respect, to the institutions of their country.

In the very next, perhaps, a furious demagogue may insist that every lesson shall inculcate the indefeasible right to rebel. And, if the poor rogues be taught any religion at all, it may be with the understanding that each and every of them, when they are big enough, will have as good a right to be paid for preaching as the parson of the parish.

What can that whole be, which is formed of such discordant elements? And would it not be better for our rulers even to enforce such a mode of instruction as might give a chance of something like a common national feeling among the people of England, instead of letting them be blown about with every wind of doctrine, as they are at present?[40]

Trollope's enthusiasm for Prussian education ('so prolific of the happiest results'), extended exceptionally to censorship of the press. Prussian efforts to spread 'the blessing of knowledge' could only be imitated successfully once the 'source whence it is to flow' had been purified.[41] This idiosyncratic stance contrasts with the more widely expressed view that any imitation of provision in an autocratic state which insisted on press censorship would not be desirable in England.

The Quarterly Journal of Education, 1831–5

Among the many means of informing an interested public about developments in education in other countries at this time was a significant publication that first appeared in 1831 under the auspices of the Society for the Diffusion of Useful Knowledge (SDUK), founded by Henry Brougham, Lord John Russell, and others, following discussions in 1826. This was the *Quarterly Journal of Education*. The society also produced a widely disseminated 'Library of Useful Knowledge' and, in 1832, its popular *Penny Magazine*. It published the *Penny Cyclopaedia* in 27 volumes over the period 1833–43, with two supplements appearing in 1845–6. The society stopped work in 1846.[42]

The *Quarterly Journal* was remarkable for its comprehensive coverage of matters of concern in education. And it took pains from the start to educate its readership about educational provision abroad, and in particular in the states of Germany. The introduction to the new journal spoke of the necessity of sharing knowledge among the 'factions, and parties, and sects' into which education was split, and argued for the importance of knowledge of foreign provision in education:

> Though the institutions of our own country fairly demand the greater part of our attention, it is of almost equal importance to show what is going on in foreign parts, and to introduce to early notice the improvements of Germany, France, and other continental nations.

It asked: 'How few even of the graduates of an English University can form any comparison between that system under which they have been trained, and the education of such places as Bonn or Berlin?' And it goes on to mention the desirability of examining what children and students were being taught elsewhere: 'It will often be in the power of the Committee to introduce new and useful works to the notice of British teachers, and to recommend additional branches of knowledge by showing what is taught in foreign schools and universities'.[43]

The first issue contains a summary of Adams's reporting on elementary education in his *Letters on Silesia* of 1804, together with information on the situation in Prussia and Bavaria. Other major articles followed, among them accounts of the University of Bonn (VI), 'The Origin of the Schools for the Lower Classes in Germany' (VIII), 'The Prussian System of Education: Seminaries for Teachers of the Lower Classes' (XII), 'German High Schools' (with a focus on Bonn and the *Gymnasium* curriculum) (XIV), 'Prussian Schools' (XIX), 'Origin and History of the University of Göttingen' (XX), and 'The Seminary for Schoolmasters at Königsberg in Prussia' (XX). In addition, there were routine short notices containing information culled from foreign publications, which kept readers informed about recent developments and gave statistical information of the kind increasingly provided at this point in the century for comparative purposes. The *Quarterly Journal* ceased publication in 1835.

At a more popular level, those wishing to be informed about educational issues generally and about provision in Prussia and elsewhere in particular could turn to the *Penny Cyclopaedia*. There they would find lengthy and informative articles on germane topics, including those on 'Education', on 'Schools, Primary' (25 pages) and on 'Universities'. The article on Prussia covers the usual ground:

> The Prussian government pays great attention to the diffusion of useful knowledge, and manifests equal zeal in encouraging the lowest as well as the superior institutions. For the education of the people, there are in all the towns elementary schools, Sunday and infant schools, schools for mechanics, &c.; in

fact, so much is done in this respect, that many persons complain of the too great extent and variety of things taught in these institutions.[44]

Under the heading 'Schools, Primary', comparisons are made with English provision and, not surprisingly for a publication under the aegis of the SDUK, the practical nature of educational provision at all levels in Prussia is emphasised:

> The advantages which the people derive from the Prussian system arise not only from the large amount of knowledge which is diffused, but also from the circumstance that a portion of this knowledge has reference to the future pursuits of the pupils. In the system of instruction in this country, the latter object is hardly ever kept in view, and the education given in British schools in general has no reference to actual life. In Prussia parents choose a school for their children, with a view to prepare them for the pursuits which are to form their future occupation.[45]

This is true also of the universities: 'The government has erected and maintains the universities for the purpose of giving an opportunity to all persons of acquiring the requisite knowledge for the performance of the duties incident to the various branches of administration'.[46]

The article also covers in detail the arrangements in place for the training of teachers: 'It is certain that the advantages which the Prussian schools have over similar institutions in this country, are mainly owing to the teachers having been trained for the business, and to the circumstance of their devoting their labours to the same school for twenty or thirty years'.[47] Provision for the regulated training of teachers was to remain on the reform agenda in England.

Select committee on the State of Education (1834)

That there was sustained interest in education in Germany at a high level and at an early and significant date in England is further shown by an investigation of a Select Committee of the House of Commons, chaired by the then Paymaster-General in the Whig government, Lord John Russell (1792–1878; later to be prime minister), on the *State of Education*. Roebuck had proposed the setting-up of a Select Committee to look into ways in which a national system of education might be established; instead the government opted to investigate the prevailing condition of education.[48] The committee's report was published in 1834, the year following the first vote of public funds to education.[49]

The evidence taken by the committee includes much reference to Germany (and especially to Prussia), and it is presented in the form of presumably near verbatim questions and answers, so that we can gain not only a clear idea of the kind of topics the committee was interested in but also something of the tone of the inquiry.

James Pillans (1778–1864), one-time headmaster of the Old School in Edinburgh and Professor of Humanity and Laws at Edinburgh University – who was known as a defender of the notion of compulsory schooling – was interviewed on 18 June 1834 and asked about compulsory school attendance:

> Have you made any observations with respect to France and Prussia [. . .], whether education is very much prized, or whether it is necessary to force and

compel parents to send their children to school?
- I should say that the law in Prussia, and not in Prussia only, but in Austria and all over Germany, is quite imperative upon that subject, but the necessity for enforcing it is very small; the people are thoroughly imbued in Germany with the principle that their children must go to school, and that regulation which looks so severe and compulsory scarcely requires to be put in execution, because the checks upon any man neglecting its provisions are so great. [. . .]

In what you have said of Germany do you speak of the Catholic parts of Germany as well as the Protestant?
- Yes; in Germany it goes down to the lowest class of both regions.

Have you been able to form an opinion whether the habit in Germany is one of old date, or whether it has been created by laws giving advantages to education and showing the benefits to be derived from it?
- I should rather say it was of late growth; I think the great law which is now in operation is as late as the year 1819 in Prussia, but I would by no means be understood to say that it then began. This was only an amendment of a former law; the practice of the general education of the people in the German States generally is much older than that.[50]

The interview with Dr Nicholas Henry (Nicolaus Heinrich) Julius of Berlin (1783–1862), a campaigner on social and prison reform who had run a journal on popular education and who was later (in 1834) to speak on education in Prussia before the committee on education of the Massachusetts legislature, contains the following exchanges, developing the committee's interest in the notion of compulsory school attendance:

What is the penalty on parents for not sending their children to school?
- To pay a fine, or they are sent to prison.

Is this penalty often inflicted?
- No, it is not often; I have seen it in visiting the prisons, in some provinces more, in some less.

What is the amount of the fine imposed?
- I am not quite certain.

Is this system agreeable to the parents generally?
- I do not know that I can say that it is in general agreeable, and that there is very little opposition.

Are they induced to send their children to school more from the fear of the penalty or the wish that they should be instructed?
- I believe as to the larger part by the desire to see them instructed.

This desire to send their children to school is engrafted on their ancient habits?
- Yes, it is.[51]

In his evidence to the committee, Lord Brougham, then Lord Chancellor, opposed compulsion, referring specifically to Prussia:

Do you consider that a compulsory education would be justified, either on principles of public utility or expedience?
- I am decidedly of opinion that it is justifiable upon neither; but, above all,

I should regard any thing of the kind as utterly destructive of the end it
has in view. Suppose the people of England were taught to bear it, and to
be forced to educate their children by penalties, education would be made
absolutely hateful in their eyes, and would speedily cease to be endured.
Those who have argued in favour of such a scheme from the example of
a military government like that of Prussia, have betrayed, in my opinion,
great ignorance of the nature of Englishmen.[52]

Elsewhere in the report the superiority of education in Germany is made very
clear by another witness (William Davis, who ran a school in Whitechapel on
Bell's system):

Are you of opinion that it is exceedingly desirable that a more extended system
of education should be established?
-   Yes, if possible.
    And that with that system of education a system of employment should be
combined, so as to give children useful habits?
-   Yes; perhaps it may not be irrelevant to observe I have known much about
    foreigners of the lowest class, who have come to England for employment,
    and I have scarcely known an instance where one of them (Germans) could
    not write his name and read his Bible.
    You mean to say that there is a much larger proportion of foreigners than
of English who can do that?
-   I have scarcely found one in my own experience, among many hundreds
    whom I have known, who could not read and write.
    Are the class of foreigners with whom you have been conversant as low as
those in this country whom you have known?
-   They come from the class of peasantry of their own country, and are here
    chiefly labourers to the sugar refiners.
    Have you found the German sugar bakers who have come to this country
better educated than men of similar stations of life, and similar occupations
in this country?
-   I should think upon the whole they are better educated.[53]

Nipperdey reminds us that what he calls the 'Prussian-German example' is
surprising and somewhat paradoxical: 'Here is a case where an authoritarian,
non-democratic state itself introduced the modern, potentially revolutionary,
elementary school system'.[54] This point was not lost on many British observers
with interest in education in Prussia. Here is an account from 1838:

It is not [. . .] of the good old parochial system of Scotland [. . .] that the
advocates of national education are enamoured. Prussia, it seems, has, in this
particular, taken the lead of all the countries of Europe; and, according to
the Prussian model, it has become fashionable to desire that the machinery
for instruction in this country shall be framed. There is something pre-
eminently ludicrous in this idea. Why, there is no government in Europe [. . .]
half so despotic as the Prussian. People do everything in Prussia by word of
command. [. . .] Is this the country of whose institutions the Liberal party
have become admirers? No; it is only the plan of education which is acted

on in Prussia that has found favour in these gentlemen's eyes – it is only in this particular that they could wish Prussia to be by England imitated. [. . .] [T]hough we are far from denying that there is a great deal about it that is excellent, we cannot conceal our astonishment that ever it should find in England patrons where it does – among the sworn enemies of arbitrary power; except, perhaps, the power of what is called the people.[55]

While this was undoubtedly a view held by some, others could see the disadvantages of not following the German example. The Member of Parliament for Waterford, Henry Winston Barron (1795–1872), for example, visited schools and universities in Holland and Germany in the summer of 1839 and reported in concise detail and with great enthusiasm on what he observed. He makes a bold attempt at quantifying attendance at schools:

> The number of children frequenting the primary schools is 2,235,359; of these, 1,159,439 are boys, and 1,075,925 are girls [sic]. This gives an average for the entire population of 1 in 6 actually attending school, which is far higher than most other nations in Europe; and, if correct data could be procured in England, I am afraid would double the attendance there.[56]

And, in rather convoluted fashion, he attempts a similar quantification of university attendance:

> The whole of the universities admit persons of every religious profession without distinction. There is an average attendance at these institutions of about 5,500 students, including foreigners; of natives, 4,700; which makes an average, in round numbers, of one person in Prussia out of 2,885 attending the universities; and it is calculated that one person of every hundred is a man in his twentieth year, this would give for all Prussia 135,000 persons of twenty years of age; and if we divide the number of students, 4,700, into this, we have 28 and a fraction. This would prove, if all the students were twenty years of age, that 1 out of 28 and a fraction were educated at the universities; but only two-sevenths of the students are of this age, therefore we must multiply by seven and divide by two, which yields 99 and a fraction; so that we can safely say that one man out of every one hundred passes through the universities of Prussia.[57]

Other observations by Barron are of interest. He vents his fury over the stranglehold of religious conformity on the English universities:

> Even in that strictly Catholic country, Austria, we see a Protestant theological faculty established in the University of Vienna. Whilst, to the shame of England be it told, that to this day her two great universities are practically closed even to a Protestant dissenter, and still more to a Roman Catholic, though these seats of learning were founded by Catholics. Here is a monopoly worse than any of those against which our ancestors fought, existing as a stain on the fair fame of England before the whole learned world, a disgrace to the nation, and a just subject of reproach by the civilized portion of mankind. England, that prides herself on her liberality, on her free institutions, excluding more than one-third of her subjects from the benefits of her national universities,

and leaving so large a portion of her people dependant for their education on the eleemosynary contributions of the philanthropist, or forcing them to fly their own country, and seek in Catholic France or Protestant Germany the advantages that are denied them at home.

Why not follow the example held out by Prussia, by Holland, and other Protestant states? Even Hanover has far outstripped her in true liberality and sound policy on this most important of all national subjects.

Both Catholic and Protestant states have vied with each other in improving the educational institutions of the people, whilst England (though far behind other countries) still makes this sacred question one of party contention, and generations are passing away in ignorance, whilst we are contending whether Catholics and Dissenters are to be forced to adopt books and forms that their contentious scruples will not permit them to use. How contrary to the spirit of Protestantism as set forth in the writers and founders of the faith! Freedom of thought, of opinion, was their doctrine; but in England now-a-days all must be instructed in the forms agreeable to the established church, or receive no education at all. Is this the liberty our ancestors contended for? This is odious tyranny in its most odious, and dangerous, and mischievous form. Talk of Papal tyranny! Why this is civil and religious tyranny of a dominant church in its worst of guises.[58]

And he concludes his observations with a passionate plea:

The few notes I have here penned were intended for my own private use and reference, at a time when education occupies so much attention, and when so many bad passions have been excited, and dangers have been anticipated and exaggerated from the attempt to give all classes in England the benefit of the same system that has wrought so much good in other states. I thought it a duty to see with my own eyes and hear with my own ears, what the results were in other states; and I can say, with a safe conscience, that I have discovered in no one instance any bad or dangerous consequences flowing from the enlarged and liberal system followed in the various states that I travelled through. I took great pains to inquire and satisfy my mind: I consulted men of all shades of opinion on other subjects, but I found them to agree on this, that marked improvement has taken place in the condition and habits of the people wherever a systematic education has been adopted by the government, embracing persons of every religion without distinction. By it religious animosities have been softened down, and in many instances, particularly in Wurtemburg and Holland, almost entirely obliterated; and in all instances, the condition and moral feeling of the people have been highly improved. In no one instance could I learn that either discontent or immorality had increased by the spread of education and an improved system. [. . .] I am far from thinking that perfection is found in any one of the states I here allude to; but I am satisfied that England has much yet to learn from many of her neighbours, and that he is her worst enemy who flatters her national vanity with the idea that other nations and their institutions are to be despised.[59]

Barron's work was to be read and used by others making comparisons with education in Germany, among them William Edward Hickson in his 1840 account of Dutch and German schools.

Publications of the Central Society of Education

The Central Society of Education, established in 1836 in opposition to the monitorial system and to the centrality of religion in education, published a series of papers which included accounts of education in other countries. A paper in the 1837 volume was concerned with elementary education in Prussia; in 1838 there was coverage of 'seminars for schoolmasters for the working classes' in Prussia; and there was a report by Thomas Wyse MP (1791–1862) on the state of education in Prussia in the publication of 1839.[60]

Wyse's account is of particular interest since it entails a detailed analysis of Prussian provision designed to counter popular notions of centralisation and government control of education:

The "New System", "the Prussian System", "the Government System", these are the appellations with which the system is honoured:- the object is clear: they are intended to mean "dangerous innovation', "foreign despotism", "ministerial interference with civil and religious liberty". And yet it is none of all these things. The system supposed to be so "new" began [. . .] as early as 1730. It is now the *old* law; the *old* system; the "custom of the land", to which the whole of the past and present generation have been born. The system supposed to be so peculiarly "Prussian", is German; and not only German, but, with the exception of England, European; nay, portions of it are to be found at the other side of the Atlantic. The system supposed to be so peculiarly "Government", is quite as much "Communal"; that is, as much managed by the people as by the State, – as much by the local as by the central power. It is to be met with in various climates, under various governments, and amidst various creeds: north and south, east and west; in monarchies, in republics; in countries solely inhabited by Protestants, solely by Catholics; and in countries inhabited by both. Prussia, so far from being the exception to the general rule, *is* the general rule. So far from "Prussian" being the proper designation, the proper designation is "Continental", as contradistinguished to English; in other words as *the system*, contradistinguished to the *no-system* of this country.[61]

Wyse describes the 'long series of authorities between the State and the school' in order to demonstrate that 'there is much less centralization in the system than is usually imagined':

1. The Council of Public Instruction, a department of the ministry, headed by a responsible officer of the Crown, representing directly the authority of the State.
2. The Provincial Consistory, an intermediate authority, representing the Church.
3. The School Commissioners, or Council of the Circle [*Kreis*], a large local authority.
4. The School Commissioners, or Council of the Commune, or a small local authority, both representing in greater or lesser mass the people.[62]

In the same vein he addresses the question of compulsory school attendance:

The Continent holds that the citizen should, by religious and moral training, by exercise and improvement of his whole nature, by knowledge and experience, be fitted to bear his part in the great family, not only to his own advantage but to that of his fellows. The Continent thinks that, for this end, means should be employed: she prepares, she offers, she gives, she enforces education. This enforcement is of various application – of various character. Sometimes it is limited to inducements only. In some States education is made a condition for admission, not only to honours and emoluments, but to rights and franchises. Some States proceed farther; and, leaving nothing to contingency, prescribe rather than invite; holding no one at liberty to remain irreligious, immoral, or ignorant. In other instances, again, the two processes are combined. Such is the case in most of the German communities.[63]

But despite his calculated defence of the system in operation in the German states, Wyse was not inclined to recommend something similar for England: 'A system may be good, and yet not good for us; or good for us, and yet not good for us at the present moment':

We are too much divided by sect and party, too suspicious of each other, too little impressed with the influence of education upon society, too insensible of the necessity of making it universal in order to make it really efficient, to suffer the introduction of a compulsory system on the German plan, however indirect or mitigated, amongst us.[64]

His intention was to challenge exaggeration, 'to measure Germany by German habits and reasonings', to show that the principles underlying education in Germany were not 'unreasonable' and that their application was not 'tyrannical'. And he shows, through a detailed account of the historical development of education from the *Principia Regulativa* of 1736 onwards, that he had a profound knowledge of his subject. Wyse is known for his *Education Reform, or, The Necessity of a National System of Education* of 1836, and for arguing (unsuccessfully) in a Commons debate in 1837 for the creation of a board of education.[65] Despite that failure, he counts as one of the more influential reform-minded politicians of his generation, as far as education was concerned, and his account of education in Prussia served to counter the arguments of those who saw dire dangers in any emulation of German approaches to education.

Committee of Council on Education (1839)

A further step towards state involvement in education can be seen in the formation of the Committee of the Privy Council on Education in 1839. The Home Secretary of the day, Lord John Russell, wrote to the Lord President of the Council indicating the Queen's concern at 'the want of instruction which is still observable among the poorer classes of Her subjects. All the inquiries which have been made show a deficiency in the general Education of the People which is not in accordance with the character of a Civilized and Christian Nation'.[66] But there was still considerable distrust of state involvement: 'It was often contended that to place popular education in the hands of the State was to introduce "Prussianism", and to take it out of the hands of the Church was to open the door to Continental licence and infidelity'.[67]

The grant of government money was to be increased to £30,000 and schools were to be inspected. Russell had also proposed the establishment of a 'normal school', 'where the young of the Established Church and of various religious sects should be educated together',[68] but this idea provoked virulent reaction.

The first school inspectors were appointed by Lord John Russell in 1839.[69] Some twelve years later the scion of nineteenth-century inspectors, Matthew Arnold, was recruited to their ranks and was to hold the post for thirty-five years.

Now that government money was being spent on education, it was considered desirable that the way it was being used should be monitored:

> Some itinerant scrutiny was needed, on a small scale, and who more suitable than a pair of shrewd and well-educated gentlemen, one a clergyman and one a layman?[70]

The phrase 'shrewd and well-educated gentlemen' is one that has a certain resonance. Percy Wilson, Senior Chief Inspector of Schools from 1957 to 1965, recalled that the early inspectors had been dubbed 'Lord John Russell's bashaws', and that this description was 'good and not discreditable'.[71] (A 'bashaw' is defined by the *Oxford English Dictionary* as 'a grandee, a haughty imperious man', and this might not quite convey the image Wilson had in mind.) The inspectors were clearly to be of considerable stature, and their duties would require them to be fair and circumspect in their judgements.[72] They were appointed only after rigorous vetting procedures.

The duties of the early inspectors were defined in a minute of the Committee of Council on Education in August 1840. Maclure[73] describes their instructions as 'notable for the modesty of the aims set forth and for the limits of the functions of the HMI'. Here is an extract:

> The inspection of schools aided by public grants is . . . a means of co-operation between the Government and the committees and superintendents of schools, by which information respecting all remarkable improvements may be diffused whenever it is sought; . . . you are in no respect to interfere with the instruction, management or discipline of the school, or to press upon them any suggestions which they may be disinclined to receive.
>
> A clear and comprehensive view of these main duties of your office is at all times important; but when a system of inspection of schools, aided by public grants, is for the first time brought into operation, it is of the utmost consequence you should bear in mind that this inspection is not intended as a means of exercising control, but of affording assistance; that it is not to be regarded as operating for the restraint of local efforts, but for their encouragement; and that its chief objects will not be attained without the co-operation of the school committees – the Inspector having no power to interfere, and not being instructed to offer any advice or information excepting where it is invited.[74]

These instructions reflect the perennial problem in the nineteenth century of coming to terms with the notion of any kind of state involvement in school provision, but they established some principles for inspection which were to hold true until quite recent times, especially in terms of non-interference, assistance, and encouragement. Clearly the early functions of the Inspectorate had principally to do with their role, as Sir William Pile (one-time Permanent Under-Secretary of State at the Department of Education and Science) puts it, as 'watchdogs'.[75]

In 1839 there appeared a report entitled *Recent Measures for the Promotion of Education in England*; its author was James Phillips Kay (1804–77). (Kay changed his name, following his marriage in 1842, to Kay-Shuttleworth, by which he is generally known, and was the first Secretary of the Committee of Council.) In the report's pages there is much reference to educational provision in other countries, Switzerland, France, Holland and Denmark among them, but there is considerable space devoted to Prussia.

The report quotes from Adams's *Letters from Silesia* to underline the early progress in education made under Frederick the Great, and it lists the measures taken in the eighteenth century, many of which would have bearing on issues under consideration in England:

> Prussia, as early as 1736, declared the elementary education of the people to be an essential part of the policy of the state. In that year she provided for the erection and repair of school-houses by the communes; regulated the duties and privileges of the teachers; appropriated portions of the church revenues to the provision of their salaries; and provided from the public funds means to meet the contingent expenses of the schools. The law underwent successive improvements in the years 1763 and 1765. These edicts also provided for the inspection and due regulation of the schools; for the transmission of reports to the Government; for the examination of teachers by the school inspectors, and for the elevation of some of the principal schools of the newly acquired territory of Silesia to the character of Normal Schools.[76]

There is also quotation from a report in the *Quarterly Journal of Education* on elementary education, which in turn draws upon Adams's early account of provision in Silesia. Such multiple cross-referencing over time is a feature of the ways in which the German example in education was repeatedly kept in the public eye during the nineteenth century. The frequent citings of the work of Victor Cousin would be another case in point, as too would be reference to Matthew Arnold's accounts of education in Germany. We shall consider below a substantial work by Kay-Shuttleworth's younger brother, Joseph Kay, on the education of the poor which drew heavily – and very positively – on the German example.

In September 1847 Kay-Shuttleworth, in a letter to Palmerston, asked for the collection of statistical data from Prussia, other parts of Germany, and elsewhere, reporting that the Committee of Council on Education had recently appointed an officer 'to collect and arrange Statistical information respecting public education'.[77]

William Dyce on schools of design (1840)

In 1840 there was published what must count as one of the very earliest officially sanctioned reports in England on particular aspects of education in other countries, anticipating the work undertaken by Michael Sadler's Office of Special Inquiries and Reports at the end of the century and the series of HMI studies that began to be published from the mid-1980s. This report, by the distinguished Scottish artist William Dyce (1806–64), Superintendent of the Government

School of Design, was concerned with 'schools of design' in Prussia, Bavaria, and France and was made to the President of the Board of Trade. The *raison d'être* of the inquiry lay in concern about competition from continental commerce and industry, a concern that was to increase in importance in the coming decades.

At the beginning of his report Dyce raises issues which others undertaking such inquiries – Matthew Arnold later in the century, for example – would have to confront:

> It is true that, complying with the letter of my instructions, I might have confined my inquiries to the internal organization merely of the schools you directed me particularly to visit; but it appeared to me, that even to render details of this kind available to your purpose, much collateral information was indispensable, of a kind which it could hardly be reckoned my business to seek for. It was necessary to view the subject of inquiry commercially as well as artistically; to consider the manufacturing and commercial conditions of the countries where schools are located, as well as the schools themselves, which it may be supposed have been intended to meet certain exigencies of industry; and this, not only to show the applicability of the means of instruction to the particular exigency of the case, but to examine what kind of influence is exerted by schools of art; or whether (and this is not an idle question) they, by themselves alone, confer the great and palpable benefits on manufactures which it has of late been so much the fashion in this country to ascribe to them.[78]

Here Dyce shows awareness of the centrality of context in such inquiries, as well as being concerned to explore the relationship between a particular type of institution and competitive economic success. In the concluding section of his report, he poses the question:

> Do the foreign schools, either singly, present a model which it might be safe to follow in organizing the Government one at Somerset-house; or collectively, do they exhibit any common character or principle which would seem to determine the precise character of the instruction which is required for the education of designers for manufacture?[79]

An account of Dutch and German schools by the educationist William Edward Hickson (1803–70), also published in 1840, was written, according to its subtitle, 'with a view to the practical steps which should be taken for improving and extending the means of popular instruction in Great Britain and Ireland'.[80] Hickson is enthusiastic about what he observed in Germany, and reports in detail (quoting liberally from Barron's text) on many aspects of educational provision, but he is cautious about the readiness in his home country to adopt some of its most prominent features. His account is structured around these overlapping questions:

'Educational administrative organization'
'How far the organization of schools, and the instruction communicated in them, should be dependent upon government?'
'Compulsory education'
'How far the state or the central authority should interfere with secular

instruction: prescribing either its extent, or the methods that should be employed'

Hickson doubts whether local authorities in England should be granted further powers to establish schools 'until education is somewhat better understood than at present. Let us, rather than multiply bad schools, wait til the want of something better is more generally felt; more progress will then be made in one year than we could now make in ten'.[81]

As to interference on the part of government, Hickson distinguishes between 'advice and example' and 'compulsory regulations': 'It is impossible to imagine what mischief could result from a government normal school, or school for the training of teachers, provided existing schools, or school committees, have the option left them of accepting, or rejecting, those teachers as they please'.[82] On compulsory school attendance he notes that even in Prussia it is difficult to enforce the law as far as rural communities are concerned:

> [The] obligation to attend school is binding from the time the child has arrived at the age of five years till it has reached fourteen, but it is not enforced till the age of seven. We were anxious to learn whether the law was really acted upon or remained practically un-enforced. We found that like other laws which require, as all laws do, the support of public opinion, it is found difficult to put in execution in the rural districts, and especially in those provinces where the Prussians are new masters, and where the grown-up generation are unable to appreciate the advantages of education.[83]

There is discussion of school choice which has resonance for problems which still exist in England today, real choice being a chimera for many families:

> [W]e would not advocate the adoption of the Prussian law, although perhaps we would adopt the principle in a less objectionable form. The Prussian law, it has been observed, leaves the parent the choice of schools; but practically the parent must send the child to one or other of those which exist in the neighbourhood, whether bad or good; and from our experience of the kind of schools which have hitherto been provided for the working classes of England, we do not believe that there is one in a thousand in which a child can profitably employ seven consecutive years of its life. After a sharp and intelligent boy has been taught to read and write, it is even mischievous to keep him shut up in a school in which nothing but reading and writing are taught.[84]
>
> It will be time enough to adopt the Prussian law, when in every parish in England there are schools, and a sufficient number of them, in which instruction shall be given of a character to deserve the name of education; till then our wisest course is to insist upon one only of the two things which we now find are by no means inseparably connected – education, and school attendance. Let us abandon the attempt to enforce attendance at school for any term of hours or years – but let no parent or employer of labour be allowed to make a profit by the labour of a child, until that child has received, either at home or at school, a certain amount of instruction.[85]

On secular instruction Hickson is clear that giving the government power over methods and content would be 'extremely injudicious':

Enough may be done by the force of example, and by training teachers upon the best methods, to render any such power unnecessary, even if it were not certain to encounter that popular jealousy which would soon be fatal to its existence.[86]

He argues for an increase in the number of trained teachers, seeing the Bell and Lancaster system as the only way to instruct 500 or 1,000 children with just one teacher. That system, tried in Holland and Germany, had been 'universally repudiated' there. In the poorer schools in those countries there was one teacher to every sixty children; a Prussian village 'never' has more than 100 pupils to a teacher; 'we visited many schools for children of the middle class, in which we found one teacher to every thirty scholars'.[87]

Part II of Hickson's study deals with physical education, religious and moral instruction, 'intellectual cultivation', and industrial training, and it shows much familiarity with the practicalities of teaching. Indeed, the principal strength of Hickson's report lies mainly in its pragmatic approach to a series of questions still at the heart of the educational debate in England towards the middle of the century. Enthusiasm for the Prussian model is not exaggerated; the lessons to be learnt from Germany are seen against what is deemed feasible in the English context.

We have noted above the enthusiastic account of education in Germany from the pen of Fanny Trollope: two further mid-century popular writers, William Howitt and Henry Mayhew, are worth mentioning, since they both devoted considerable space to education in their various books on Germany.

William Howitt

William Howitt (1792–1897) was a dabbler in many fields, pharmacy, politics, language study, publishing, spiritualism and animal welfare among them – and he travelled widely. In 1840 he moved for three years to Heidelberg[88] 'for the sake of his children's education'.[89] Based on his experiences in Germany he wrote three substantial books in which educational description figured prominently: *The Student-Life of Germany* appeared in 1841, and this was followed in 1842 by *The Rural and Domestic Life of Germany* and in 1844 by *German Experiences*. The first of these was written as if 'from the unpublished MS of Dr Cornelius', presumably for the sake of authenticity and a slight distancing from the more exotic descriptions the work contains of various aspects of German student life, guaranteed to shock or titillate a sober-minded Victorian audience.

'No country has so many and such excellent universities as Germany,' says Howitt, 'and the proofs of their advantages exist in the great number of illustrious learned men and authors, which quench their thirst of knowledge at these immortal wells of science; men, whose creations daily more and more receive abroad their just recognition, and in no country more than in England'.[90] This, unfortunately, comes at the end of a book devoted for the most part to descriptions of the excesses of university life in Germany. One British traveller had once written mysteriously of 'that *order* which pervades every thing in Germany – matrimony and the universities excepted',[91] and it is from Howitt that we can appreciate precisely what might have been meant by such a remark. He takes pleasure in describing in the closest detail the customs and traditions of the various clubs, societies and fraternities, emphasising the drinking songs, ceremonies and routines, and the practice of duelling. There is very little on the wider context of education, but one chapter – on the 'General System of German Education', attempts an historical analysis and concludes 'that Germany bears away the crown of school economy from all other countries, is not to be denied'; what is more, 'Germany propels at the highest speed its people towards intellectual consciousness. It possesses a moral vigour which no other nation of the earth possesses, and the giant arms of German art and science embrace the whole surface of the globe with an all-living power'.[92] This is surely hyperbole – but it is indicative of the growing interest in what had been achieved in basic educational provision in Germany, in contrast to the slow progress in England. *The Student-Life of Germany* clearly focuses on the exotic; Howitt's later works are rather more developed.

His most interesting thoughts on education in Germany are contained in his third book with a German theme, *German Experiences*. Here we see a revealing stance on the undesirability of any state control of education in England, particularly in respect of the working class; and we see too Howitt's view that the Prussian system of popular education could have little effect, since there was, he argues, no freedom of expression possible in Germany. This did not mean, however, that Howitt felt that an education which would allow the masses to articulate their views would be desirable; on the contrary, he regarded this as a very dangerous proposition. 'Before I went to Germany,' he writes, 'when I heard of the King of Prussia establishing a system of universal popular education, I thought he must be mad, or dreadfully short-sighted'.[93] And though he castigates the influential Scottish writer Samuel Laing (1780–1868) for some misinformation on student life in Germany – 'these are the mistakes of a *traveller*,' he says; had Laing been a resident like himself such errors would have been avoided – he quotes approvingly a passage in which these views are reinforced. Laing had written: 'Who could suppose while reading pamphlets, reviews, and literary articles out of number on national education, and on the beautiful system, means, and arrangements adopted by Prussia for educating the people, and while lost in admiration in the educational labyrinth of country schools and town schools – common schools and high schools – real schools and classical schools – gymnasia – progymnasia – normal schools – seminariums – universities – who could suppose that with all this education, no use of education is allowed – that while reading and writing are enforced upon all, thinking and the communication of thoughts are prevented by an arbitrary censorship of the press [. . .]?'[94] Another contemporary writer, Robert Vaughan, could write of education in Prussia: 'We do not scruple to say, that we look with much misgiving on the Prussian education system, and that we do so in part, on account of the relation in which it stands to a scheme of government which has superseded all liberty, civil and religious'.[95]

The German system, Howitt argues, 'would fall into the minds of our working classes, not like an additional drowsiness on a drowsy generation, but like a spark into a train of gunpowder'.[96] Small wonder, then, that England lay so far behind Germany in the provision of basic education, if observers like Howitt saw so much danger in government intervention. 'It was rung from side to side of the island,' he writes, 'that Germany is outstripping us in the race of knowledge; that the flame was spreading, and would spread, all over the continent; that we were the last in the race of nations; and that our neglect of the *people* in the matter of information was a national disgrace'[97]. But desirable as the education of the working class might prove to be, it was to be the people themselves rather than government that should provide it: 'A GOVERNMENT EDUCATION of the people of England will never be obtained'.[98] 'The free spirit of England and private interests will never permit government here, as in Germany, to take charge of, regulate, and enforce the education of *every* class of the community';[99] 'A NATIONAL EDUCATION in England MUST PROCEED SOLELY FROM THE NATION. [. . .] A NATIONAL EDUCATION must be carefully contra-distinguished from a GOVERNMENT EDUCATION. Yes, the education of the people must come, as all our other institutions have come, *from the people*'.[100] It could be argued that Howitt was right; we have avoided speaking of 'state' schools in England, preferring to refer to those schools under the control of local education authorities as 'maintained schools', and there has of course been a long tradition of diversity of provision by the churches and the local councils. But for all that Howitt could see advantages in the diversity of strictly non-government provision, others could identify the dangers of the narrow sectarianism evident in the church schools. Friedrich Engels's *The Condition of the Working-Class in England in 1844* describes the situation in the year Howitt's book appeared, and there we can read that 'the bourgeoisie has little to hope, and much to fear, from the education of the working-class' and that 'each [sect] would gladly grant the workers the otherwise dangerous education on the sole condition of their accepting, as an antidote, the dogmas peculiar to the especial sect in question'.[101]

On a more positive note, however, Howitt saw some advantage in the educa-tion of the class of people just above the working classes: 'The shop and humble citizen class make good use of their schools. They are the only class in Germany which could be said to be better educated than the parallel class in England; and it is principally amongst this class that the spirit of more active trade, of manufacturing, and of political liberty appears. Everywhere I have found this class extremely well informed, full of zeal for liberty, and of personal integrity'.[102] With the increasing trade rivalry between the two nations, such attention to the education of a significant group of providers of wealth and prosperity grew, with Michael Sadler referring during the First World War to Germany's endeavours not to neglect what he called 'second rate intelligence'.[103]

Howitt's work of 1844 is something of a polemic, but it is based on direct expe-rience and intimate knowledge, and it is also important as an early attempt at comparison – 'What is really the comparative state of *real* education between the working classes of Germany and our own?', he asks.[104] And he seeks genuinely to learn lessons and to look for the possibility of transfer of ideas or for reasons for not emulating a foreign example. Chapter X is entitled: 'How Would the Prussian System of Popular Education Operate in England?'

Henry Mayhew

Henry Mayhew (1812–87) is remembered principally for his widely read works on the poor of London. He exemplified a form of what has been called 'philan-thropic journalism', with the poor as its focus, which was much in vogue around the middle of the century and which gained impetus through the phenomenally popular writings of the novelist Charles Dickens. He developed his expertise in this area to such an extent that he can be counted as a pioneering sociological observer.

Mayhew lived abroad for a time, writing *The Lower Rhine* in 1856 and *The Upper Rhine* in 1857. In 1862 he lived in Eisenach and Jena, mainly to research the early life of Luther, and as a result he wrote a substantial work devoted to Germany, *German Life and Manners* (1864).

In *The Upper Rhine* he had written satirically about the supposed superior classical education of the ordinary German:

> "'Every baker in Germany,' said [. . .] Mr Cobden, "can serve you with bread in Latin, as well as his own language."
>
> Now this was intended to give the English people a sense of the high state of education prevalent throughout Germany. [. . .]
>
> The statement is, however, simply untrue. "*Salve, magister*," we said to the *Deutscher* who brought our batch of "*milch brodchens*" [sic] (milk breadlets) [. . .].
>
> The "*Bäcker*" threw up his floury eyebrows and shook his head as he answered, "*Ich verstehe nicht Englische*" [sic]. [. . .]
>
> Moreover, when we spoke to the Germans themselves as to the classical acquirements of their butchers and bakers, they laughed'.[105]

This – for all that it is interesting as an *aperçu* on the wisdom of the day – would place Mayhew firmly in the travellers' tales category of early accounts of Germany. (The inaccurate German is as in the original.) But in his more developed work of 1864 Mayhew devotes much closer attention to analysis of education in Saxony. (Saxony, incidentally, had been singled out by Horace Mann, Secretary of the Massachusetts State Board of Education, as standing – together mainly with Prussia – 'foremost in the education of the people'.)[106]

Mayhew devotes four chapters to schools, and his emphasis is firmly on practical aspects of the educational provision he observed. In the first he praises the free and open access to the schools in Eisenach training those who wished to become schoolmasters: 'in this [. . .] respect, [. . .] the Germans are far ahead of our own countrymen.'[107] He makes a nice distinction between the *Gymnasium* and the *Realgymnasium*: 'the one [is] more *nominalistic* in its character, dealing with words and languages rather than things; and the other principally *realistic* in its objects, attending more to the study of things than the words which stand for them'.[108] He does basic calculations of costs, is astounded at how cheap one Kindergarten in the town could be (he says the equivalent of a twelfth of a farthing per week!), lists curriculum content, details of examinations and holidays, etc., and attempts some crude comparisons with England, concluding – remarkably and on the basis of his own prejudice alone – that 'despite all this education, we are satisfied that an English mechanic, who can just manage to read his Sunday newspaper, is a more handy, a more inventive, and a more worldly-wise man than the most learned German professor we ever encountered in the Thuringian capital'.[109]

Mayhew's next two chapters are concerned with the 'currend' school, deriving from his interest in Martin Luther, and to the *Forstschule* (school of forestry), which he describes in considerable and critical detail. He turns next to university life, and in five chapters covering some 120 pages ('Student Life at Jena', 'On the Beer-drinking Customs at Jena', 'Of the Drinking-bouts of the Jena Students', 'Of the Duels at Jena' and 'Three Fights in Jena') he covers in lurid detail the topics which William Howitt had delighted in describing in his book of two decades earlier.

One example of Mayhew's attempts at comparative analysis is worth quoting, to demonstrate some crude, if well-meaning, techniques at calculation which are still with us in many studies today:

There are altogether twenty-seven Universities distributed throughout Germany, at which, in round numbers, some 20,000 young men are continually studying. [. . .] Now, the population of all Germany, may be roughly estimated at 40,000,000 souls; and of these a fourth part, or 10,000,000 may, perhaps, be taken as the entire body of youths under twenty-one years old. So that dividing the gross number of males who are under age by the entire body of youths studying at these Universities, we find that one boy in every 500 receives a College education in Deutschland. We cannot tell what may be the proportion in England, and indeed, we know of no official returns that would enable us to come to such a conclusion. At Cambridge and Oxford [. . .] the number of students may be taken roughly at 1500, respectively, or at 3000 altogether; and perhaps, with the other Colleges throughout the country [. . .], the sum of the University students in England may be roughly taken at 7000, or one-third those of all Germany. But then it should be remembered that the population of England alone (for we are excluding even Wales from the calculation) is but little more than one-third of the people throughout Deutschland; so that the proportion of those receiving a University education with us may be said to be about the same as it is in the Fatherland, or as one youth in every 500.[110]

Mayhew goes on to demonstrate his belief in the superiority of university education in England; his remarks reveal much of his true intent:

The German students must not, in any way, be confounded with those of the higher English Universities; for the youths at the Deutsch [sic] Colleges are, for the greater part, the sons merely of second-rate middle-class families, such as publicans, butchers, chandler's-shopkeepers, chemists and druggists, well-to-do peasants, and the like. Indeed, owing to the cheapness of matriculating at such institutions in Deutschland, the class of youths who attend them approximates more to the university students of Scotland, where it is the ambition of every small farmer to make a "minister" of some one of his sons; for the German "boys" in no way resemble the "men" at Oxford and Cambridge, whither, owing to the great expense of the course of study, only the children of the richest in the land can be sent.

The reader, therefore, [. . .] must bear this distinction continually in mind; otherwise, when he learns that it is the custom of these "boys" to sit at their convivial meetings in their shirt-sleeves, and to do certain other acts of which the lowest Oxford or Cambridge "man" could never be guilty, he may fancy we are painting a general coarse picture, from some extraordinary vulgar exceptions.[111]

This can only be taken to mean that exclusivity equals superiority; it reveals too that Mayhew's perception of the idea of university education in Germany was severely limited. Here there is no mention of the excitement felt by an earlier generation of observers – Coleridge and Crabb Robinson and many others among them – at the advances in German science (*Wissenschaft*) and at the obviously different concept of a university that had emerged in Germany at the beginning of the century and that was now approaching its period of greatest prominence.

The Great Exhibition

One way in which the achievements of other nations could be brought to the attention of a wide public was through the device of the exhibition. Exhibitions are essentially heuristic, providing direct evidence of advanced accomplishment, and through them nineteenth-century visitors were able to gain a clear sense of advancement, of some of the tangible results of education and training.

The Prince Consort played an important part in the planning for what was to become the 'Great Exhibition of the Works of Industry of All Nations' of 1851, visited by over six million people. This showpiece of the nation, the first in England to present products of other countries – about half of the exhibits were from abroad – helped in some measure to compensate for the disappointing role of the mechanics' institutes and schools of design (as we have seen from Dyce's report of 1840) and to stimulate inventiveness and, ultimately, educational reform. There were to be some 36 international exhibitions from 1851 to 1900.[112] They provided a novel and popular opportunity to bring to the attention of large audiences the advances in manufacturing that individual nations were making. While in 1851 the ascendancy of Britain as an industrial nation was obvious, with the exhibits of the German states appearing somewhat fragmented,[113] Germany as a whole was nevertheless well represented, and later exhibitions would continue to illustrate Germany's increasing strength as an industrial nation, adding to the evidence of German achievements contained in the reports of the Royal Commissions of the 1860s and later.

Royal Commissions, 1861–8

Three important Royal Commissions on education, generally known by the names of their chairmen, reported during the 1860s. The Newcastle Report (1861) dealt with the state of popular education in England; the Clarendon Report (1864) inquired into the state of the nine great public schools, and the Taunton Report (1868) looked at education in schools not covered by the Newcastle and Clarendon reports. Between them, therefore, the reports cover all sectors of educational provision. This flurry of official reporting in the decade leading up to the 1870 Education Act is another measure of the state's increasing engagement with all aspects of education, and it provides further substantial evidence of interest in education in Germany.

The Newcastle Report (1861)

Towards the end of the 1850s there was serious concern that elementary education would have to be put on a firmer footing. As we have seen, various attempts over many years to legislate for improvement had failed, principally as a result of denominational controversies. In 1858 a Royal Commission was appointed 'to inquire into the state of Popular Education in England, and to report what Measures, if any, are required for the extension of sound and cheap elementary instruction to all classes of people'.[114] The Newcastle Commission, set up in 1858 and named after the Duke of Newcastle, who chaired it, reported in 1861 and included in its deliberations accounts of education in France, French Switzerland and Holland written by Matthew Arnold (1822–88) and a paper on Germany written by Mark Pattison (1813–1884), Fellow and later Rector of Lincoln College, Oxford. Arnold and Pattison had been appointed as assistant commissioners. A piece in the *Westminster Review* by Pattison describes the controversy surrounding the decision to report on education in other countries – 'It was obvious', the article says with palpable irony, 'that a body charged with the task of reporting the state of popular education in England had nothing to do with France or Germany': apparently Disraeli wanted to stop the foreign part of the inquiry – but the author concludes that

> whatever doubt there may have been beforehand as to the utility for home purposes of an examination of foreign systems [. . .] must be entirely removed by the Reports which are now laid before the public. We find the same difficulties, the same prejudices, the same conflict of interests, as in our own country; and we read here the various expedients which have been resorted to to meet and smooth them down.[115]

In his *Westminster Review* piece Pattison goes on to make some sage remarks about the efficacy of foreign comparison, with particular reference to Germany:

> To hold up foreign fashions as models for imitation is one thing; to study them carefully as materials for assisting our judgment is quite another. Rightly understood and used, the experience of Germany may be made our experience. We may reap the fruits of it without the cost of the experiment – *felix quem faciunt aliena pericula cautum*. True it is, that great care and judgment are requisite to enable us to make the proper application of another nation's historical experience. The analogy between any two countries is so complicated with differentiating peculiarities, that most men, impatient of toil, reject all foreign precedent at once as inapplicable.[116]

In its report, the Newcastle Commission uses the German example to argue *against* compulsion, because compulsion, whatever its practical advantages, can only succeed with the will of the people:

> Any universal compulsory system appears to us neither attainable nor desirable. In Prussia, indeed, and in many parts of Germany, the attendance can scarcely be termed compulsory. Though the attendance is required by law, it is a law which entirely expresses the convictions and wishes of the people. Such a state of feeling renders the working of a system of compulsion, among a people living under a strict government, comparatively easy. Our own condition [. . .] is in many respects essentially different. But we also found that the results of this system, as seen in Prussia, do not appear to be so much superior to those which have been already attained amongst ourselves by voluntary efforts, as to make us desire an alteration which would be opposed to the feelings, and, in some respects, to the principles of this country.
>   An attempt to replace an independent system of education by a compulsory system, managed by the Government, would be met by objections, both religious and political, of a far graver character in this country than any with which

it has had to contend in Prussia, and we have seen that, even in Prussia, it gives rise to difficulties which are not insignificant. And therefore, on the grounds of a long-established difference between our own position and that of the countries where a compulsory system is worked successfully; on the grounds of the feelings, both political, social and religious, to which it would be opposed; and also on the ground that our education is advancing successfully without it, we have not thought that a scheme for compulsory education to be universally applied in this country can be entertained as a practical possibility.[117]

Mark Pattison had been appointed through an intermediary at Balliol College, William Charles Lake, later Dean of Durham, who was a member of the Newcastle Commission. He wrote to Pattison:

The great result we hope for from the foreign part of the Report is such an account, very clearly given, as will set the present state of working of foreign education before the parliamentary and popular mind. . . . The only point I think you must be on your guard against . . . is the danger not perhaps so much of *hasty* theorizing, as of an undue admixture of theory in your Report. Your critics on all sides admitting fully your ability charge you with a certain amount of 'crotchettyness' and even in this matter I have been warned 'only to prevent Pattison from letting crochets get hold of him'.[118]

Pattison's contribution on Germany contains a salutary warning about the usefulness of foreign models:

The same difficulties in the way of national education with which we have to contend have to be met in the several countries of Germany, only under conditions so altered and infinitely varied, as to afford a most instructive lesson. Their experience has been longer than ours, and has in some points passed through stages we are only approaching. It is, indeed, true that the legislation in any country is always determined by its own necessities, and is not influenced by the knowledge of what is being done in another. In this country we are little likely to err on the side of a hasty imitation of foreign modes, or to adopt a usage from a neighbouring country, forgetful that its being successful, there is no guarantee that it will thrive when transplanted to our climate. But when debating how we shall legislate, we cannot afford to ignore the vast storehouse of experience which the history of the last fifty years of primary instruction in Germany offers. Much rather is every one who has any information on foreign systems to give, called upon to come forward with it, not as precedent to be followed, but as material for deliberation.[119]

Pattison mentions that he was given a far-reaching brief for his investigation: 'The field of inquiry pointed out to me . . . was so vast that I conceived I was to regard [the] letter of instructions as offering me a choice of topics, information with respect to any of which might be useful for the purposes of the commission'.[120] Later in his report he quotes an example of the questions he was asked to address. He was to 'attempt to form general opinions as to whether the general character of the people appears to have been distinctly altered by an advance or decline of education'.[121] (His response to this, incidentally, was 'I must confess that I cannot find any one of the national characteristics of any part of the German populations which I can on reliable grounds trace to the methods or the matters taught in the schools'.)

Pattison's report is in three parts: (1) exterior organisation of education (church, state, district inspector, local inspector, funding, local boards, compulsory attendance, voluntary effort); (2) matters taught in elementary schools (religious instruction, other subjects); (3) the teacher, qualifications and training (examination, training in the seminary, preparatory training; recent reform, the *Nebenseminar, Fortbildung*).

His report is in the finest tradition of scholarly analysis and argument. It embraces some one hundred pages of text and remains a valuable source on the outsider view of education in Germany in the middle decades of the century.

* * * * *

A further official circular of July 1867 elicited among other returns a long letter from a representative in Berlin on compulsory school attendance. It reads in part:

> The theory of the Prussian system in making primary education compulsory appears to have been founded upon the recognised fact that great apathy as regards the education of their children prevails among the poorer classes. As a preliminary step therefore it was necessary to get rid of it, and as it did not seem possible to do so by mere inducement it was resolved to establish a compulsion which should be judiciously and carefully applied, the odium attached to which would gradually diminish as the advantage accruing from it became apparent, and thus render its application necessary, only in a modified form. Such a result would, it seems to have been thought, be attained by creating a direct local interest in the management of the primary schools by rating, so that parents as well as local authorities should find themselves associated with the state in carrying on the great work of social improvement. The Report under consideration [the Prussian government's Report on Elementary Education in the Prussian States for the years 1862–1864] leaving no doubt as to the successful result of this theory. It must be borne in mind moreover that compulsion is applied directly, and not upon the principle which the Colliery Acts in England seek to apply. Children are not punished because their parents may have refused them instruction, for the prohibition to work after a certain age unless provided with a certificate that they can read and write, which by the wilful neglect of the parents they may not be able to obtain, virtually amounts to a punishment, but on the contrary the parents are punished if they neglect to have them duly instructed. The direct application of the principle of compulsion therefore, as far as Prussia is concerned would seem to be attended by a better result than could be obtained by any other method, which must more or less leave to the parents an option on the question of the education of their children, and thus give place for that apathy so fatal to educational progress, and which it is the main object of the system to overcome.[122]

A report on technical education in Bavaria, written in December 1867 in connection with the same circular, provides some basic factual description typical of the kind supplied:

In the first place there exists the Institution of Popular or National Schools (Volksschulen) for boys and for girls, attendance at which is obligatory on all children – from their 6th to their 12th year inclusive – whose parents are unable or unwilling to provide them with any other or better description of Education.

There are further, as forming the next step in the system of Popular Education the Sunday and Holyday Schools (Sonn- und Feiertagsschulen) which children, after leaving the weekday National Schools, are bound to attend, until they have completed their 16th year.

In the former order of Schools the education afforded is of a simple and elementary character, consisting (besides instruction in Religion) of Reading, writing, German Grammar, etc, Arithmetic and geography, with sewing, knitting etc for girls: In the Sunday and Holyday Schools instruction of a somewhat superior description is given, the subjects taught comprising, in a higher degree, all those prescribed for the weekday national Schools, and in addition, drawing, the elements of Geometry, Chemistry, Practical Mechanics etc for Boys; and various descriptions of female work for girls.

The annual payment for each scholar at both descriptions of school is extremely small, varying from 24 to 36 kreutzers (8d. to 1/- Sterling) per Quarter, and in cases where poverty is pleaded by the parents, the children are admitted free of all charge.[123]

Also included with the records that contain these reports is a very lengthy draft translation entitled 'Draft of a Law on the System of Popular Schools in the Kingdom of Bavaria, with Statement of Reasons, 1867'. This document demonstrates the extraordinary lengths to which officials were willing to go in their efforts to collect the fullest information possible about what was happening in Germany. It is a tediously long and painfully constructed translation, which must have consumed an enormous amount of time to put together. We cannot know if anyone ever read it – if anyone did it is testimony to the dogged application of the nineteenth-century bureaucrat.

The Clarendon Report (1864)

The Clarendon Commission was concerned with an investigation into the nine great public schools: Eton, Winchester, Westminster, Charterhouse, St Paul's, Merchant Taylors', Harrow, Rugby, and Shrewsbury. Its focus was on their 'revenues and management' and on studies and instruction.

The report discusses at an early point the need for some boys who lacked aptitude for classical languages to 'deviate' into 'modern' or 'practical' studies, and in this context the experience of France and Germany was relevant; there 'provision is made for giving such boys as these an entirely distinct education'. In Germany, in contrast to the bifurcation permitted in the French *lycées*, 'the business of preparing boys for the universities is left to the *Gymnasien*, and that of educating them for other careers is assigned to the *Real-schulen* [sic], which are wholly distinct and separate establishments'.[124]

Volume II of the Clarendon Report contains extensive appendices, including an eleven-page 'Account of the Higher Schools in Prussia' put together by the commission's secretary, Mountague Bernard, on the basis of information provided by the Prussian Minister of Education.

The *Gymnasien* and *Realschulen*

do not differ in the principles on which their respective *curricula* are framed; that principle being, in each case, to aim at the thorough preparation and cultivation of the mind for the future work, whatever that work may be, rather than at the imparting of such knowledge as may be immediately and practically useful. They are not Fachschulen – not mere places of training for particular callings or professions. And they are "before all things, German and Christian".[125]

The account covers the other types of school in Prussia and the subjects taught, and the relative lack of private schools:

> The scarcity of private schools is attributed partly to the greater security which the public ones afford to parents for the efficient teaching and superintendence of their children; partly to the advantages in the way of admission into the civil service and the army, which are obtained by resorting to the Public Schools.[126]

The importance of the '*Maturitäts-prüfung* or *Abiturienten- prüfung*' for admission to the university is covered, as are statistics of those completing the *Gymnasium*. The functions of the state are described, and extracts are provided from an official document relating *inter alia* to admission and qualifications, subjects of instruction, and 'manner of teaching'. The latter section contains an important recognition by the Prussian Ministry of defects in the teaching style adopted in some schools:

> It is a frequent subject of complaint, that whilst in the elementary schools a remarkable advance has been made during the present century in the method and practice of instruction, this improvement has not extended to the higher schools. The younger masters in the *Gymnasien*, it is alleged, do not pay sufficient attention to the difficult art of teaching; . . . they are too apt, instead of thoroughly grounding their scholars, to overwhelm them with a mass of undigested knowledge which they cannot assimilate; and they try rather to lecture like University Professors than to teach like schoolmasters; their instructions want life and animation; they fail to accommodate themselves to the capacity of young minds, and they are unable to penetrate, keep on the alert, and handle successfully large masses of boys; and they are too apt to attribute the unsatisfactory results which too often follow, especially as regards proficiency in the classics, in German, and in history, to the stupidity and idleness of their pupils instead of the right cause.[127]

Such criticism in the 1860s demonstrates a deviation from the Humboldtian ideal of the humanistic *Gymnasium*. The way in which dull pedantry and pointless routine had permeated the *Gymnasium* curriculum was much later caricatured by Heinrich Mann in his novel *Professor Unrat* (1905):

> The class had been busy with Schiller's *Jungfrau von Orleans* since Easter, for three-quarters of a year. Those who were repeating a year were even familiar with it since the year before. They had read it forwards and backwards, learnt

scenes by heart, provided historical explanations, done poetry and grammar on it, translated its verse into prose and the prose back into verse.[128]

Extracts from regulations on the final school examination and on the examinations for teachers are also provided, and the account ends with some general observations, describing the historical development of educational provision in Prussia, focusing on the overcrowded curriculum of the *Gymnasien* and the development of the *Realschulen* ('the most important, perhaps, of the changes that have taken place in the present century'), covering the salaries of teachers and the nature of centralised control:

> The amount of Government interference and control, and the uniformity which it creates and enforces, are deemed, even in Prussia, to have been carried too far, and the tendency of recent measures has been to give greater liberty both to local authorities and to rectors of schools. It appears, however, to be true that even under the present highly centralized system there is more than we might suppose of variety and freedom. Different schools have their different traditions, and are moulded and influenced by the personal characters and exertions of their rectors and teachers.
>
> [. . .]
>
> Making allowances for some defects which are inseparable from so large, complicated, and elaborate a system, and for others which the authorities are endeavouring with good hope to remove, it works well, we are told, in the opinion of the Government, and appears to be approved by the public. The number of boys attending school increases fast; the number of schools increases; and comparing the two classes together, the *Gymnasien* multiply faster than the *Real-Schulen*, in spite of the disposition prevailing in the present day to depreciate classical learning.[129]

The Clarendon Commission recommended, in line with developments in Prussia, the introduction of more 'modern' subjects into the curriculum, while arguing for the continuing centrality of classical languages and literature. Its deliberations have been seen as part of the advocacy of reform 'from a European point of view and within the context of comparisons with Europe which rarely showed English schools, of any kind, in a favourable light'.[130]

The Taunton Report (1868)

The Taunton Commission was charged in December 1864 with the task of reporting on 'the education given in schools not comprised within Her Majesty's two former Commissions'. It was chaired by Lord Taunton and included in its membership the Liberal William Edward Forster (1818–86), who was to see the 1870 Education Act through Parliament. The first chapter of the commission's report, 'Of the kinds of education which appear to be desirable and attainable', contains coverage of education in the United States (New England), Canada, Scotland, France, and Germany (Prussia); on each of these countries assistant commissioners were asked to report, and their substantial texts were included in an appendix.

The commission outlines provision in Prussia, using for the most part Matthew Arnold's report printed in full in volume VI of the commission's multi-volume report. It concludes:

When we view it as a whole, the Prussian system appears to be at once the most complete and the most perfectly adapted to its people, of all that now exist. It is not wanting in the highest cultivation like the American, nor in dealing with the mass of the middle classes like our own; nor does it run any risk of sacrificing everything else to intellectual proficiency like the French. It is somewhat more bureaucratic in its form than would work well in England, but it is emphatically not a mere centralized system in which the Government is everything. [. . .] In Prussia the education department is simply the instrument which the people use to procure the fulfilment of their own desires. The Prussians believe in culture, and, whoever may have originally created the educational machinery, that machinery has now been appropriated by the people themselves.[131]

The commissioners charged Matthew Arnold with the task of writing a report on 'the system of education of the middle and upper classes which prevails in France, Germany, Switzerland, and Italy'. His brief was to cover a wide range of topics: (1) laws for the provision of schools for the people; schools provided by voluntary efforts; legal obligations on parents to have their children educated; penalties for not doing so; whether the obligation to attend school has any effect on juvenile delinquency: 'You will state not only the provisions of the law on these subjects, but also the manner in which it is enforced, and the extent to which it is practically operative'; (2) central and local financial support for schools; (3) relations between central and local government in terms of administration; (4) internal (school) organisation; (5) educational results; (6) provision for religious instruction.[132] We shall consider Arnold's findings on Germany in detail below.

The Taunton Report's recommendations had largely to do with endowment and organisational and administrative questions. The notion of establishing a 'normal' school for the training of secondary teachers was rejected.

Matthew Arnold and education in Germany

Matthew Arnold is celebrated as one of Britain's foremost poets and essayists of the mid-Victorian age. He was the son of the famous Headmaster of Rugby School, Dr Thomas Arnold (1795–1842), who transformed Rugby into one of the best-known 'public' schools in England and whose views on education were widely publicised and discussed. He had introduced the teaching of German at Rugby in 1835[133] and he had been much influenced by disciples of 'Turnvater' Jahn (1778–1852) in his personal interpretation of the 'muscular Christianity' which became an important aspect of the ethos of the public schools in England.[134]

For more than thirty years (1851–83) Matthew Arnold combined his literary activities with the demanding post of inspector of schools, and he produced a body of work which did much to focus attention in England on what was being achieved in the education systems of France and Germany. His reports on elementary schools in England, covering the thirty-year period 1852 to 1882, were thought to be so useful that they were published shortly after his death and later reissued. They are noted for their style and clarity: 'beautifully written, crystal-clear and luminously persuasive', as A. L. Rowse puts it.[135]

As part of his official duties Arnold spent time on the Continent in 1859 (for the Clarendon Commission) and 1865. From his first visit, and based on his report as an assistant commissioner, there emerged the text published as *The Popular Education of France* (1861), which also included sections on Holland and Switzerland; later (1864) he returned to the subject of France in *A French Eton, or Middle-Class Education and the State*. Following his second round of travels in 1865, when he went to France, Germany, and Italy to report on behalf of the Taunton Commission, he produced *Schools and Universities on the Continent* (1868), the German parts of which were reissued in 1874 as *Higher Schools and Universities in Germany*. Reference here will be to the 1868 text throughout, rather than to that included in volume VI of the Taunton Commission's report.

Arnold writes of the 'preponderating importance of Prussia at the present time'[136] and of the excellence of its schools. He was able to visit all of the more important schools in Berlin and to observe classes, and so he takes the Prussian example as a proxy for the whole of Germany.

He devotes much space to an analysis of the various types of secondary school and their curricula, placing them in their historical setting and showing a detailed knowledge of the forces that had shaped them. He provides full statistics, recording that he found for the year 1865, 'I will not say in the public schools of England, but in all the schools which by any straining or indulgence can possibly be made to bear that title, 15,880 scholars. In the public higher schools and preparatory schools of Prussia we find 74,162 scholars'.[137]

He describes the legal framework for the provision of public schools, establishing that they are state institutions under the supervision of the state, that teachers are state functionaries and that sufficient provision had to be made for the education of the young. 'It would be a mistake to suppose', he writes, 'that the State in Prussia shows a grasping and centralising spirit in dealing with education; on the contrary, it makes the administration of it as local as it possibly can; but it takes care that education shall not be left to the chapter of accidents'.[138] He had in mind here the principal weakness in provision in England, still with us in the first decades of the twenty-first century.

The *Abitur* examination (*Abiturienten-Examen*) meets with his full approval: it was, he felt, an entirely fitting form of assessment for schools of such evident high standing. He quotes with admiration Wilhelm von Humboldt on a proposal not to require Greek except for those destined for holy orders: 'Es ist nicht darum zu thun, daß Schulen und Universitäten in einem trägen und kraftlosen Gewohnheitsgange blieben, sondern darum, dass durch sie die Bildung der Nation auf eine immer höhere Stufe gebracht werde'.[139] These perceived high standards lead him to remark that 'it is common to meet in Germany with people of the tradesman class who even read (in translations, of course) any important or interesting book that comes out of another country, a book like Macaulay's *History of England*, for instance; and how unlike this state of culture is to that of the English tradesman, the English reader himself knows very well'.[140]

He covers the training and examination of teachers, and here includes some remarks doubting the acceptability in the English context of a minister of education with powers like those enjoyed by the Prussian Minister; yet he argues that those powers, as far as he could tell, were being exercised responsibly: 'When a nation has got the belief in culture which the Prussian nation has got, and when its schools are worthy of this belief, it will not suffer them to be sacrificed to any other interest; and however greatly political considerations may be paramount in other departments of administration, in this they are not'.[141] He goes on to describe the Prussian system as he observed it – using his skills as an inspector of schools – in operation in various schools, among them the Friedrich-Wilhelms Gymnasium (where he heard a lesson on the *Philoctetes* of Sophocles given in Latin to the top class, the pupils replying in Latin), the Gymnasium zum grauen Kloster, and the Joachimsthalsche Gymnasium.

Chapter XX of *Schools and Universities on the Continent* is devoted to universities. Arnold calculates that, taking the whole of Germany there was at the time about one matriculated university student per 2,600 inhabitants – this in contrast to England, where the figures were one to every 5,800. These figures are again slippery, since the population sizes are no longer roughly comparable and we do not know if he included Wales – but it was clear to Arnold that the German universities were educating more students and doing so in a quite different way from England. He sketches the main features of university structure and operation, eschewing all reference to student societies, drinking and duelling, and summarises the essential features: '*Lehrfreiheit* and *Lernfreiheit*, liberty for the teacher and liberty for the learner; and *Wissenschaft*, science, knowledge systematically pursued and prized in and for itself, are the fundamental ideas of [the] system'.[142] University education in England was a routine, made such by a lack of 'science', in which respect England had 'need to borrow' from Germany. And he concludes with his famous dictum: 'The French university has no liberty, and the English universities have no science; the German universities have both'.[143]

Arnold ends his chapters on Germany with a prophetic statement:

> What I admire in Germany is, that while there too industrialism, that great modern power, is making at Berlin, and Leipzig, and Elberfeld, the most successful and rapid progress, the idea of culture, culture of the only true sort, is in Germany a living power also. Petty towns have a university whose teaching is famous throughout Europe; and the King of Prussia and Count Bismarck resist the loss of a great *savant* from Prussia, as they would resist a political check. If true culture ever becomes at last a civilising power in the world, and is not overlaid by fanaticism, by industrialism, or by frivolous pleasure-seeking, it will be to the faith and zeal of this homely and much ridiculed German people, that the great result will be mainly owing.[144]

In his concluding remarks to the reports as a whole – in which, *inter alia*, he opposes the teaching of languages for speaking purposes, supporting the view that 'the speaking of foreign languages tends to strain the mind, and to make it superficial and averse to going deep in anything'[145] – Arnold sets out the main problems facing education in England, in contrast to the successes he had perceived in Germany:

> Our dislike of authority and our disbelief in science have combined to make us leave our school system, like so many other branches of our civil organisation, to take care of itself as best it could. Under such auspices, our school system has very naturally fallen all into confusion; and though properly an intellectual agency, it has done and does nothing to counteract the indisposition to science which is our great intellectual fault. The result is, that we have to meet the calls of a modern epoch, in which the action of the working and middle class assumes a preponderating importance, and science tells in human affairs more and more, with a working class not educated at all, a middle class educated on

the second plane, and the idea of science absent from the whole course and design of our education.[146]

The excellent *Journal of Education* reported following Arnold's death in 1888 that 'if England had, like Prussia, a Minister of Education, independent of Parliament, the office might have been conferred by public acclaim on Mr Arnold, but we doubt whether he would have accepted it. He knew too well his own powers, and again and again, when asked to take a share in active life, or help to carry out the reforms that he himself had suggested, he pleaded the privilege of the critic to be an onlooker, and refused to leave his coign of vantage'.[147] On his retirement Arnold had confessed that the profession he had had for so long was 'a "Hobson's choice", adopted under stress of matrimony, and for a time at least, almost insupportably irksome'.[148] He had not been without his critics. At a meeting of teachers in December 1886 he 'was called a distinguished amateur, an educational tourist; he was rated for his anti-patriotic bias; he was said "not to understand the quantitative relations of things, and to build lofty theories not founded on any substantial statistical basis". It was shown that even the fragmentary facts that he has collected are not all accurate'.[149]

But Arnold set the agenda for a debate that was to dominate over several decades, as England struggled to legislate for something approaching a national system of education. Through his deep and scholarly understanding of what had made the German education system what it was he was able to produce a powerful set of arguments by contrast for England. Connell[150] sums up the three areas in which, according to Arnold, education in England was 'making an inadequate response to the requirements of the times': it was lacking in responsible organisation; it was failing as a 'humanising agent'; and 'it lacked a social consciousness'. The *Journal of Education* felt that 'under any other Government [Arnold] would have been dismissed ten times over for his outspoken criticisms. [. . .] [I]n his riper years he has been the spoilt child of the Department, sent on foreign tours, and permitted, if not encouraged, to criticise his masters on two continents'.[151] The freedoms he enjoyed to report without fear or favour allowed him to establish a case for change which would be used by others as England moved inexorably towards a system of education in which the state would play a proper part.

'I hope with time to convince people', Arnold wrote in a letter of April 1868, 'that I do not care the least for importing this or that foreign machinery, whether it be French or German, but only for getting certain English deficiencies supplied'.[152] University and public school teachers, however, were annoyed at being 'constantly told that all good things in education were made in France and Germany'.[153] So frequent were allusions to Germany that a one-time Master of Sidney Sussex College, Cambridge is said to have exploded: 'A Prussian is a Prussian and an Englishman an Englishman and God forbid it should be otherwise!'[154] A later commentator could say, with evident frustration at the reminder of German achievements in educational provision: 'If we wish to introduce the German educational system into Great Britain, and to make it a success, we must begin by turning Englishmen into Germans'.[155]

Arnold remained a prophet whose views were fated to be more felt in later generations, when he influenced administrators and policy formers like Michael Sadler and Robert Morant at the Board of Education in London. We shall return to him briefly in Chapter Four in connection with a report he was commissioned to write in 1885 on elementary education in Germany, Switzerland, and France.

Towards the 1870 Education Act

The 37 years between the first vote of government funds to education in England and the landmark 1870 Education Act saw a steady progression towards acceptance of the state's responsibility for oversight of something approaching a proper system of education. This was achieved through slow but systematic parliamentary investigation, aided by growth in the number of elementary schools and an increasing general desire for popular education. Throughout, and especially in connection with the work of the Royal Commissions, the Prussian example in education was paraded before those charged with the formation of policy. Contributing to the debate on the state of education in England were a number of proto-sociological studies in which education and society found a prominent place.

Frederic Hill (1803–96), a scion of the philanthropic Hill family, was an active educationist, producing in 1819, together with his three brothers, *Public Education: Plans for the Liberal Instruction of Boys, in Large Numbers*. He published his thoughts on national education in 1836, with a substantial chapter on Prussia. He writes of Cousin's report, remarking its influence on developments in France and reflecting that any government statements in Prussia must be viewed against the background of censorship of the press. He quotes figures showing that only one in a hundred children were without schooling in Prussia which, 'if true, show that Prussia stand[s] pre-eminent for the education afforded to her youth'.[156] He wonders, however, quite what is taught, since he regards Cousin's report deficient in describing the content of teaching and its results:

> It is not enough to inform us that so many children are at school, and that such and such subjects are laid down in the course of instruction; – nay, it is not enough to do what Mons. Cousin has done, (and in this his report is very superior to the sweeping statements and vague generalities which are so frequently put forth,) to point out the machinery provided for carrying the regulations into effect. The first question that presents itself – that about which all must be most anxious – that which alone can attract the earnest attention of the many to the examination of the general system – is, "*What are the results produced?*"[157]

The remainder of his coverage consists largely of quotation *in extenso* from Cousin's report, divided into sections on compulsory education, school funding, courses of instruction, religious education, and normal schools.

An informed observer of the German scene in the late 1830s, the long-lived Bisset Hawkins (1796–1894), author of the first book in English on medical statistics, reported in full detail on educational provision in Prussia in his study of 1838. He recounts the usual information and adds:

> It is in vain to seek for results in the works of those who have only studied the plan in its program, and in decrees, and who have not looked into the farmhouse, the barrack, the manufactory, and the cottage, for the measure of its realisation.[158]

His view was that he had not succeeded 'in discovering that the Prussian peasant or artisan is better informed, or more moral than his neighbours; his manners are not superior, nor does he appear to solace his hours of leisure more than others, with study, or books'. He finds reverence for the Christian religion admirable, and concludes that it is difficult to ascertain the degree to which military training rather than schooling contributes to the formation of character.[159]

The Scot Samuel Laing (1780–1868), author of studies of conditions in Norway and Sweden, had spent eighteen months in Kiel to learn German. He warns in an account of 1842 against confusing means and ends, echoing the concerns of Frederic Hill:

> This is the people whose educational system, spirit, and institutions are held up as a model by the liberal, the pious, the benevolent of other countries, who are anxious for the diffusion of education; but who mistake the means for the end, the almost mechanical arts of reading and writing for the moral elevation of character which education should produce.[160]

In his *Observations on Europe* of 1850, Laing concentrates on university students in Germany, making comparisons which serve to illustrate the enlightened style of university education in Scotland.

Joseph Kay was a lawyer and economist; his study (of 1850) of the social condition and education of the people is an enthusiastic outpouring of praise for what had been achieved in particular in education in Germany. The sections on foreign countries begin with a long panegyric:

> I purpose now to give a simple statement of the really wonderful efforts which Germany, Austria, Switzerland, France, Holland, Denmark, Norway, and Sweden are making to educate their people. Whether the methods, by which any of these different countries are carrying out their great design, are in any way applicable to this country or not, I shall not stop to consider, my desire being merely to show how different countries, – with different degrees of political freedom, with different political constitutions, whose people profess different religious tenets, where Protestants of different sects, Roman Catholics, and Jews are mingled up in every kind of proportion, – have all managed to overcome difficulties precisely similar to those, which stand in our way, and have all agreed to labour together to educate their poor. For it is a great fact, however much we may be inclined to doubt it, that throughout Prussia, Saxony, Bavaria, Bohemia, Wirtemburg [sic], Baden, Hesse Darmstadt, Hesse Cassel, Gotha, Nassau, Hanover, Denmark, Switzerland, Norway, and the Austrian Empire, ALL the children are actually, at this present time, attending school, and are receiving a careful religious, moral, and intellectual education, from highly educated and efficient teachers. Over the vast tract of country, which I have mentioned, as well as in Holland and the greater part of France, *all* the children above six years of age are daily acquiring useful knowledge and good habits under the *influence* of moral, religious, and learned teachers. ALL the youth of the greater part of these countries, below the age of twenty-one years, can read, write, and cipher, and know the Bible History, and the history of their own country. No children are left idle and dirty in the streets of the towns – there is no class of children to be compared, in any respect, to the children who frequent our "ragged schools" – all the children, even of the

poorest parents, are, in a great part of these countries, in dress, appearance, cleanliness, and manners, as polished and civilised as the children of our middle classes – the children of the poor in Germany are so civilised that the rich often send their children to the schools intended for the poor; and, lastly, in a great part of Germany and Switzerland, the children of the poor are receiving a *better* education than that given in England to the children of the greater part of our middle classes! These facts deserve to be well considered.[161]

This is pure hyperbole. But he moves on to a detailed and measured account of the organisation of education in Prussia (in six chapters) and in other German states, as well as in Austria, Switzerland, France, Holland, Denmark, Sweden, and Norway. As far as Prussia is concerned, he covers the political and legal framework for educational provision, the position of teachers and their education, school inspection, the parochial schools, and the statistics of education.

At an early point he attempts to counter common criticisms of the German example:

> It is very strange . . . to hear the unfounded and untrue aspersions, which are cast upon all these noble efforts. When one speaks in England of German education, one is sure to be assailed by cries of "Centralisation," "Irreligion," "No local liberty of action," "No union between the schools and the churches," "All done by the state," and so forth. Now I assure my readers that all these are only so many untruths, or most unwarrantable exaggerations.[162]

And he addresses the question of reliance on local philanthropy with excoriating criticisms of teachers:

> I know there are many in our land who say, "But why have any system at all? Is it not better to leave the education of the people to the exertions of public charity and private benevolence?" Let the contrast between the state of education and social condition of the poor in England and Germany be the answer. In England it is well known *that not one half of the country is properly supplied with good schools, and that many of those, which do exist, are under the direction of very inefficient and sometimes of actually immoral teachers.* In Germany and Switzerland, *every* parish is supplied with its school buildings, and *each* school is directed by a teacher of high principles, and superior education and intelligence.[163]

This is a theme Kay develops later, on the basis of his visits to schools:

> A short time ago I visited two large schools, situated in a great and populous parish in the south of England: one belonging to the National Society, and the other to the British and Foreign School Society. [. . .] The teachers were men, who deserved no better description, than that of half-educated peasants.[164]

In one of these schools he found

> All the poor children standing, ranged round the walls, although there were plenty of desks in this school, and delivered to the charge of poor ignorant little boys of nine or ten years of age, who knew little more than the children themselves did. These so-called monitors were pretending to teach geography,

while their poor scholars were leaning against the walls, playing tricks with
one another, talking, and doing anything but learning; whilst the noise of all
the different classes shouting at the same time, and in the same room, was so
great, as to render almost inaudible the instruction, which the teacher himself
was conveying.[165]

When he contrasted these schools with those he had observed in Germany
he 'could not help feeling that if this be what we mean by EDUCATION,
then indeed it is a dream to expect to raise the character of the people by its
means'.[166]

Kay also covers in outline provision in Bavaria, 'Wirtemberg', and Baden,
and he provides two comparative tables which place provision in England into
sharp contrast with that in other European countries. The first (Table 1 below)
lists, somewhat strangely, the proportions of pupils in elementary schools, and
the second (Table 2) compares countries according to basic statistics and a list
of criteria including teacher training, religious education, and availability of
school buildings.

Kay's tables are an interesting example of early attempts at systematic comparison of educational data: his liberal use of exclamation marks ensures that
the contrast is made clear.

* * * * *

The long period from the first modest government funds allocated to education
to the climate of change which led to the 1870 Education Act in England saw an
uninterrupted tendency to refer to what was happening in Germany. The influence of Victor Cousin's detailed report was obvious in the early years, and it was
still being referred to twenty-five and more years after its publication.

What is particularly remarkable is the extent of official efforts to gather
information on the German example to be used in the context of investigation of provision in England and any recommendations that might emerge
from it. Those efforts ranged from the simple collection of statistical data to
the commissioning of detailed reports on the state of education in Germany.
The involvement of figures of the intellectual eminence of Mark Pattison and
Matthew Arnold gave such investigations an outstanding imprimatur.

We see the debate about state intervention and control veering between
positive endorsement and extreme caution on the basis of evidence from
Germany. Many commentators could appreciate that while the Prussian state
did not represent an ideal model of government, extraordinary progress had
been made in educational provision. Just what the lessons were for England was
always somewhat uncertain. There was both unbridled enthusiasm for emulation
of the Prussian system and cautious warning against copying aspects of a system
rooted in another culture – and especially one in which the government had
such a stranglehold on the people. Censorship was a major concern. By as early
as 1840 elementary education in Germany had reached what Andy Green calls
'its acme of illiberal, centralized efficiency'.[167]

Once policy makers in England had taken the decision to introduce compulsory
schooling interest in conditions in Germany came to focus more on the economic and military rivalry between the two nations, with Germany looking
dangerously powerful following the creation of the German Empire in 1871.

Table 1 The proportion of scholars in elementary schools, to the whole population in different European countries

Scholars Inhabitants				
Berne, Canton of Switzerland	1843	1	in every	4.3
Thurgovie	1837	1		4.8
Vaud	1844	1		5
St Gall	1843	1		5.5
Argovie	1843	1		5.5
Neuchatel	1838	1		6
Lucerne	1844	1		6
Schaffhouse	1844	1		6
Geneva	1844	1		6
Zurich	1838	1		6.3
Fribourg	1839	1		6.5
Solothurn	1844	1		7
Saxony	1841	1		5
Six departments of France (each)	1843	1		6
Wirtemberg	1838	1		6
Prussia	1838	1		6
Baden (Duchy)	1838	1		6
Overyssel (Province of Holland)	1838	1		6
Drenthe	1838	1		6
Friesland	1838	1		6.8
Tyrol	1843	1		7.5
Norway	1837	1		7
Denmark	1834	1		7
Holland (generally)	1838	1		8
Bavaria	1831	1		8
Scotland	1842	1		8
Bohemia	1843	1		8.5
Austria Proper	1843	1		9
France (generally)	1843	1		10.5
Belgium	1836	1		10.7
ENGLAND	1850	1		14

(Source: Kay, *Social Condition and Education of the People*, vol. II, p. 539)

Table 2 Showing the comparative state of the Education of the Poor in several of the European Countries.

Name of Country	Population	Number of Normal Colleges for the Education of Teachers	Number of Schools for the poor open to the inspection of Government	Children of different religious sects educated together	The Teachers supported in honourable and independent situations by Government	No one but a person of high character and attainments ever allowed to be a Teacher	The Government has a veto on the appointment of Teachers whose characters and attainments it does not think sufficiently high	All children are *obliged* by law to attend School between the ages of seven and thirteen	Government takes care that school-houses shall be provided for all the people	The different religious sects unite in assisting Government to promote the education of the people	All the parishes well supplied with school-room
Wirtemberg	1,600,000	3	All the schools	Yes	Yes	Yes	Yes	Yes	Yes	Yes	Yes
Bavaria	4,000,000	8	7,353	Yes	Yes	Yes	Yes	Yes	Yes	Yes	Yes
Grand Duchy of Baden	1,335,200	3	1,971	Yes	Yes	Yes	Yes	Yes	Yes	Yes	Yes
France	34,000,000	92	59,838	Yes	Yes	Yes	Yes	No	Yes	Yes	Yes
Denmark	2,100,000	5	4,600	Yes	Yes	Yes	Yes	Yes	Yes	Yes	Yes
Hanover	1,700,000	6	3,428	Yes	Yes	Yes	Yes	Yes	Yes	Yes	Yes
Holland	2,600,000	2	2,882	Yes	Yes	Yes	Yes	No	Yes	Yes	Yes
Prussia	14,100,000	42	23,646	Yes	Yes	Yes	Yes	Yes	Yes	Yes	Yes
Switzerland	2,200,000	13	All the schools	Yes	Yes	Yes	Yes	Yes	Yes	Yes	Yes
Saxony	1,719,000	8		Yes	Yes	Yes	Yes	Yes	Yes	Yes	Yes
England & Wales	17,000,000 population *rapidly* increasing	Only 12 worth mention!!	Not 4,000!!	No!	No! Quite the contrary	No! Quite the contrary	No!	No!	No!	No! Quite the contrary	No! Great numbers of districts without any schools at all, or insufficiently supplied

(Source: Kay, *Social Condition and Education of the People*, vol. II, p. 540)

Chapter 4

Towards a National System of Education in England, 1870–1918

I. The spectre of Germany, 1870–1902

In Prussia, which is so often quoted, education is not flourishing because it is compulsory, it is compulsory because it is flourishing.

Matthew Arnold, 1867[1]

The German secondary school is really one of the most effective factories in the educational world.

Cloudesley Brereton, 1913[2]

The year 1870 saw Prussian victory in the Franco-Prussian War and a treaty of alliance between the North German Confederation and Bavaria (Baden and Württemberg having previously negotiated similar treaties). This paved the way for the unification of the German states with the creation of the German Empire under Wilhelm I early in 1871. The long march of German military might and technological and commercial power was given a new impetus. And a strong state-supervised and compulsory education system was firmly and very evidently in place.

Progress towards a national system of education in England, however, had

> followed the familiar pattern of poor law and public health reforms: commissions of enquiry, followed by public pressure from the new electorate and by parliamentary legislation setting up locally elected boards and a means test. [. . .] The more rapid growth of popular education had been prevented partly by the clash between Church and Dissent, partly by the apathy of the people.[3]

But there was now a clearly emerging change in the political will, which was in due course to find expression in the 1870 (Forster) Education Act.

At the time of the Forster Act there were said to be some 4,300,000 children who should have been attending school. About 1,300,000 of these were going to schools run by the voluntary organisations and another 1,000,000 or so were pupils at various private schools.[4]

One measure of educational progress in Prussia, testing the notion of compulsory school attendance, would be the number of army recruits who in 1871 were recorded as not having been to school. Of the 88,382 recruits enrolled in that year, 3.42 per cent (3,019) had had no schooling. There was considerable variation between the provinces, with Posen recording a high of 15.59 per cent and the 'old' provinces appearing to be less satisfactory.[5] In Germany as a whole the number of illiterate recruits was to decline from as few as 23.7 per thousand in 1875–6 to an insignificant 0.45 per cent in 1900–1.[6] In England and Wales the literacy rates of brides and bridegrooms (judged crudely by the ability to sign a marriage register) increased from around 80 per cent in 1870 to well over 90 per cent in 1900.

In 1870 there was still much to be achieved in England to come near to educational provision in Germany. But the 1870 Act was a significant step forward.

The 1870 Education Act

After the long period of debate about the desirability of a national system of compulsory education the 1870 Elementary Education Act was far from being the final solution to the problems: although it brought much consensus, it was also surrounded by bitter controversy which cut across party lines. The Radical Liberal MP John Bright (1837–89) was so disappointed with its provisions that he described it as 'the worst Act passed by any liberal parliament since 1832'.[7] Gladstone had made uncomfortable concessions on the bill, and the result was a compromise which did not fully satisfy either supporters or opponents. The Act's architect was W. E. Forster (1818–86), Vice-President of the Council, brother-in-law of Matthew Arnold, a friend of Thomas Carlyle and of another Germanophile, the poet and politician Richard Monckton-Milnes (1809–85), who had spent time at the University of Bonn.

One of Gladstone's biographers recalls the schoolboy howler that the Franco-Prussian War 'caused' the 1870 Act and reminds us that Gladstone's remark in the *Edinburgh Review* of October 1870 – which caused the error – appeared after the war had begun. (The Act was introduced some months before the outbreak of hostilities.) Gladstone had written that 'the conduct of the campaign, on the German side, has given a marked triumph to the cause of systematic popular education'.[8] The remark showed, however, the continuing awareness of the significance of what the Germans had achieved in education.

In his speech introducing the bill in February 1870 Forster described the scale of the deficiency in educational provision:

> Only two-fifths of the children of the working classes between the ages of six and ten years are on the registers of the Government schools, and only one-third of those between the ages of ten and twelve. Consequently, of those between six and ten, we have helped about 700,000, more or less, but we have left unhelped 1,000,000; while of those between ten and twelve, we have helped 250,000, and left unhelped at least 500,000.[9]

The situation in Liverpool and in Manchester was described in detail to highlight further the magnitude of the problem:

> It is calculated that in Liverpool the number of children between five and thirteen who ought to receive an elementary education is 80,000; but, as far as we can ascertain, 20,000 of them attend no school whatever, while at least another 20,000 attend schools where they get an education not worth having. In Manchester — that is, in the borough of Manchester, not including Salford,

there are about 65,000 children who might be at school, and of this number about 16,000 go to no school at all. I must, however, add that Manchester appears to be better than Liverpool in one respect, that there are fewer schools where the education is not worth having.[10]

Forster emphasised the importance of the proposals in the bill and the potential cross-party support they demanded:

> There never, I believe, was any question presented by any Government to this House which more demanded to be considered apart from any party consideration; nor do I believe there ever was a House of Commons more disposed so to consider it than the House I am now addressing.[11]

He mentioned the situation in Germany when speaking of compulsory school attendance:

> I believe that last year I stated in this House that in America, although they had a compulsory provision, it was so rarely put in force as to be of no effect. Further study of the matter has convinced me that, while it is as seldom put in force in America as in the parts of Germany where a similar provision exists, yet it is acknowledged to have had a great effect, since it embodies a moral force which has made education more universal. And there is the important fact to be remembered — that in no country has education been really a success in which this principle has not at one time been acknowledged, and that remark applies to Scotland as well as to the New England States, and to Germany.[12]

In the debates surrounding the Act, the question of standards as compared with Germany was not forgotten. John Morley, in his 1873 account of 'The Struggle for National Education', recalled a speech drawing comparisons with Saxony and Prussia by the Liberal MP Anthony Mundella (1825–97), later to be Vice-President of the Committee on Education (1880–5):

> Arithmetic was taught in the schools of Germany to an extent far beyond that which was deemed necessary here. In Saxony, the pupils before leaving school, were not only called upon to read fluently, and write a good readable hand, but they were also required to write from memory in their own words a short story which had been previously read to them; and the children besides were instructed in geography, singing, and the history of the fatherland, as well as in religion. We had never yet passed 20,000 in a population of 20,000,000 to the sixth standard in one year; whereas old Prussia without her recent aggrandizement passed nearly 380,000 every year.[13]

The measures introduced by the Act included the mapping of school districts, each with a school board (and the creation of additional boards where necessary), the ability for boards to require children to attend school from age 5 to 13 and to fine parents if their children did not attend, and the right of parents to withdraw their children from religious instruction (which should include 'no catechism or religious formulary' distinctive to any particular denomination.) Non-denominational religious teaching was to be confined to board schools, with the Church of England schools continuing to provide denominational teaching. (These latter schools were still educating some half of the nation's elementary school pupils in 1900.)

The Act's importance has been summarised as follows:

> [T]he Elementary Education Act of 1870 was one of the most important events in Britain's history. By the end of the century it had laid the firm foundations of a national system of elementary education, and had even made it possible to envisage the establishment of a similar system of secondary education. True, the Act had to be modified and reinforced in the decades following 1870 by more generous provisions encouraging free schooling, compulsory attendance and the development of voluntary and board schools alike; but it had acknowledged the ultimate responsibility of the government for the education of the people; it had made it possible for those of very different views to obtain or supply education in ways generally in accordance with their principles and consciences; and it had helped to establish the status of teachers as men and women who might well feel disposed to co-operate with the clergy, but who were free to insist upon the dignity, value and independence of their own professional commitments.[14]

The Forster Act did not achieve compulsory school attendance immediately. It took the 1876 Act to establish school attendance committees where there were no school boards, and only with the Act of 1880 was it made compulsory to compel attendance. The school leaving age was universally raised to eleven in 1893 and to twelve in 1899. The attendance figure was about half of the population by 1876[15] and had reached over 80 per cent by the end of the century, thanks to the efforts of school attendance officers.[16]

* * * * *

Joseph Payne (1808–76), Professor of the 'Science and Art of Education' in the College of Preceptors, London, wrote an account of his visit to German schools undertaken in the autumn of 1874. Payne focused his attention on the Kindergarten, the primary school, and the training college in North Germany in order to discover what methods and theories were being used for the education of children aged between three and eight. For Payne, this stage in a child's development was swallowed up in England in the elementary school, where the emphasis was on instruction rather than education:

> The question . . . whether we shall educate with a view to instruction as in Germany, or instruct with a view to education as in England, is, I venture to think, answered by the facts. No sane person will challenge a comparison between the average results of German primary education and of ours.[17]

Payne had written on Pestalozzi, Fellenberg, and Froebel, and was in particular interested in the application of Froebel's theories in the Kindergarten. He visited schools in Hamburg, Berlin, Dresden, Weimar, Gotha, and Eisenach, and aimed to report on the detail of teaching methods and classroom activity and to investigate any shortcomings. Though not every lesson he observed was successful, most impressed him, despite a tendency (which he noted also for England) to make teaching and its results 'prematurely regular and systematic'.[18]

This particular study is interesting as an academic educationist's attempt to explore theory as it is manifest in schools. The detail of his coverage of classroom practice reveals a deep understanding of the principles which teachers were attempting to implement in their practice. He concludes:

> The adoption of Pestalozzi's principles by the Governments of Prussia, Saxony, Baden, Würtemberg, &c., has only been a matter of time, and to their adoption we may fairly ascribe the enlightened teaching, with its excellent results, in the common schools of Germany. When the different States shall add (as Saxony has done) Fröbel's methods to those of Pestalozzi, the arrangements for elementary education will probably be as complete as it is possible for ordinary human ingenuity to make them.[19]

The efficacy of the German example, as far as early childhood education was concerned, was evidently very clear to Payne.

* * * * *

In 1879 the Clerk to the Birmingham School Board, George Davis, produced a report on schools in Germany and Switzerland. He had devoted four weeks (his summer holiday) to a visit to Germany to discover whether German schools were 'really so much better than the English'. Among other cities, he visited Hamburg, Berlin, Dresden, Halle, and Stuttgart, and he covers in his report information on teaching staff, organisation, school buildings, and discipline.

He recognises the high level of training of German teachers compared to their English counterparts:

> Our young Assistant Masters and Mistresses have very rarely received a training that can at all be compared with that which I have described as being the *universal rule* in Germany. Our Assistants are rarely so well educated, either as scholars, or as teachers.[20]
>
> Every class is taught by a trained and certificated teacher, the enormous difference between the ordinary staff of a German school and an English school will be strikingly apparent.[21]

He is sceptical throughout about the effects of the Revised Code in England (which introduced the notion of 'payment by results', based on pupils' performance in reading, writing, and arithmetic at three levels or 'standards'), preferring the German approach to the course of instruction in schools:

> The German course of instruction is a syllabus of work; and is intended to show what the teachers are to teach and the scholars are to learn. The standards of the English Code do not profess to be anything of the kind. They merely prescribe a number of mechanical tests to enable Her Majesty's Inspectors to determine whether certain grants should be paid from the Public Treasury.[22]
>
> The German teacher . . . is taught to enter upon his work as an educationist. He has to study the best methods of teaching in order to make the children intelligent; and his salary in no way depends upon "passes" and grants. Nothing that is purely mechanical, and does not appeal to the reason and

intelligence of a child, would be tolerated. All the instruction given is by means of conversational lessons, which interest the children, train the reasoning faculties, and expand the mind. The minds of the children are being constantly influenced and developed by the mind of the teacher.[23]

He is impressed by facilities for physical education, and he praises standards of discipline and children's willingness to be at school:

> I was particularly struck with the happy faces, nice manners, and good order in every school I visited. The whole system of organisation and teaching tends to the cultivation of good manners and to the prevention of scenes of disorder.
>
> [. . .]
>
> It is impossible to find anywhere the class of children who cause the greatest trouble in our English schools. I refer to those rough undisciplined boys and girls of from ten to twelve years of age, who are driven into school by our visiting officers, having never attended school before, and whose previous training has been obtained in the streets. Such a class of children does not exist in Germany.[24]

And in his summary he makes a number of points which provide contrast with provision in England. 'Education is much more highly appreciated in Germany than in England', he says: 'In Germany nothing is allowed to stand in the way of education':[25]

> There can be no doubt that the state of education in Germany is better than in England, and that the average German boy of fourteen is considerably in advance of the average English boy of the same age.[26]
>
> The high estimation in which teachers are held by the people of Germany must have a very great effect in increasing the influence which those teachers can obtain over their scholars.[27]
>
> If one of our best teachers were required to give a special lesson on a particular subject, and a German teacher were also required to give a lesson on the same subject, I do not think there would be very much difference in the value of the lesson given, nor even in their style. The difference is chiefly in this – that the German teacher has been accustomed *all his life* to give *every* lesson in the same excellent way, and carefully to arrange all his lessons, and even the details of each separate lesson, so as to form part of a systematic whole.[28]
>
> Whenever a visitor goes into a German school, the very first thing shown to him is their apparatus for teaching. We have no apparatus to show.[29]

And he concludes:

> Let us do our best to secure skilful teachers and intelligent teaching. As we fill our schools with able teachers, so we shall be able to adopt the class-room system, and to improve our methods; and as we succeed in improving the attendance and making the teaching intelligent, we shall approach, and I hope equal, the Germans in their results.[30]

Davis's report includes school plans, an etching of a German school desk, full details of the course of instruction in elementary schools in Hamburg, school timetables, and information on teaching methods. His views are especially interesting inasmuch as they reflect concern about the effects of the Revised Code on instruction in England (largely concerns about teaching to the test) and because they come from an administrator who had had useful teaching experience and so was able to appreciate the differences that existed in the schools between the two countries. Many of the positive features of his observations were still evident in German schools a hundred years and more later, even down to an interesting feature he noted about the design of classrooms:

> The class-rooms . . . are rectangular, with the windows in one of the longer sides. The desks are arranged parallel to the shorter sides, and are always turned in the direction which gives the children the advantage of having the light on their left hand.[31]

His report is significant in terms of how the German example in education was used at a more parochial level, in his case to inform educators and administrators in Birmingham about those features of educational provision which were contributing to perceptions of the superiority of education in Germany.

Royal Commission on Technical Instruction, 1882–4

With the rapid growth of Germany as an industrial nation there was an increasing awareness in Britain first of the commercial and later of the military threat which that growth represented. In 1881 a Royal Commission on Technical Instruction was given the brief

> To inquire into the Instruction of the Industrial Classes of certain Foreign Countries in technical and other subjects for the purpose of comparison with that of the corresponding classes in this Country; and into the influence of such Instruction on manufacturing and other Industries at home and abroad.[32]

The commissioners were chaired by the Liberal Member of Parliament – born in Germany – Bernhard Samuelson (1820–1905), who in 1867 had undertaken a comparative report of technical education in Europe. They visited a quite remarkable range of institutions in France, Switzerland, Germany, Austria, Belgium, Holland, and Italy. In Germany – and here we must remind ourselves that Alsace was part of Germany at the time – they looked at schools and other educational establishments in Mulhouse, Guebwiller, Strasbourg, Heidelberg, Reutlingen, Stuttgart, Munich, Nuremberg, Chemnitz, Freiberg, Dresden, Meissen, Berlin, Düsseldorf, Elberfeld, Gladbach, Remscheid, Barmen, Crefeld, Bochum, Iserlohn, Cologne, Bonn, Höhr Coblenz, Aachen, Sarreguemines, and Hanover. They examined among other things cotton spinning and weaving in the Rhine Provinces, calico printing in Alsace, the hosiery and glove trades in Saxony, the wool industry in the Rhine Provinces and Westphalia, the silk industry in Crefeld, technical education for printers in Alsace, engineering and machine making in Alsace and Prussia, the engineering and mechanical industries of Bavaria and the iron industries of Westphalia. They visited Siemens and Halske in Berlin and Hartmann's works in Saxony.[33]

The report identified two significant deficiencies:

In two very important respects [. . .] the education of a certain proportion of persons employed in industry abroad, is superior to that of English workmen; first, as regards the systematic instruction in drawing given to adult artizans, more especially in France, Belgium and Italy; and secondly, as to the general diffusion of elementary education in Switzerland and Germany.[34]

The Samuelson Report is a pre-eminent example of the thoroughness with which the foreign example – in a very wide variety of manifestations – could be used to inform policy-making processes at home. It also, incidentally, proposed that there should be held in 1884 an 'exhibition of the school-work of all nations', as 'an appropriate illustration of the account of foreign schools' contained in the report. This idea was realised in the International Health Exhibition of 1884, which covered many practical aspects of education, including demonstration classes in cookery and illustrative material from other countries, among them France, Germany and Japan. (This was a notion developed also – if only parochially – in the Paris Exhibition of 1889, which included much material to illustrate the work of elementary schools.[35])

* * * * *

Also in 1884 there appeared a 'brief practical account' of higher (i.e. 'secondary') education in Germany and England by the headmaster of a grammar school in Rochester, Charles Bird.[36] Bird had the specific intention of making critical remarks and suggestions with reference to the organisation and curriculum of English schools.

He laments the haphazard provision in secondary education: schools are 'planted over the country with about as much regard to national wants as if they had been dropped from a pepper-box'.[37] They are almost exclusively for boys and they are expensive. 'Few realize to what an extent we are surpassed by Germany'.[38] 'English schoolmasters do not fully realize how inferior we are to the Germans in educational matters'.[39]

Bird's is a largely descriptive account, with a concentration on the individual subjects taught. He writes enthusiastically about buildings and funding, and notes what George Davis was to record in his report, that the classrooms are 'lighted from the left side only'.

His enthusiasm for what he had observed (in his case in Stuttgart only) is clear from a summary statement:

The perfection and thoroughness of the German system of education contrasts very strongly with our own. In a German state the Minister of education ("Cultus Minister") is the head of a department which controls the whole of the educational machinery, from the people's schools at the bottom to the universities at the top. By this arrangement the schools work in harmony, each along its own line, neither overlapping on the one hand, nor leaving blank untouched spaces on the other.[40]

This uniformity and 'completeness' observable in the system was to remain a feature attractive to reform-minded commentators in England.

The Cross Report

By the 1880s it was felt necessary to investigate whether sufficient progress was being made in the provision of elementary education in England following the 1870 and subsequent Acts.

In November 1880 the London School Board (which had been elected in November 1870) wished to find out about aspects of educational provision in certain foreign countries, in order to assist its own work. It had struggled with problems of truancy and general non-attendance, one of its members reporting in early 1871 that only 66 per cent of children attended school regularly and that 'many of the parents did not care whether their children attended or not'.[41]

The board's request reads:

The School Board for London are now desirous with a view to possible improvements in their own work, to ascertain how compulsory attendance at School is enforced in some Continental States, and, in particular in Austria, Prussia, Bavaria, Denmark, Switzerland, and Italy. They would be glad to learn

The actual laws affecting the attendance of children at School, and (2) the machinery by which these laws are carried out.

It is [on] this latter point that the Board particularly wish to obtain information.[42]

The reply from Berlin provides an example of the kind of information that was collected:

. . . although for the moment there does not exist an Educational Code for the whole of Germany, the law applicable to Prussia may be taken as representing the practice followed in the remaining States of the Empire.

In the Kingdom of Prussia compulsory Education is enforced, not necessarily however at school, if requisite proofs can be produced that a child is being properly educated at home.

The law states that children must be sent to School after they have completed their fifth year, should the parents be unwilling or unable to attend to their education in their own hands. Formerly the period during which compulsory education lasted was from the beginning of the sixth to the end of the twelfth year. It has however been extended to the completion of the fourteenth year.

In the case of girls compulsory education is not enforced till they have completed their sixth year; and this same rule as to age applies to boys also if they live in villages which are more than a quarter of an hour's distance from the school, girls under similar circumstances not being required to attend till they have completed their seventh year.

The machinery for giving effect to the Law is the following:

Every year a notice is issued and displayed in some public place calling upon all Parents to send to school such of their children as have reached the age prescribed by law for this purpose.

After a certain time the Police auths. who are furnished with Lists of all inhabitants and the returns of births and deaths, visit the different district schools and enquire what children are in the schools.

Should it be discovered that any children are absent who have arrived at the age for attending, the Police go to the Parents' house, and should the latter be unable to present a certificate showing that the children are obtaining the necessary education at home, the police can interfere and oblige attendance; the Parents, if refusing to comply with the law being liable to a fine varying in amount from one to five shillings.

Should the offence be repeated, a heavier fine can be imposed or the Parents can be imprisoned.[43]

Following this localised interest in what was happening in education in other countries the Education Department in Whitehall wrote in October 1885 to the Secretary of the Treasury proposing that Matthew Arnold be appointed to undertake an investigation of elementary education in Germany, Switzerland, and France, focusing on four points: the quality of the education provided; its free provision; the training and emoluments of teachers; and the enforced attendance of children at school.[44]

A letter was sent to Matthew Arnold on 3 November 1885.[45] It constitutes a very full brief for the precise nature of the comparative investigation that was being proposed:

You have already been informed that my Lords have appointed you to make a special Report on certain points connected with Elementary Education in Germany, Switzerland, and France. But I am to point out that of these countries Germany and Switzerland are the most important.

The chief points are these,-

1. You are aware that the subject of Free Education is now exciting much attention: As to this you will ascertain whether gratuitous education is confined to Elementary Schools or extends to other Schools or Colleges; what reasons induced the State to establish the gratuitous system; in what way (directly or indirectly) the lower classes of society are made to feel the weight of the expenditure on Education; in what way the dirty and neglected children in large towns are dealt with – and especially whether all descriptions of children are mixed in the same School-room; whether there is a legal prohibition against charging fees in Public Schools even if Parents and Children are willing to pay; whether the attendance of children has increased or diminished since the establishment of Free Schools.
2. My Lords are anxious to ascertain the quality of the education furnished in the Elementary Schools – particularly in the case of children between 10 and 14.

For this purpose, it will be necessary that you should request some Masters and Mistresses to set a certain number of papers in writing and especially Arithmetic, so that a comparison may be instituted between the results obtained in the foreign schools with the results obtained in English schools.

It will, or course, be necessary to state the ages of children whose papers are to be examined and compared: These specimens – worked in the foreign schools – will form a most important part of your inquiry.

It will also be necessary to compare the curriculum pursued in foreign schools with the curriculum set forth in the Code.

3. With respect to Teachers – distinguishing males and females – you will ascertain from what class of society they come: How, where, and for how long they are trained; and whether the teachers in all Public Schools are certificated as such. You will also ascertain their annual emoluments, and whether they are entitled to retiring pensions and upon what conditions.
4. You will ascertain whether any law exists to enforce attendance – the nature of this law; whether it requires attendance every time the School is open; how many times the School must be open; and especially whether it is necessary for a child to pass a *particular standard of examination* before being allowed to go to work; and whether the right to labour is simply a question of age.

You will also ascertain what penalties are prescribed for breaking the law and if it is rigorously enforced; and lastly, what excuses for non-attendance may be pleaded.

Arnold spent some time away from his duties as inspector of schools in order to conduct his inquiries on the Continent, much to the chagrin of his superiors. His personal file contains letters criticising his protracted absence, as well as complaints from Arnold that he could not manage financially on the extra sum he had been allowed to cover his expenses:

> I find in making up my accounts that I am absolutely out of pocket by my foreign journey, owing to the insufficiency of the allowance of one guinea a day for personal expenses to cover the recent cost of living at the great hotels in the chief foreign capitals. When I tell you that my bedroom – small single room on the third floor – cost me twelve francs a day at Paris, and even more – eleven marks or shillings – at Berlin, you will understand that this must be so.[46]

Arnold produced a closely argued 25-page report, 'Special Report on Certain Points Connected with Elementary Education in Germany, Switzerland and France' which was presented to both Houses of Parliament in May 1886. In it he covers, as his brief required, four main concerns: free education; quality of education; status, training, and pensioning of teachers; compulsory attendance and release from school. Like all of Arnold's work it is meticulous and elegant in its preparation and argument. In his conclusions he argues for the retention of school fees and passionately for the development of secondary education. And in terms of general comparisons of popular education, he finds England wanting:

> [. . .] the things on which we pride ourselves are mere machinery; and what we should do well to lay to heart is that foreign schools with larger classes, longer holidays, and a school-day often cut in two [. . .] nevertheless, on the whole, give, from the better training of the teachers, and the better planning of their school course, a superior popular instruction to ours.[47]

In the same year Richard Laishley of the New Zealand Department of Public Instruction published a report on educational provision in various European states for the New Zealand General Assembly. He described education in the countries in question (Great Britain, France, Switzerland, Italy, Germany, Belgium, and the United States) in clear tabular form. The entries for Germany are included as Appendix 1 below as representing the state of education in Germany at the time of Arnold's report. His analysis of the strengths of educational provision in Germany are usefully summarised:

> The results of what I have heard, seen, and recently read induce me to believe –
>
> 1. That the Germans, in pursuance of a policy to become the strongest of all nations, by excelling in civil as in military affairs, have concluded that, in order to secure the most successful results possible from national education, thorough discipline of mind and body is indispensable: and to facilitate this that there must be at least –
>   a. consideration for the feelings of all in religious matters;
>   b. local government, including regulation of religious instruction (subject to the protection of minorities), of direct local taxation, of expenditure, and of administrative details;
>   c. religion (subject to the conscience clause provisions) considered as the primary subject on elementary school programmes;
>   d. compulsory attendance laws;
>   e. thorough qualification of all teachers for private, as well as for public, schools;
>   f. and recognition of the great importance of gymnastic exercises.
>
> So that in Germany, as in Switzerland, we find friction, as between the State and the citizens in religious matters, provided against; religion, universality, thoroughness in detail, thrift and adaptation to local circumstances, provided for by local government and compulsory school attendance laws; physical strength and vigour promoted by gymnastic exercises; and discipline established and maintained, and correct information imparted, in the best mode possible, by thoroughly qualified teachers.
>
> The consequence is education – not merely instruction – is carried out under most favourable circumstances, with no thwarting undercurrent of religious or local influences.
> 2. That pre-eminent attention is paid to scientific knowledge in all the higher institutions, and to the study of philosophy in the universities, and –
> 3. That extreme exactness and minuteness are insisted upon.[48]

Such a checklist of advantages, coming from an observer from way beyond the confines of Europe, serves to reinforce the advantages of educational provision in Germany as perceived by commentators with easier access to the country.

* * * * *

In March 1887 a further circular was sent out via British representatives to the governments of Austria, Belgium, Denmark, France, Germany, Holland, Italy, Norway, Sweden, and Switzerland, in connection with the work of the Royal Commission on the Elementary Education Acts. Its report was published in 1888 and known as the Cross Report after a former Home Secretary, Lord Cross (Richard Assheton Cross, 1823–1914), who chaired the commission. As far as Germany was concerned, information was sought from

Bavaria, Frankfurt am Main, Hamburg, Prussia, Saxony, and Wurtemberg. This circular, entitled 'Schedule of Inquiries as to the Present Systems of Primary Education now in force in the leading Countries of Europe and in certain British Colonies', embraced some 57 questions, many of which were divided into several sub-sections.[49]

Here is the circular in full:

Schedule of Inquiries as to the Present Systems of Primary Education now in force in the leading Countries of Europe and in certain British Colonies

  I. The information asked for relates to Primary Education: that is, to elementary schools or higher elementary schools, and *not* to secondary schools.

 II. The answers to these questions, more especially where measures of money are concerned, should be given, not only in terms of the Country, but also in all cases in their English equivalents.

III. The answer to each question should be written in as short a form as possible in the blank space immediately opposite.

IV. It is particularly requested that this Schedule may be returned with as little delay as possible to The Secretary, Royal Commission on the Elementary Education Acts, 8, Richmond Terrace, Whitehall, S.W.

Name of Country _____

Inquiries

  1. What is the date of the School Law now in force?
  2. What is the Estimated Population of the Country?
  3. Give the number of Children –
     • Of School Age – i.e., from – to – years of age.
     • On the School Rolls of
       Public schools – i.e. under Public Management
       Non-public schools – i.e., under Private or Voluntary Management
       c. In Regular Attendance
  4. Is Elementary Education Compulsory?
  5. If so,
     • Between what ages?
     • What minimum of Attendances satisfies the law?
     • What penalties are imposed for Non-Attendance?
     • What Exemptions are allowed?
     • How and by whom is Compulsion enforced?
  6. Are there any Rewards on the part of State or the Locality for Good Attendance?
  7. Is there any class of Vagrant or Destitute children where the ordinary school system fails to reach? If so, how is that class dealt with?
  8. What are the prescribed Hours per day and per week of School Attendance? Do they vary with the age of the scholar or with the season of the year?
  9. For how many Days during the year must the School be Open? Is this minimum usually exceeded, and by how much?
 10. Is there any system of Half-Time or Partial Exemption from attendance of scholars for the purpose of enabling them to go to work?
     a. If so, what is the system?

  b. What is the Law as to Juvenile Labour?
11. Whose duty is it to determine what is a Sufficiency of School Accommodation for each locality? At whose cost is such accommodation provided, and what securities are taken for the suitability of the buildings?
12. Is School Accommodation provided for the total number of children of school age? If not, for what proportion? and what surface and cubic space per scholar on the roll are required?
13. In districts supplied with schools by Voluntary Means are schools under Public Management also provided?
14. Is there any Regulation enforced upon Schools Not under Public Management -
  a. As to the State of the Premises?
  b. As to the Proportionate Number of Teachers and their possession of Diplomas or Certificates of Competency?
  c. As to the Curriculum of instruction?
15. Is the Curriculum of Elementary Instruction prescribed by the State or otherwise? If otherwise, state how.
16. Do the Schools of the State give Religious as well as Secular instruction? and, if so, of what nature? By whom is it given?
17. If not, are the School houses used out of School hours for Religious Instruction?
18. Is any provision made for Moral Training of the Children in the Schools by the ordinary Teachers in the ordinary school hours? If so, state what means are taken to secure it.
19. Is the Religious Instruction Obligatory on all the scholars? If not, what provision is made for the Religious Instruction of the minority?
20. Are the Teachers in the Schools exclusively Lay?
21. Does the Curriculum of Secular Instruction vary in different schools, and under what circumstances?
22. Is there any difference between the Curriculum of Urban and Rural Schools?
23. Give the curriculum for (a) a Village school of less than 100 scholars; (b) for a Town school of 200 or more scholars.
24. How far is (a) Drawing,
  (b) Needlework,
  (c) the Use of Tools,
  (d) Cookery,
  a compulsory or optional Subject of Instruction?
25. Is there any system of Gymnastics or of Physical Training in use in the Schools?
  a. If, so, describe it.
  b. Is it obligatory?
  c. How much time is given to it?
  d. Is it used for Girls as well as Boys?
26. Is a Second Language taught in any of the Elementary Schools, and if so, which and to what extent?
27. To what extent do Infant or Kindergarten Schools exist? At what age do children begin to frequent them? Are they a part of the public system?

28. What is the ordinary practice in respect to the Promotion of Scholars? Are all the members of the same class promoted class by class periodically, or are exceptions made in any cases? If so, on what grounds, and to what extent?
29. Are the Elementary Schools Mixed or Separate for boys and girls? If mixed, are they taught by men or women? To what extent are women teachers employed in primary schools?
30. What are the qualifications as to age, attainments, teaching power, and moral character required in the case of Teachers employed in Elementary Schools?
31. What is the number of scholars on the roll assigned to one teacher (i.) by the school, and (ii.) in actual practice?
32. Are all the Teachers Adult, or are there others employed in teaching?
33. Is there any system of (a) Night or (b) Continuation schools?
34. How far is attendance in such schools compulsory, and during what ages, for males and females respectively? How often do they meet in the year? Are there Fees? How are the expenses met?
35.   i. Is any instruction, (a) Religious or (b) Secular, given in the Public Elementary Schools on Sunday?
    ii. If so, what is the Religious teaching?
    iii. By whom is it given?
    iv. If so, what is the Secular instruction?
    v. Is there any Technical instruction in these schools on Sunday?
    vi. By whom is it given?
    vii. Is attendance at the instruction compulsory?
    viii. At what hours is it given?
    ix. By whom are the expenses met?
    x. If by fees, state amount per scholar.
36. In the ordinary Elementary Schools, how are Teachers Appointed and Removed? Has the Teacher any Appeal against Dismissal?
37. Give the Scale of Salaries of Teachers, male and female, of all grades -
    i. Together with their other emoluments,
    ii. Stating if a house and firing,
    iii. Or any other advantages,
    iv. Are attached to the office.
    v. Do they discharge any paid civil or ecclesiastical offices in addition to their school-work?
38.   i. How are Teachers Trained?
    ii. At whose cost?
    iii. At what age do they enter training colleges?
    iv. What is the length of the course of instruction?
    v. How are they educated before entering the colleges?
    vi. Are they generally drawn from the same class as the children who use the Schools? If not, from what class?
    vii. Is the supply of qualified Teachers sufficient or excessive?
39. Are there any untrained Teachers employed, and if so, what qualifications are they allowed to teach?
40. Are the Training Colleges institutions exclusively for the professional training of Teachers? Do teachers obtain their general education by previous attendance at higher Schools or universities?

41. Do the Students live in the Colleges, or do they only attend there daily for instruction?
42. Is there any provision in the Training Colleges for Religious or Moral training?
43. Are the Colleges connected with any particular Church or Religious denomination?
44. Are the Elementary Schools inspected by the State or by the Local authority? If by both, how do the two kinds of Inspection differ?
45. Who appoints the Inspectors?
    a. What are their special qualifications?
    b. What are their salaries?
    c. Are they drawn from the ranks of elementary teachers?
46. How often are the Schools Inspected? Is any record made of the result of the Examination of Individual Children?
47. Is Elementary Education maintained from Public Funds or from Voluntary Contributions, or from both sources combined? State the proportion of each.
48. Under what circumstances, and on what conditions, are Grants made to a Locality or School from National or from Local Sources?
49. Is any extra assistance given to Poor Districts?
50. What is the Cost of School Maintenance per scholar in attendance, in (i.) elementary and (ii.) higher elementary schools, excluding the cost of administration?
51. Is Elementary Instruction Gratuitous? If paid for by the Parents, what are the fees? How are Arrears of Fees collected?
52. What is the usual Rate of Wages for (a) Skilled or (b) Unskilled labour?
53. Is there any Public Aid for Feeding or Clothing Indigent Children who attend the elementary schools? Is there any provision for admitting such children free?
54. What is the Total Number of the children under Instruction in the Elementary Schools of the State, and what is the Cost per Child-
    a. To the Parents?
    b. To the Locality [?]
    c. To the State?
55. Is there a Public System of Secondary Education in the Country?
56. Is it Gratuitous? If not, what does each scholar pay?
57. Is there any system by which poor and deserving scholars are enabled to rise from Elementary Schools into the Higher Schools?[50]

The main purpose of these questions can be synthesised as follows:

- basic statistical information
- compulsory nature of the education system and school attendance details
- public management of schools and financial questions
- curricular provision, especially relating to religious education
- teachers and their qualifications and terms of employment
- school inspection
- provision of secondary education.

The British Ambassador to the German court in Berlin, Sir Edward Malet (1837–1908), reported back to the Marquess of Salisbury (at that time both Prime Minister and Secretary of State for Foreign Affairs):

> I have now the Honour to enclose copy and translation of a Note I have this day received from Count Bismarck pointing out that, owing to essential differences between the Educational Systems of Great Britain and Germany it would be almost impossible to supply answers in detail to these enquiries.[51]

Bismarck's letter effectively asked the commission to do its homework on the basis of published information:

> According to the reply of Herr von Goßler [Prussian Minister of Education] which is now to hand, fulfilling the wish of the British government would encounter considerable difficulties, since the conditions which seem in the questions asked to be decisive are quite different from those which prevail in Prussia and equally in the other German states. The difficulties would be even greater if, as could be concluded from the inclusion of a special questionnaire for Frankfurt, it was expected on the British side that the very detailed questions could be answered for every district and every big city in Prussia or in Germany. It will, however, be an easy matter for the British government or the Royal Commission on Education to gain the desired information on elementary education in Prussia from the documents which are now included.
>
> [Present author's translation][52]

The British *chargé d'affaires* in Munich made a not unreasonable request; having taken advice about the completion of the schedule, he reported:

> if these queries are received by the School Department through the regular channel, the Ministry for Foreign Affairs, they will be happy to give complete answers to the questions placed before them, but, it appears to them more practicable if these questions were rendered into German, in that there appeared to be intricacies of expressions which might puzzle the Department and only obstruct the return of answers, should the original queries be set before them.[53]

Despite these reservations about the questionnaire, a lot of material was eventually collected – even it transpired from Prussia, where Sir Edward Malet took great pains to respond following an admonition from the Foreign Office in London – and this enabled the commissioners to produce in an appendix a comparative table divided into seven groups:

> Compulsion: yes/no; between ages? attendance required?
>   Instruction gratuitous?
>   Primary schools maintained by: state? local authorities? voluntary action?
>   Religious teaching given?
>   Continuation or Night Schools: yes/no; system? compulsory?
>   Training Schools supported by: state? voluntary action?
>   Training College: day? boarding? religious instruction given?[54]

The responses for Prussia were:

Compulsion: yes; 4 to 14; 8 years
  Instruction free, generally. In some places parents pay 4 to 8 marks per annum
  Primary schools maintained in principle by the communities and patrons. State provides salaries and pensions for teachers; Church co-operates from church funds
  Religious teaching given by teacher, compulsory
  Continuation or Night Schools: Continuation schools in the country, and for artizans [sic]
  Training Schools supported by state
  Training College: day – one-third; boarding – two-thirds; religious instruction given.[55]

At an earlier point in the Cross Report information from the foreign returns is presented in connection with a discussion of religious education.[56] A comprehensive presentation of all the returns received was published as a special volume of the Cross Report.[57]

Diversity of provision was still strongly defended, however. During a conference of the Teachers' Guild which took place in Oxford in April 1893 one delegate reported a conversation he had had some twenty years earlier with a German professor who was investigating schools in England. He asked him what advice he would have for English teachers: 'You have great variety; keep your variety; don't copy our dull uniformity'.[58]

Michael Sadler and the availability of information on Germany

In the last quarter of the nineteenth century there were not surprisingly much greater opportunities generally to discover information about other countries. One means by which those directly involved in the teaching profession and others with a concerned interest in educational issues could be kept informed about educational developments abroad was through the pages of the *Journal of Education*, a successor to the *Scholastic Register* (1874–7) and the *Scholastic Register and Educational Advertiser* (1869–74) and published from 1879. As was the case with the *Quarterly Journal of Education* (1831–5) the *Journal of Education* is a remarkably rich source of information on all aspects of development in education in Britain and elsewhere. The writing is of the highest standard: elegant and of an intellectual sophistication that would be unimaginable in a similar publication in modern times. There was an assumption that the readership was well read and competent in Latin and Greek and also in French and German. Allusions to German literature and philosophy were common in editorial comment, and it was clearly not deemed necessary to translate German words and phrases and even whole sentences quoted from literary sources. Correspondents wrote frequent short but detailed reports on the minutiae of the educational scene in all parts of Germany, and there were often more substantive articles which described particular features of education in the German states at generous length. Over the ten-year period 1884–93, for example, the journal reported at length, among very many other topics, on German examinations (1884), the free schools of Berlin (1886), the curriculum of German high schools for Girls (1886), 'some German schools' (1887), a visit to a German district school inspector (1888), a German *Volksschule* (1889), Heidelberg schools (1889), the new Prussian law on elementary education (1890), Herbart's life and system (1892), and the training of teachers in Germany (1892–3).

But alongside sophisticated journalistic coverage of this kind and that provided in other periodicals and in the press, another series of publications stands out. These are the remarkable studies on aspects of education in other countries produced by the Office of Special Inquiries and Reports under the directorship of Michael Sadler from 1895 to 1903. The first volume, published in 1897, contained twenty-five papers, seven of which concerned education in Germany:

The Realschulen in Berlin, and their bearing on modern Secondary and Commercial Education

(Sadler)

The Ober-Realschulen of Prussia, with special reference to the Ober-Realschule in Charlottenburg

(Sadler)

The Prussian Elementary School Code

(translated by Twentyman)

The Continuation Schools in Saxony

(Dale)

The School Journey in Germany

(Dodd)

The Teaching of the Mother Tongue in Germany

(Dale)

Holiday Courses in France and Germany for Instruction in Modern Languages

(Marvin & Morant)

The ninth volume, of over 600 pages (1902), was devoted entirely to education in Germany. Its contents are very wide-ranging:

The Unrest in Secondary Education in Germany and Elsewhere

(Sadler)

Note on the Revised Curricula and Programmes of Work for Higher Schools for Boys in Prussia

(Twentyman)

Higher Schools for Girls in Germany: An Introductory Sketch

(Lyster)

The Smaller Public Elementary Schools of Prussia and Saxony, with Notes on the Training and Position of Teachers

(Field)

Note on Impending Changes in the Professional Training of Elementary Teachers in Prussia

(Twentyman)

School Gardens in Germany

(Rooper)

Impressions of Some Aspects of the Work in Primary and Other Schools in Rhineland, etc.

(Hughes & Beanland)

The Continuation Schools in Berlin

(Bertram, translated by Twentyman)

Note on the Earlier History of the Technical High Schools in Germany

(Twentyman)

Recent Developments in Higher Commercial Education in Germany

(Sadler)

On the Measurement of Mental Fatigue in Germany

(Parez)

Report of the Congress on the Education of Feeble-minded Children at Augsburg, April 10–12, 1901

(Eichholz)

On the Education of Neglected Children in Germany

(Rathenau)

The series diminished in scope after Sadler's resignation and its eventual discontinuation (though the board would still publish a series of 'educational pamphlets') was a matter of regret: even in the late 1940s attempts were being made to reintroduce it in some form.[59]

A full account of elementary schools in Prussia appeared in 1881 from the pen of the academic and journalist John Laidlay Bashford (who was to teach at the University of Berlin from 1882 to 1890), intended to be of interest to those concerned with 'National Education' in England. Bashford's study is largely concerned with a detailed analysis of the curriculum, but it also argues strongly for compulsory education for boys in England after completion of the 'ordinary course required by the Education Act', along the lines of the free Saxon *Fortbildungsschulen* (continuation schools), providing four or six hours of tuition a week on weekday afternoons or evenings or on Sundays:

> The difficulties at first of introducing this new school were very great, for as in England when attendance at school became compulsory, the parents of children complained because they said their children were taken away from them when they might be helping their parents towards the support of the family, so in Saxony the employers of labour complained that their apprentices were taken away from them, and the boys too did not like being forced to go to school again. But in so short a period as five years much of this opposition has disappeared. Employers are beginning to see that that which benefits the pupil, in so far as it makes him more intelligent for his work, benefits them also, so long as he remains an apprentice. And the boys themselves look upon attendance at the Fortbildungsschule as part of their duty as young citizens, and those who choose to do so can reap great advantages from their work there.[60]

To these benefits such further education adds a moral dimension in terms of respect for others and of self-respect, and makes profitable use of leisure time. He concludes:

May the time soon come in England when parents of the poorer classes will acknowledge the benefits conferred on them by the State, and look upon the education of their children as a duty every citizen owes to his country![61]

We shall return to the subject of continuation schools below.

The Bryce Commission (1895)

Towards the end of the nineteenth century increasing attention was gradually being paid in England to provision in secondary education.[62] The first stirrings of what was eventually to become in the twentieth century a demand for 'secondary education for all' can be found in various initiatives in which Michael Sadler played a part, though at this early stage secondary education was still essentially for children of the middle and upper classes. In 1893 Sadler was instrumental in the setting-up of a significant conference on secondary education in Oxford,[63] and he was to become a member of the Bryce Commission, which reported in 1895 on the organisation of secondary education. In line with the previous tradition of Royal Commissions on education, it reported at length, with a substantial main report and a further eight volumes of minutes of evidence, memoranda, reports of assistant commissioners, and statistical tables. Among the memoranda is an account of the registration and training of secondary teachers in Germany by J. J. Findlay (1860–1940), who had spent time in 1891–3 as 'a student of education in Germany'[64] and had a doctorate from the University of Leipzig, and who was later Professor of Education in the University of Manchester. In addition, Sadler contributed a report on the leaving examination in the secondary schools of Prussia.[65] And there were responses to a general circular sent out by the commission from Bavaria, Hesse, Prussia, Saxony, Saxe-Weimar-Eisenach, and Wurtemburg, as well as from British colonies, the United States, and several other European states.[66]

The general circular sent to European countries asked for information on a range of topics germane to the commission's inquiries:

1. What proportions of the secondary schools in your country are provided by the State and by private enterprise respectively?
2. In the case of secondary schools provided or aided by the State what proportion of the total cost of education is covered by the scholars' fees? On what principle is the proportion determined?
3. How best may provision be made for the passing of scholars from –

   a. Primary to secondary schools;
   b. One class of secondary school to another?
   c. Secondary schools to the universities;
      and for giving aid to poor scholars of promise.

4. What has been found to be the best way of bringing technical into proper relation with general education in your secondary schools?
5. What provision exists for the training of secondary school teachers? How far is such training provided in connection with the universities?
6. It has been said that there has been recently a tendency in some countries for a large number of scholars, whose circumstances in other respects seemed to indicate some form of manual labour as their natural destination, to quit secondary schools with a dislike or unfitness for manual labour,

and with little prospect of obtaining any other kind of employment.
Is that statement true as regards your country? If so, to what cause do you attribute this result, and what steps should be taken to prevent it?

7. Has there been any material change in your system of secondary education since 1865, particularly as regards the training of teachers, the relation of the State and the teacher, and the organisation of primary in relation to secondary education? If so, on what grounds has such change been effected, and how is it working?

8. Has there recently been any considerable increase in the number of private schools in your country? If so, to what cause do you attribute this increase?[67]

For Germany replies were received from Bavaria, Hesse, Prussia, Saxony, Saxe-Weimar, and Wurtemberg, with individuals in Saxony providing by far the most detail. The Prussian return is short and factual, referring the commission to various official published sources. Together the replies present a remarkably positive picture of provision throughout the Empire, contrasting sharply with what was available in England at the time. An extract from the reply of Professor Friedersdorf of Halle to question 3 will serve to illustrate the contrast:

There is no difficulty about the transfer of pupils from elementary to higher schools, because the subjects taught in the lower classes of secondary schools are generally the same as those taught in the four upper forms of an elementary school. Thus children who have been in the four classes pass without difficulty into the lower classes of a secondary school.

Those children who do not wish to attend an elementary school can attend the three classes of the preparatory divisions attached to the higher schools.

b. Promotion from class to class in the same school is decided by the teacher of the class in conference with the head master, on the results of examination.

c. Transition from the highest class of a school to the university is effected by means of an oral and written examination conducted by the head master and staff of a higher school, under the direction of the Royal Council of Education for the province.

Poor scholars are assisted

1. by free education in higher schools. In State schools fees are remitted to 10 per cent of the scholars. In other establishments the per-centage is a little lower.

2. by scholarships, *i.e.* the interest on capital devoted to the needs of poor scholars.

3. by the provision of books, &c. free of charge.[68]

The Bryce Report's main proposals were for a central authority for education (which became a reality in the 1899 Act, establishing the Board of Education) and for the establishment of local authorities for secondary education. It led to the provisions in the 1902 Education Act (the Balfour Act).

* * * * *

We shall see that Weimar Germany attracted particular attention as a result of achievements in physical education – an attraction that extended into the years of National Socialist hegemony. But other aspects of educational health and hygiene in Germany were not neglected. Here, for example, is an extract from a report from the London County Council on bathing arrangements in schools in Germany and Holland, published in 1906:

> For twenty years school cleansing baths have been an institution on the Continent. There is no doubt on the part of teachers or doctors as to the great benefits, both direct and indirect, which result from their use. There is immediate and noticeable improvement in the school air. German schools beat our schools generally, but are remarkable for the badness of their school air. The improvement in this, however, is remarked on by every one in the schools.
>
> There is a noticeable improvement in the quality and cleanliness of the underclothing of the children, and improvement, too, in self-respect. All teachers speak of this. In England many children have clothing sewn on. The diminution of vermin is said to be also noticeable, absence of irritability and greater ability to do school work being claimed as a result of the weekly bath.
>
> These developments in school bathing have been taking place during the past generation, and nothing has been heard of them in England till the question arose indirectly out of the "Cleansing Scheme" in London. It is so generally known and recognised abroad that even Germans have long ago ceased to write papers or hold discussions on so commonplace a proceeding as the school shower bath.[69]

This kind of study of the detail of provision in Germany was also typical of the work of Michael Sadler's Office of Special Inquiries and Reports, to which we shall return below.

Technological advance in Germany

[W]hen the advantages afforded by the schools for technical instruction are considered; that is to say, those found in schools for teaching the theory (and, in part, the practice) of architecture, construction, civil and mechanical engineering, chemistry, agriculture, metallurgy, mining and other arts and sciences, we can only wonder that the Englishman has been able, even in some degree, to hold his own against the competition fostered by every educational advantage carefully applied to economical results.[70]

This view of 1874 gives an indication of the wide coverage in educational provision in Germany of some of the subjects which might contribute to economic success. Humboldt's universal concept of *Allgemeinbildung* eventually had to give way in part to the more practical consideration of training people to work in the industrial society of the second half of the nineteenth century. Humboldt had warned against the dehumanising processes of 'technocracy and bureaucracy' (*Technokratie und Bürokratie*)[71] and he had refused to see the virtues of more utilitarian approaches to the curriculum: for him the school should first and foremost equip the child with the necessary foundations of knowledge to be able to go on to acquire further knowledge and develop particular expertise.[72] But by the end of the century Georg Kerschensteiner (1854–1932) could define three aims of every school in rather different terms: (1) to prepare for, or to provide vocational training; (2) to teach civic duty through vocational training; (3) to teach the moral values of the community.[73]

In the 1840s an eminent German chemist polarised the issue by attacking 'overgrown humanism which stands above all else against the progress of natural science and scientific medicine': this would be 'a thing that will be looked back on half a century hence with shame and a smile of pity'.[74] With the increasing awareness of the need to develop a more modern and realistic approach to the education and training of young people, modern subjects, *Realien*,[75] were introduced into school curricula, and the second-tier secondary schools, the *Realschulen*, began to grow in importance.

Attention was increasingly paid to the experiments of Pestalozzi and later to the theories of Herbart and Froebel, and progress was made in the formal training of teachers. Wilhelm Rein (1847–1929), a follower of Herbart, ran a successful teacher seminary at Jena from 1886 and based his approach on Herbart's five steps. German educators at all levels were receiving increasing recognition outside Germany as the best instructors in Europe. This was despite the fact that their schools lacked the educative (*erzieherisch*) aspects of the approach favoured by the followers of Pestalozzi and Herbart and put into practice in schools in England like Abbotsholme, which attracted wide interest from the Continent from its foundation in 1889. Cecil Reddie (1858–1932), headmaster of Abbotsholme, made the contrast between the *Erziehungsschule* (*Lebensschule*) and the *Unterrichtsschule* (*Lernschule*) – the 'educative school' ('life school') as opposed to the 'instruction school' ('learning school'):

> If Germany, on the one hand, teaches us the best method of instruction, we on the other hand can, I think, furnish you with a picture of harmonious education. Let us continue the best German school-*instruction* with the best all-round English school-*life*. Then we shall have the perfect Educative School as it appeared to the imagination of a Herbart or a Ruskin.[76]

The type of *Realschule* known as *Realschule erster Ordnung* had been in existence in Prussia since 1859 and had given instruction in Latin while abandoning Greek in favour of mathematics and science. This development led to a clash between the defenders of the classical *Gymnasien*, who believed that the benefits of traditional training in the humanities would be eroded, and the proponents of the *Realschulen*, who wanted the leaving certificate of such schools to be on a par with the *Abitur* for university entrance. In the years following 1871 the humanists found it increasingly difficult to defend their position: Germany had now entered a second phase of fervent nationalism and was becoming a first-rank industrial and commercial power. The future prosperity of the country lay in scientific and technical progress, and this in turn depended on the educational provision of the state.[77]

Wilhelm II intervened in the debate at the school conference of 1890, quoting his own unhappy experiences at the hands of the classicists. His education, he said, was not a national education: it was unsuited to the modern age; it was concerned with classical antiquity without being truly humanistic; it was training in grammar aimed at the Latin essay in the leaving examination.[78] For a long time, he had been concerned with the thought of making the school 'useful' (*nutzbar*) in order to counter the forces of socialist and communist ideas. Fear of God and love of the fatherland were to be encouraged: the ethical aspects of religious education should come to the foreground, the history of the fatherland should be emphasised, including the role of the Prussian kings in furthering the interests of the workers.[79]

By the time of the school conference of 1900 the leaving certificates of the *Realgymnasium* and the *Oberrealschule* were recognised as equivalent to those of the *Gymnasium* in indicating attainment of the *Hochschulreife*, the qualification for university entrance.

Modern studies thus grew considerably in the schools during the second half of the nineteenth century, and rapid progress was made too in the development of higher education, particularly in the technical and scientific fields, and in vocational training.

Britain was still behind in terms of educational provision for the second phase of the industrial revolution, a situation that has been described as 'one of the strangest paradoxes of modern history':

> that on the one hand, a liberal society standing out from all others in the eighteenth century for equality and mobility of status, should have lost something of these during the very period of its progressive political democratization; while on the other, a far more authoritarian society, characterized in its pre-industrial period by a clearly defined, fairly rigid hierarchy of rank, should have developed a more open structure, without corresponding political change.[80]

Germany had founded an impressive range of *technische Hochschulen* (technical universities) in the 1820s and 1830s which after 1871 had facilities for 6,000 students, with a considerable surplus of places over available applicants.[81] 'A veritable cult of *Wissenschaft* and *Technik* developed'; 'The People came to gape at the Hochschulen with the awe usually reserved for historical monuments'.[82]

A consequence of the increased provision of scientific and technical education for the industrial age was the need to train young people for specific trades and occupations, and Germany entered a new phase of vocational training in which rapid and important advances were made. A key figure here was Georg Kerschensteiner.

Technical schools had begun to emerge in the late eighteenth century, and trade schools (*Arbeitsschulen*) started to be developed at the end of the Napoleonic wars. Humboldt and the New Humanists, with their insistence on a non-utilitarian approach to education, had caused a setback in the growth of such schools, but by the 1870s it was recognised that post-elementary education should be provided for all children, with considerable attention to training in specific skills useful in civic life. General continuation schools began to be introduced. These schools provided further general education together with training in functional skills – compulsory attendance at continuation schools (for three years for boys) was introduced in Saxony in 1873 and other areas followed this example.

In Munich – and in the face of considerable opposition – Kerschensteiner established a continuation school system which was to attract widespread attention. By 1907 compulsory attendance had been introduced for all skilled workers until the age of eighteen. The educational provision of the continuation schools reflected Kerschensteiner's view that 'vocational training leads to character training':[83] civics became an important subject in the curriculum since Kerschensteiner believed that the main aim of education was to produce 'selfless, moral citizens whose greatest desire it was to uphold the moral pillars of the State and of their fellow men'.[84]

An account of the continuation schools in Berlin, published in Sadler's series, summarised the aims and functions of the continuation schools:

> [The compulsory Continuation Schools] are to be attended by such young people between the ages of fourteen and sixteen or fourteen and eighteen as cannot show that they have already attained the highest standard of the Continuation School, or that they are attending some other school of a similar or higher grade. Non-attendance is punishable by police regulations. The curriculum is prescribed and occasionally adapted to the occupations of the pupils, and generally assumes four to six hours of instruction a week. Special stress is laid upon the ethical influence on the pupil. The instruction constitutes a prolongation of compulsory school attendance in two directions; it compels the pupils to learn and the parents (or principals, or employers) to give the apprentices (or employés) the necessary free time.[85]

As we shall see, the Lewis Committee was to recommend compulsory attendance at day continuation classes in England.

What was special about advances in science and technology in Germany was an accompanying focus on the *application* of new knowledge and on the training that would facilitate such application. Table 3 below shows something of the huge gap in the numbers of trained chemists and engineers in Britain as compared with Germany over the period 1910 to 1921.

Germany had clearly laid the ground for such achievement in training by the last decades of the nineteenth century, while in Britain the comparative lack of support for science and technology was generally lamented, attention often being drawn to the better example from Germany. A British geologist could report that on one occasion before the First World War a British Treasury official had said that he would be glad to talk to him about the needs of geology but 'begged that the example of Germany might not be mentioned'.[86] Germany's ability to compete with Britain, despite its later industrialisation, was especially evident in the growth of its chemical, pharmaceutical, and electrical industries. This growth was boosted in the form of state financing of education to support industry, reckoned to be over six times that of support in England in 1900.[87]

Economic growth in Germany was rapid from about 1860, and – according to Bairoch's calculations (see Table 4) – was to overtake that of the United Kingdom by 1910.

Table 3 Comparative numbers of trained chemists and engineers, Britain and Germany

	Germany	Britain
University students, 1913	c. 44,000	c. 26,700
Trained chemists, 1910	5,500	1,500
Engineers with higher education	65,202 (1914)	48,000 (1921)

(Derived from Sanderson, *Education and Economic Decline in Britain, 1870 to the 1990s*, p. 19)

Table 4   Gross National Product (in Purchasing Power Parity), Germany and United Kingdom, 1830–1913, calculated in millions of 1960 US dollars

	1830	1840	1850	1860	1870
Germany	7,235	8,320	10,395	12,771	16,697
UK	8,245	10,431	12,591	16,072	19,628

	1880	1890	1900	1910	1913
Germany	19,993	26,454	35,800	45,523	49,760
UK	23,551	29,441	36,273	40,623	44,074

(Source: Derived from Bairoch, 'Europe's Gross Domestic Product, 1800–1975', table 4, p. 281)

Bairoch places the UK third in Europe in terms of size of total GNP in 1830, with Germany in fourth position. By 1913 Germany was in second place, with the UK third. (Russia was the country with the largest volume of GNP.) Economists admit that measurement of this kind is difficult and can be misleading, but it is clear that growth in Germany was impressive in comparison to that of the UK in the final decades of the nineteenth century. It is not surprising that observers in England sought to learn lessons from German success as the new century dawned.

Attraction of the reform movement in modern language teaching in Germany

There had been serious efforts to reform modern language teaching before the publication in 1882 of Wilhelm Viëtor's pamphlet *Der Sprachunterricht muss umkehren* ('Language Teaching Must Change Direction'), but Viëtor (1850–1918) is seen as having stimulated a movement that was to be widely felt in England. In this particular area of the school curriculum the German example, manifested as the 'reform method', was to encourage a reinvigorated approach to the teaching of modern foreign languages.

Viëtor's work is a polemic, relying heavily on the work of the eminent British philologists Henry Sweet (1845–1912, who had studied in Heidelberg) and A. H. Sayce (1846–1933). The subtitle of his text was *Ein Beitrag zur Überbürdungsfrage* ('A Contribution to the Question of Overload' [in the curriculum]) and so it was designed to address the problem of imbalance in the German school curriculum, which required *Gymnasium* pupils to spend 7,000 hours on language learning over a five-year period.[88]

Some of these lessons, Viëtor says, might be given up if new methods of language teaching could be adopted that would make more profitable use of time.

A contribution to volume 3 of Sadler's series of special reports on educational subjects by Mary Brebner (published in 1898) looked specifically at modern language teaching in Germany. (There were three further pieces on the same subject.) Brebner was able to identify the essential features of language teaching according to the new method:

- Only oral teaching at the beginning
- The foreign language used as much as possible
- Whole or partial exclusion of translation into the foreign language, except in higher classes

Table 5   Number of language lessons in German secondary schools

	Gymnasium		Realgymnasium		Oberrealschule	
	Overall	**Language**	**Overall**	**Language**	**Overall**	**Language**
1856/59	268	165	285	127	-	-
1882	268	159	280	135	276	112
1891	252	143	259	120	258	106
1901	259	150	262	124	262	106

(Source: Viëtor: *Der Sprachunterricht muss umkehren,* 3rd edn, p. 35)

- Minimal translation from the foreign language
- Extensive use of pictures in younger classes
- Use of *Realien*
- Conversation based on reading
- Use of reading to learn grammar inductively[89]

In the coming years these features were to find expression in manuals and text-books in England, for example in J. Stuart Walters's *A Reform First German Book* of 1914, which claimed to be '"live", vivid – [treating] of the actualities of both life and language' and which used pictures to encourage facility of expression.

In the same volume of Sadler's series Fabian Ware begins an article on the teacher of modern languages in Prussian secondary schools with a damning comparison with the situation in England:

> It has been remarked by foreign critics of our educational institutions that English secondary schools are a hundred years behind those of Germany in their organisation and curricula. The two systems of schools are, however, so absolutely different, they are so entirely a result of distinct national forces, that it is futile to attempt to compare them with mathematical precision. The future alone can determine the relative value of the education which each has furnished during the nineteenth century; the comparison of common educational factors is all that is at present possible. To one such factor public attention in England has been particularly directed during recent years, and Germany's superiority in modern language instruction is now generally recognised.[90]

Modern language teaching had had and continued to have severe critics in England. As we have seen, Matthew Arnold had been sceptical of its value, arguing in 1868 that 'learning to speak foreign languages, showy as the accomplishment always is, and useful as it often is, must be regarded as a quite secondary and subordinate school aim'.[91] The introduction of modern languages in Oxford was hotly contested, the first degree examinations taking place only in 1905.[92] And a Cambridge academic is quoted as arguing in 1917 'as a genuine and patriotic Englishman' that 'the teaching of foreign languages was futile and to be deprecated in the highest degree'.[93]

But the principles of the German reform method were clearly very influential in the teaching of modern languages in schools; in the history of modern language teaching in England the principles of the 'direct method', existing as it did alongside the more traditional 'grammar-translation' method, were to be felt into the 1960s and beyond.

The education of girls

In the long period with which we have been concerned so far insufficient attention was given in England to approaches to the education of girls in Germany. Mary Lyster's account of the higher schools for girls (*höhere Mädchenschulen*), published in volume 9 of the series of Special Inquiries and Reports, provided a historical account of these schools within the context of the development in Germany of education for girls during the nineteenth century.[94] A substantial study of the higher education of women in Europe was published as volume 16 of W. T. Harris's widely read American 'International Education Series' in 1901 and included much criticism of German provision, with a few plaudits for what had been achieved in England. 'While I am sure that the English schools might borrow from Germany in regard to ethical education,' the author says, 'the German schools might be induced to borrow from England in the matter of intellectual education'.[95] Girls in German schools were said to be good in literature, history, and modern languages, 'less than mediocre' in composition, and 'below par' in logical thinking. A study of 1905, by Isabel Rhys, described the curriculum of the *höhere Mädchenschule* in Munich as follows:

Table 6 Curriculum of the *Höhere Mädchenschule* at Munich

Subjects	Classes						Total
	I	II	III	IV	V	VI	
(a) Compulsory–							
1. Religion	2	2	2	2	2	2	12
2. German	5	4	4	4	4	4	25
3. History	-	1	2	2	2	3	10
4. Geography	2	3	2	2	2	1	11
5. Arithmetic and Geometry	3	3	3	3	3	2	17
6. (a) French	5	5	5				15
7. (b) English	-	-	3	6	6	6	3
							(18 combined)
8. Natural Science and Domestic Economy, leading to	2	2	2	2	3	2	13
9. Hygiene and Preparation for life	-	-	-	1	1	1	3
10. Sewing	2	2	2	2	2	2	12
11. Drawing	2	2	2	2	2	2	12
12. Gymnastics	2	2	2	2	2	2	12
13. Singing	1	1	1	1	1	1	6
Total	26	26	30	29	30	28	151
(b) Optional–							
1. French or English	-	-	-	2	2	2	6
2. Shorthand	-	-	-	-	2	2	4
3. Cookery	-	-	-	-	-	3	3
Total	27	27	30	31	34	35	164

(Source: Rhys: *The Education of Girls in Switzerland and Bavaria*, p. 60.)

The curriculum here does not include Latin or Greek, which were the domain of boys' schools.

There is particular admiration for teacher training and for the straightforward way in which the vexed issue of religious education is handled:

> Bavaria provides an object lesson in its solution of the problems of sectarian teaching. [. . .] Two hours per week are allotted to religious instruction, and when the time arrives, the several priests or pastors mount the stairs to their respective rooms, one class of girls perhaps sending a contingent to each denomination. [. . .] At first sight it seems a pity to introduce such differences of faith into the school, but after all it is exactly what happens outside the school; the differences exist, and the frank recognition of them does away with all contention as to the religious teaching.[96]

And there is much discussion of the dominance of men: a male teacher was observed giving a series of lessons on 'Preparation for Life'. 'A man teaches the girls their future duties in the home, and tells them what views they ought to hold as to the position of women' . . .[97]

The author wonders why the 'higher' (i.e. secondary) education of women had been neglected:

> It is difficult to understand all the objections to the higher education of women in Germany; it is partly no doubt because men fear the increase of competition which would result from opening the profession to women; partly from the idea that advanced study will unfit women for their position in the home. It is admitted that there are exceptional women who are fitted to be doctors or authors, and that for them perhaps this higher education is necessary, but for the ordinary girl it is not considered either necessary or good.[98]

Criticism of the dominance of men in girls' education in Germany was frequently made: some twenty years later a British observer could write:

> We find that those in charge of female education are, to a large extent, men. [. . .] The whole organisation of life is indeed conceived from a masculine standpoint, and carried out by masculine officials. In the public schools maintained by the State, from the elementary (*Volksschule*) up to the *Höhere Töchterschule* (equivalent to our High School for Girls) the Heads or Directors are men, to whom the highest pay, with the highest responsibility, is given. Below the Head, is a mixed staff of men and women, taking the various subjects which are regarded as respectively suitable to masculine or feminine capacity. The corresponding *Gymnasium*, approximately equivalent to an English boys' Grammar School, is, of course, entirely staffed by men.[99]

Isaac Kandel would report in 1910 that there was concern in Germany at the rapid feminisation of the elementary schools, given a general increase in the number of women teachers (though Germany lagged behind France, England and the United States in terms of the proportion of women to men teachers.[100])

Rhys criticises the dull teaching of history, covers in detail the teaching of modern languages (which uses the inductive method), and describes how the curriculum provides a good general education (with no 'preparation for technical occupations'), on which 'special knowledge' can be built.

What is clear from such coverage in English-language sources is that there was in Germany a system providing for the separate education of girls beyond the *Volksschule*, while in England, though there had been advances, the educational opportunities for girls generally had been mixed and left to a great extent to chance. Opportunities for secondary education were limited. In 1895 less than a quarter of pupils in endowed schools were girls.[101] In Germany, by contrast, the *höhere Mädchenschule* had been developed with enthusiastic support in the German states since the 1870s[102] and it provided an example of what was possible for the widespread education of girls beyond the elementary school.

The German example was not lost on the pioneers of girls' education in England. Dorothea Beale (1831–1906) had visited Germany and Switzerland in the 1850s and observed ways of teaching mathematics that could be emulated in her first school. She introduced German in place of Latin when principal of Cheltenham Ladies' College, whose preparatory section was run in accordance with the methods of Pestalozzi and Froebel, arguing that German was 'far more valuable'.[103] Frances Buss (1827–94), the headmistress of the North London Collegiate School from 1850, had taught in her mother's school (founded in 1845) which was run on Pestalozzi's principles. We have seen in Chapter 2 that the Shirreff sisters were dedicated adherents of Froebel.

Publications on education in Germany around the turn of the century

We have noted the important publications of the Office of Special Inquiries and Reports which included so many contributions on German education. In particular the series provided an opportunity for Michael Sadler to write at length and in remarkable detail on the basis of his expert knowledge of educational developments in Germany.

One of the most prominent German writers on educational topics at the end of the nineteenth century was Friedrich Paulsen (1846–1908). His two-volume *Geschichte des Gelehrten Unterrichts* is an indispensable source on the history of schools and universities in Germany from the Middle Ages to his own time. A short work on the German universities appeared in English in 1895, and a more substantial study was published in English translation in 1906, with a preface by Michael Sadler.[104] A long review of the German version by Mabel Bode had appeared in hard covers in 1905.[105] In addition, Paulsen's popular *German Education, Past and Present*, published in German in 1906, was made available in English translation in 1908. These publications are significant in terms of the availability of information on education in Germany to a British readership seeking reliable accounts of recent developments and their historical background.

A work by Professor Wilhelm Lexis of Göttingen appeared in English translation in 1904. Titled *A General View of the History and Organisation of Public Education in the German Empire*, it includes vast amounts of statistical information on the universities and all types of schools. John Burnet called it 'a handy work . . . which has been translated into something resembling English'.[106]

To them we might add a number of works on aspects of education in Germany by various authors, including American observers of the German scene:

Levi Seeley's *The Common-School System of Germany* (1896), Charles Copland
Perry's *Reports on German Elementary Schools and Training Colleges* (1887), James E.
Russell's much cited *German Higher Schools* (1899), J. W. A. Young's *The Teaching of
Mathematics in the Higher Schools of Prussia* (1900), and Frederick E. Bolton's *The
Secondary School System of Germany* (1900). A work by the Minister of Education
for Ontario, George W. Ross, *The Schools of England and Germany*, had appeared
in 1894. These and a growing number of similar publications served to provide
a rich source of information for policy makers and others contemplating change
in England.

Education was covered too in general accounts of Germany, such as Williams's
"Made in Germany" of 1896, in which there is fulsome praise for technical education, making the distinction between ideas/theories/knowledge and their
application:

> The attention paid by the State in Germany to Education – and particularly
> to Scientific and Technical Education – is matter of common knowledge the
> world over, though the knowledge has not yet effectually dislodged the notion
> that the Germans are a people devoted to dreamy philosophy or plodding
> research into remote by-paths of knowledge; a people addicted to the piling
> up of facts of little use to any one, and least of all to their compilers. There
> are dry-as-dust enthusiasts everywhere, and Germany has her share of them;
> but the scientific training of the mass of her people is not dry-as-dust at all. It
> is severely practical. The Technical Education to be obtained in Germany is
> thorough, and thoroughly scientific; *but it is meant for application.* Active use,
> rather than abstract mental improvement, is the main object kept in view; so
> it produces, not "superior" shopwalkers and "soulful" governesses, but artisans
> and engineers of the best class, men who know the why and the wherefore of
> their work, and do it well.[107]

This classic statement of what Germany was achieving, in such stark contrast to
England, reflects concerns about the focus of education in England that would
remain on the policy agenda for a century and more.

* * * * *

By the end of the century Germany had clearly evolved an education system
that was the envy of many other advanced nations. Two periods of nationalistic
fervour had been motivators in the system's development, and in addition the
remarkable growth of Germany as an industrial power was a spur to educational
reform, providing the country with a serious approach to vocational education
and training which is still in force today. Its present manifestation owes much to
the forward outlook of the late nineteenth- and early twentieth-century planners.
Sadler, writing of the 'ferment' in education at the time (1903), summarised the
merits of German education in enthusiastic terms:

> The German system excels in the grade of academic and of higher technological
> instruction. It also excels in the provision of cheap, standardised, well-staffed
> and easily accessible secondary day-schools for boys, where much is taught
> (perhaps a little too much taught) that equips a man to take a well-informed

and intelligent part in modern trade and professional life, and prepares him to submit to the further discipline of special technical training. A third, but not the least important, excellence of German education is to be found in the combination of well-informed municipal initiative with expert supervision on the part of the State. At the present time this is perhaps the most remarkable characteristic of the whole system, and evidence of its success may be seen in the widespread appreciation, among parents of all classes, of the importance of well-chosen curricula, of sound rather than showy teaching, and of prolonged courses of intellectual discipline.[108]

This is a verdict that British ministers of education would have been happy with a hundred years and more later, had it been made of the system which they were still struggling to improve.

Much had been achieved in England during the nineteenth century. The groundwork for a modern system had most certainly been achieved – a cultural historian has argued that 'the Victorians invented education as we understand it today'[109] – and it is clear that the example of Germany had served in a variety of ways to stimulate debate about the possibilities for development since the early 1800s. The huge deficiencies, however, were in secondary school provision for all but well-off families and in technical and scientific education and training. As Hobsbawm puts it:

There is no reason why British technical and scientific education should have remained negligible, in a period when a wealth of rich amateur scientists and privately endowed research laboratories or of practical experience in production clearly no longer compensated for the virtual absence of university education and the feebleness of formal technological training. There was no compelling reason why Britain in 1913 had only nine thousand university students compared to almost sixty thousand in Germany, or only five day students per ten thousand (1900) compared to almost thirteen in the USA; why Germany produced three thousand graduate engineers per year while in England and Wales only 350 graduated in *all* branches of science, technology and mathematics with first- and second-class honours, and few of these were qualified for research. There were plenty of people throughout the nineteenth century to warn the country of the dangers of its educational backwardness; there was no shortage of funds, and certainly no lack of suitable candidates for technical and higher training.[110]

These were fields in which Germany had made enormous strides, and the comparison became particularly acute as competition between the two nations increased. England had failed to make use of science, as a British academic put it in 1898:

Our manufacturers have remained unfettered by any scientific system in their factories, while their German rivals have laboratories and expert scientists as permanent parts of their factories, and are thereby outstripping us in their schools, as long as we hold that it is the business of our teachers to force knowledge into scholars' minds, and not to be fettered by any scientific knowledge of the nature of those minds.[111]

Table 7   Comparative progress between 1871, 1876, and 1880

Year ending 31st of August	Children of school age, between 3 and 13, less one seventh not supposed to attend Public Elementary Schools	School Accommodation	No. on Registers	No. present at Examination	No. in average daily attendance
1871	4,604,544	2,085,414	(Not stated separately for England and Wales)	1,509,288	1,231,434
1876	-	3,426,318	2,943,794	2,412,211	1,984,573
1880	5,151,781	4,240,753	3,895,824	3,268,147	2,750,916

Percentage in average attendance in 1871 (calculated on present school population): 23.90
Percentage of gain between 1871 and 1880: 29.49
Percentage not in average attendance: 46.60
(Source: Adams: *History of the Elementary School Contest in England*, p. 343.)

Even in terms of elementary school attendance, advances had been slow in England, despite the legislation. In 1882 Francis Adams produced a table showing progress in school attendance between 1871 and 1880:

Clearly there was still much to be achieved in terms of realising the goal of universal compulsory elementary school attendance.

What Matthew Arnold had identified as the two main obstacles to England's learning with profit from the foreign example still remained. He had written in 1868:

> There are two chief obstacles, as it seems to me, which oppose themselves to our consulting foreign experience with profit. One is, our notion of the State as an alien intrusive power in the community, not summing up and representing the action of individuals, but thwarting it.
>   [. . .]
> The other obstacle is our high opinion of our own energy and prosperity. This opinion is just; but it is possible to rely on it too long, and to strain our energy and our prosperity too hard.[112]

Ambiguity about the role of the state and complacency about Britain's standing and prosperity had served to hinder the kind of progress made in Germany. And there were still doubts about what might actually be learnt from Germany. The Scottish classicist John Burnet was to write towards the end of the First World War that

> ever since the time of Matthew Arnold our own controversies have taken shape under the influence of German ideas, whether these were regarded with admiration or the reverse. It is now high time for us to make up our minds what our attitude to German education is to be. The present state of the world calls for a thorough examination of everything we have been accustomed to take for granted.[113]

The new century would see a diminution of general enthusiasm for things German, but there would still be much lingering fascination with what was happening in education in a country with which Britain would soon be at war.

II. From Balfour to Fisher, 1902–18

Prussia, that Mecca of nineteenth-century educationalists.

John Roach, 1960[114]

The nineteenth century much overestimated everything German.

A. L. Rowse, 1976[115]

Michael Sadler was without doubt one of the most knowledgeable observers of education in Germany during the final decade of the nineteenth century. His investigations in the Office of Special Inquiries and Reports provided a body of information on Germany that has been unsurpassed since that time and that clearly fed into policy discussion at the highest levels of decision making. His particular forte was attention to detail, an attribute that is very much in evidence in a text in his hand preserved in the National Archives, a 'Memorandum on the Constitution & Financial Powers of Local Educational Authorities in various countries'.[116] This large format document comprises 78 folio sheets ruled into two columns, and it covers France, Belgium, Prussia, Bavaria, Saxony, Baden, Switzerland, The Netherlands, Norway, the Dominion of Canada (with separate entries for various provinces), the Commonwealth of Australia (various states), New Zealand, and the United States of America (various states and cities). The first column in each case deals with the constitution of the local authority and the second with its financial powers. Here there is extraordinary detail on the precise responsibilities of the Prussian local authorities. This kind of information on provision in other countries was needed as ideas were being developed in England on the nature of local control in education, exemplified in the work of the Bryce Commission (as we have seen) and eventually in the 1902 Education Act (the 'Balfour Act').

In a speech introducing the provisions of the 1902 Education Bill, Balfour made comparisons with Germany and other countries:

> For my own part, reasoning either from theory or from the example of America, or Germany or France, or any other country which devotes itself to educational problems, I am forced to the conclusion that ours is the most antiquated, the most ineffectual, and the most wasteful method yet invented for providing a national education.[117]
> [...]
> To the educationist I think I need make no apologies and offer no excuses. From him I anticipate, and I believe I shall obtain, the heartiest support. He has long seen a vast expenditure of public money, which has yet left this country behind all its Continental and American rivals in the matter of education. He has seen a huge average cost per child in our elementary schools, and yet at the same time many of those schools half starved, inadequately equipped, imperfectly staffed. He has seen in the last ten or fifteen years a development of University life by private liberality which has no parallel except in America, which has covered, and is still covering, our great industrial

centres with Universities and University colleges where the very highest type of University instruction is given by men well qualified for their duty. He has seen technological institutions which I am afraid do not yet rival those which America and Germany have produced, but which yet in their measure and within their limits are admirable. He has seen them erected at a vast cost in every great industrial centre. Yet these University colleges and these great technological institutions do not, cannot, and never will effect all they might do so long as our secondary education, which is their necessary preparation, is in the imperfect condition in which we find it.[118]

Haldane spoke in the debate from his own detailed knowledge of German provision:

The right hon. Gentleman, I was glad to see, has introduced the Universities into the scheme. To my mind that is of great importance. From America and Germany we may learn how to take the best brains of the country and permeate the country with them. The University is the dominant feature of the education of those countries. They work downwards. We have never sought to connect our parts of education, but have left a position of dry isolation between them.[119]
  [. . .]
  Allusion has been made to the great commercial problem which is an important element which we cannot afford to make less. On the other hand we ought not to lower our standards of culture, and for that purpose it is necessary that we should do what has been done successfully abroad, and that is we should co-ordinate the three systems of education, the tertiary, the secondary, and the primary, and also provide on the other hand for the double aim of culture on one side and the application of knowledge to industries on the other. That has been successfully done in Germany. There, in the primary schools, all subjects are pursued together, but when you get to secondary education you either go into the Gymnasien, or you go into schools where there is no Latin taught, and lay yourself out for ending your career in a tertiary institution. We have no provision for the double aim in this country, or for the co-ordination of the two classes.[120]

And the needs of industry were addressed by another participant in the debate, the conservative MP Sir Albert Rollit (1842–1922):

I agree also with the hon. Member that the great want of our country at the present time is first, general education up to a certain and a high point, but especially specialised education, which fits our people to compete with other countries which have given such vast advantages to what I may call their captains of industry. Industrial works in Germany and America are frequently filled with the most highly trained men as managers and heads of departments; there are works having the services of twenty or thirty and more doctors of science, to whom they liberally, wisely, and economically give an interest in the inventions made during the industrial processes. That is a point at which we ought to aim more than we have done.[121]

The foreign example is used here (in Steiner-Khamsi's term) to 'scandalise' the situation at home, to point to a superior situation in the United States and in Germany. And the perception of that superiority had to do both with the technical detail of provision and its management structures and with concerns about competitiveness, about economic rivalry.

Sadler left the Office of Special Inquiries and Reports in 1903. Until his death in 1943 he continued to write on education, devoting much attention to Germany. During the period with which this chapter is concerned there are three texts which stand out. In 1912 he wrote on the history of education in Germany in a collection of papers on *Germany in the Nineteenth Century;*[122] in 1915 he contributed a chapter on 'The Strength and Weakness of German Education' to a volume on *German Culture,*[123] and in 1916 he wrote a remarkable article in *The Times* headed 'Need We Imitate German Education?'[124]

Sadler's chapter of 1912 on the historical development of education in Germany is characteristic of his usual scholarship, tempered by somewhat haughty comment. A section of it is reproduced in Appendix 2 below. In this text Sadler attempts a comparative periodisation of educational development in Germany and Britain (as discussed in Chapter 1), seeks to argue that the two systems are 'more closely akin' than either is to that of France, and that administrative development in Germany resulted from 'the political need for a highly developed State organisation, military in some essential parts of its structure and authoritative in its control over social and industrial developments'.[125]

'German education,' he writes in the 1915 article, 'has long been in many respects an example to Great Britain. Seen in the light of the war, it is also a warning'.[126] Its 'elaborate organisation' had weakened its moral independence, it 'has made the educational system of Germany a weapon in the hands of the dominant power in the State' and caused the minds of individuals to be 'too susceptible to current intellectual fashions', lacking in independent criticism and resistance to government control.[127] The lessons for Britain lay in avoiding excessive bureaucratic control and 'administrative tidiness' and preserving variety, with each school having 'a personality of its own'.[128] This is a view which mirrors present-day policy making in England, based on the principles of choice and diversity and responsible freedoms.

The piece in *The Times* makes a measured statement of the strengths and weaknesses of education in Germany:

No one whose words have weight has ever said that German education is perfect. It has great faults as well as great excellence. It makes use of all second-grade ability, which in England is far too much of a waste product. But something in the atmosphere of it makes the German too ready to obey.

It goes on:

Whatever we may feel about its capital defect – its idol-worship of the State and the subordination of conscience to system and success – German education has high merits. These have been made clearer than ever by the experience of the war. German education has made the nation alert to science. It has made systematic cooperation a habit. It has taught patriotic duty. It has kept a whole people industrious. Combined with military training, it has given them the strength of discipline. It has made profitable use of second-rate intelligence. It has not neglected the mind.

Sadler's reference to 'second rate intelligence' has a powerful resonance. The point is that while the Germans had been assiduous in developing the academic secondary school to prepare an elite for access to the universities, attention had also been paid to those who did not aspire to academic or high-level professional careers. The group Sadler has in mind are those who will drive the wheels of industry and commerce, who will constitute the technicians and middle managers with responsible positions contributing to economic success. The modern division of secondary school types into 'basic' (*Hauptschule*), 'modern' (*Realschule*) and 'academic' (*Gymnasium*) reflects a differentiation between skills, with those in the *Realschule* being the equivalent of Sadler's 'second rate intelligence'. As we shall see, the failure in England after the Second World War to develop the technical school concept was a missed opportunity to emulate the success of the German *Realschule*.

Sadler's balanced view of the achievements of education in Germany can be seen alongside those of Victor Henri Friedel in his book *The German School as a War Nursery*, translated from the French and also published in 1918, with an introduction by Sadler.[129] Friedel's study is a detailed indictment of the militaristic tenor of education in Germany. Sadler's introduction describes the context of German education and looks, uneasily, for explanations and solutions, with a prescient expectation that with a political revolution there would be an educational revolution and Germany would look to the United States for its models.

For Sadler and others who had been enthusiastic about the German model in education, coming to terms with what had happened to turn the German school into a 'war nursery' was clearly problematic, and it was hard for them to focus on the positive features of the system. Sadler's piece in *The Times* is a bold attempt to draw attention to some aspects of educational provision that might still have lessons for policy in England.[130]

Towards the 1918 Education Act

The 1917 Lewis Committee on 'Juvenile Education in Relation to Employment after the War' had a brief to consider what provision should be made for the education of children and young people after the war, with particular regard to those employed 'abnormally' during the war or who could not find employment, or who needed special training.[131]

It recommended compulsory attendance at day continuation classes for those aged 14 to 18 for at least eight hours a week for forty weeks a year, arguing that this would go some way towards providing the juvenile training which had been severely disrupted during the war. Education in the day continuation schools was to be both general and vocational:

> Although . . . at any rate in the earlier years, Continuation Classes should give a general and not a technical education, we think that they may with advantage from the very beginning have something of a vocational bias. This will not mean very much more than that the children will be as far as possible classified according to their occupations, and that four or five alternative courses will be planned, in which subjects will be differently grouped and differently treated, so as to give them some kind of living relation to the occupations of the children taking them.[132]

There was an aim too to contribute by this means to industrial efficiency:

> Over and above the four years' prolongation of formal education which they
> imply, we believe that compulsory Continuation Classes will carry on the moral
> and disciplinary influence of the Elementary School, will conduce to a far
> higher standard of physical well-being, will increase the industrial efficiency
> of the mass of the population, and will give those able to profit by it full
> opportunity for the beginnings of a valuable technical training.[133]

The Fisher Act of 1918 was intended to give effect to the committee's recommendation on day continuation classes. H. A. L. Fisher (1865–1940), introducing the
Education Bill in August 1917, argued in favour of the principle of compulsory
continuation school attendance, emphasising the value of 'the education of the
whole man, spiritually, intellectually and physically':

> The compulsion proposed in this Bill will be no sterilising restriction of whole-
> some liberty, but an essential condition of a larger and more enlightened
> freedom, which will tend to stimulate the civic spirit, to promote general
> culture and technical knowledge, and to diffuse a steadier judgement and a
> better-informed opinion through the whole body of the community.[134]

In the event the proposal came to nothing, but the principle of compulsory
attendance at continuation schools, as developed in Germany from the 1870s
onwards, was widely enough accepted for it to be officially recognised, even if it
was not actually implemented.[135]

Michael Sadler, by now Professor of Education in Manchester, had edited
a comprehensive volume on continuation schools in England and abroad in
1907, and in 1910 the Board of Education published a report on continuation schools in Germany. It began by describing the variety of provision and
influences – religious, economic, social-political – which had brought the
German continuation schools about and which had resulted in 'a feeling of
discomfort, as if this lack of orderliness, so uncongenial to the national tem-
perament, were a matter for reproach'.[136] The author of the report made clear
the board's familiarity with the detail of legislation and administration relating
to continuation schools in the German states, and there is ample evidence of
this in a well-informed historical account of their development, and in complex
appendices describing provision in various cities of Germany. We can see in
the account the beginnings of the modern vocational education system of
Germany. Here is a description of the duties of the pupil/apprentice:

> The occupation once chosen and entered upon, and the indentures, if any,
> of apprenticeship having been signed, the boy will for the next two, or proba-
> bly three, years attend the Continuation School for four or six hours a week.
> [. . .]
> Whatever the calling of the boy, mechanic, clerk, or messenger, his individu-
> alist impulses are aroused. Because he sees that no subjects are superfluous,
> and that all are practically useful to him, he believes in the school. The
> German knows that the good workman, with a proper pride in his work and
> skill, makes the good citizen. As the boy grows older, say in his last year at the
> Continuation School, he will gain something of the altruistic point of view.

He will understand from the lessons on citizenship (*Bürgerkunde*), which are an essential and obligatory part of the course of every group, not only that he has duties and rights but that his craft or his trade guild has an honourable history, that it is but one of many forms of labour, that he is but one of an ordered community, State and Empire, and that the welfare of all is bound together.[137]

And the duties of the employer are described with an equal sense of admiration:

The Imperial Labour Law (*Reichsgewerbeordnung*) puts on the master the duty of providing that his apprentice shall learn his trade from him, and that he shall attend the Continuation School, and, this is the basis of the *Ortsstatut* or byelaws of those towns which have established compulsory attendance. The Imperial Law may thus be said to lay down the principle of the moral obligation of the employer, and the municipal byelaw to enforce his active concurrence. He is held chiefly responsible for the regular attendance at the Continuation School of the boys whom he employs, and a public opinion is formed against those masters who willfully resist the law. Compulsion of the employer there must be in the last resort, but this alone cannot breathe life into any organisation. He has to be brought to see that his interest is served by the trade and commercial schools. He must be made to believe in the public policy.[138]

The report concludes with the belief that

The real and organic connection existing or aimed at in Germany between the compulsory Continuation School on the one hand and the life of the pupils who are leaving the Elementary School, and on the other the trades and industries of the place, should not be less possible of attainment in this country.[139]

A commentator reporting on the education of a marine engineer in Germany at a conference in 1915 described the contrasts between the approaches of Germany and England:

While the German engineer 'lacked the adventurousness and inborn inventiveness' of his British counterpart, 'education had made the German an engineer; what he lacked in mechanical genius he made up for in education'.[140]

* * * * *

The coverage of education in Germany in books published in English before and during the First World War demonstrated increasing concern about its nature, with much discussion of the concept of *Kultur*.[141] Prior to the outbreak of war, Barker in his *Modern Germany* (1907) was warning, in a chapter on 'Education and Mis-Education', that the educational organisation of Germany was an 'absolutist machine', that German secondary schools were 'cramming establishments of the worst kind', and that German education had been 'overvalued and much misunderstood' in Britain. Berry's *Germany of the Germans* (1910), though favourably inclined towards schools in Germany, describes the universities as 'intellectual hothouses' with no character-building function: 'the German universities do not impress as being the centres of national refinement and culture'. Charles Tower,

GERMANY

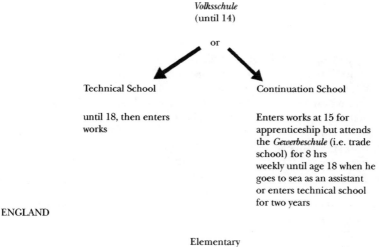

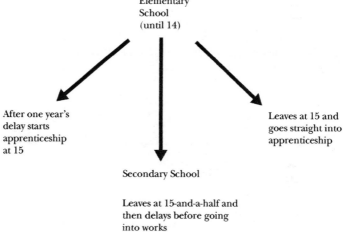

FIGURE 4   Paths to becoming a marine engineer, Germany and Britain. Source: Roderick & Stephens: *Scientific and Technical Education in 19th Century England*, p. 88 (adapted)

in his *Germany of To-Day* (1913), argued that the German school system was 'not educational in the best sense' and that German university life had 'lost its social character'. During the war there was, for example, Henry de Halsalle's *Degenerate Germany* (1915), in which the 'beer-duels' of German students were highlighted with evident disapproval; or Smith's *The Soul of Germany* (1916), where German schools are described as 'intellectual barracks' and universities as 'high schools of Kultur and brutality', or Curtin's *The Land of Deepening Shadow: Germany 1916* (1917), with a chapter on 'Puppet Professors' (the German professor as a 'semi-deity'); or Morrison's *Sidelights on Germany* (1918), with its discussion of 'war pedagogy'. We have mentioned one of the more scholarly accounts, that by the Scottish classicist John Burnet (1863–1928), *Higher Education and the War*, published in 1918, which contains a more serious discussion of what might be understood by *Kultur*.

* * * * *

The 48 years from the Education Act of 1870 to the end of the First World War saw the consolidation of an English interpretation of 'national education'. From legislation for compulsory attendance to a (still today unfulfilled) commitment to continuing education up to the age of 18, and from precarious provision of elementary education to a system based on local authorities, education in England had been slowly transformed. A series of important commissions had shown successive governments' determination to progress the cause of education, and the German example had figured prominently in the investigations that were a significant part of their work. Increasing industrial and military rivalry between the two countries acted in England both as a stimulus to observe and seek to understand the nature of German success in education and a disincentive to follow approaches which had resulted in the more negative features of German culture. With the cessation of hostilities and the abdication of the Kaiser, there could be a period of respite and reflection, with, as we shall see, renewed opportunity to investigate some progressive ideas in educational provision in the new republic.

But first I shall interrupt the chronological narrative with a sketch of some features of the German university that are important within the context of British interest in education in Germany.

Chapter 5

Excursus: Aspects of the German University

'You'll have those universities of yours about your ears soon, if you don't consent to take a lesson from Germany'.

Anthony Trollope, 1857[1]

It is astonishing that British scholars and politicians should still be found speaking of 'our intellectual debt to Germany' . . . But theories made in Germany have so long been accepted at the valuation of their authors both in this country and in America, where the younger generation has sat obediently at the feet of Teutonic professors, that it has become difficult to see them in their true light. It is worth while, therefore, examining what Germany has really done for culture and scientific progress.

A. H. Sayce, 1914[2]

During the period with which this study is concerned the German university veered between being an object of extraordinary admiration and attracting the widespread opprobrium of the civilised world.

At the beginning of the nineteenth century England had only its two ancient universities: Oxford and Cambridge. Scotland, by contrast, had four long-established universities: St Andrews (1413), Glasgow (1451), Aberdeen (1495), and Edinburgh (1583). Oxford was emerging from what is widely accepted as an undistinguished period of its history: 'No one would claim, though some did, that eighteenth-century Oxford could rival Leiden or Göttingen, Edinburgh or Glasgow as a centre of intellectual dynamism', as the editor of the eighteenth-century volume of the *History of the University of Oxford* puts it.[3]

In Britain by the early 1840s there was a well-established interest in the German universities. At this point in the century England also had the very young University of London, which consisted thus far only of University College (founded in 1826 and dubbed the 'godless institution of Gower Street'[4] or the 'German' university) and King's College, dating from 1828; there was also the University of Durham, founded in 1832, which received its Royal Charter in 1837. Germany, in contrast to England's three universities, had many institutions of considerable renown, and German advances in modern scholarship were attracting the attention of academics and others throughout the Western world.

It had been fashionable for many decades for young British scholars to spend some time studying in Germany, where the intellectual atmosphere was perceived to be more exciting than that in the duller halls of Oxford and Cambridge. Samuel Taylor Coleridge, for example, sailed for Germany in 1798 in order to learn German and to sit at the feet of philosophers in Göttingen. He was received by Christian Gottlob Heyne (1729–1812) 'a little, hopping, over-civil, sort of a Thing who talks very fast & with fragments of coughing between every ten words'[5] – and he delighted in writing home with a list of the great professors he was encountering during his studies. One of Coleridge's most recent biographers describes the impact of the German experience on him: 'This intensive period at Göttingen [. . .] gave him a sense of sharing in the intellectual life of Europe, of being part of a broad community of world-renowned scholars, which shaped much of his subsequent writing, and distinguished him sharply from the purely provincial aspect of English thought'.[6]

Another influential figure from the early years of the century was the man of letters Henry Crabb Robinson (1775–1867), who spent five years in Germany to make up for the deficiencies of his education in provincial England. At school he 'could learn nothing, for nothing was to be learnt', he tells us, and he became one of the best-informed Englishmen of his generation as far as knowledge and appreciation of German scholarship and culture were concerned.[7] He met Goethe, Schiller, and Herder, and studied under Fichte, Schelling, and the Schlegel brothers in Jena. On leaving Jena in 1805 he could write: 'It was my good fortune to come to Jena while the ancient spirit was still alive and active, and I saw the last not altogether insignificant remains of a knot of public teachers who have seldom been surpassed in any university'.[8]

These early examples of enthusiasm for the German university are among many we could cite. The standing and influence of the German universities encouraged imitation later in the century in the United States, to the extent that the Johns Hopkins University became known as 'Göttingen in Baltimore'. The University of Chicago was founded with a graduate research centre along German lines.

With the founding of the University of Berlin in 1810 ('an Idealist show-piece'[9]), new impetus was given to the notion of a modern university, incorporating Humboldt's vision of academic freedom (*Lehr- und Lernfreiheit*), and the essential duality of teaching and research. To these Röhrs[10] adds 'the relative independence of the university' and 'the political relevance of the idea of education'. The excitement felt by many foreign observers at the reconceptualisation of the university through the establishment of the Friedrich-Wilhelms-Universität was still obvious much later in the century. Writing in 1879, a British author could comment enthusiastically: 'The Berlin University is quite a modern institution. No black-letter learning has been fostered in its halls. No early traditions linger around its precincts';[11] and he could conclude, with Jena in mind: 'No other city can offer such an advanced scientific education as Berlin, the advantages derived from which are more worthy of commemoration than the follies of a student's life in a provincial town'.[12]

This growing awareness of the status of the German university, especially following the founding of the University of Berlin, but as a result too of the reputation of Göttingen and other established institutions, created in increasing numbers of young Britons (and Americans) a desire to spend time studying in Germany, attending the lectures of a German professor who was at the forefront of scholarship in his subject. In many a memoir later in the century we find accounts of the writers struggling with the German language and ultimately benefiting from the advances in the sciences and the humanities spearheaded by the German professoriate. Here is Richard Burdon Haldane (Lord Chancellor 1912–15 and again in 1924), who went to Göttingen for four months or so in 1874 to study philosophy and theology, with geology 'as a by-study':

When I matriculated at the University of Göttingen it was to enter as a student under Lotze. [. . .] I used at times to hear other great teachers. Ritschl was there, and von Jhering, whose books on Jurisprudence I was to study later. Wöhler, the discoverer of synthetic urea, although he no longer lectured, was also a familiar figure in the streets. Gauss and Riemann were dead, but Göttingen remained a great home for mathematicians . . .[13]

Göttingen clearly had a long-lasting effect on Haldane's intellectual development:

A German university had led him out of the perplexity of youth into the assurance of manhood. A German professor had demonstrated to him how to combine intellectual rigour with moral principle. [. . .] Kant, Hegel, Schopenhauer and, above all, Goethe – shone a light ahead for his career.[14]

In August 1911 he was lecturing on 'The Growing Influence of German University Methods'.[15]

One more example among many will suffice to exemplify the pull of the German universities. H. A. L. Fisher, historian and politician (architect of the 1918 Education Act), also studied in Göttingen, in 1890:

During the last two decades of the nineteenth century the German universities enjoyed a wide reputation for freedom, courage, and learning. To sit at the feet of some great German professor, absorbing his publications, listening to his lectures, working in his seminary, was regarded as a valuable, perhaps as a necessary passport to the highest kind of academic career. Every year young graduates from our universities would repair to Berlin and Heidelberg, to Göttingen and Bonn, to Jena and Tübingen. The names of the German giants, of Ranke and Mommsen, of Wilamowitz and Lotze, were sounded again and again by their admiring disciples in British lecture-rooms. We learned that the great figures of the Augustan period of German literature had been followed by two generations of perhaps even more remarkable men, who had given new life to every branch of human knowledge.[16]

The enthusiasm and respect for German scholarship shown in their early years by two individuals who were to become such significant public figures are indicative of the power of the German example in education. Those who preceded and followed them will have brought back notions of what was different from the norm 'at home' and would have had their thinking influenced by their very different experiences in Germany. (It is estimated that some 9,000 American students crossed the Atlantic to study in Germany during the nineteenth century.[17])

The Humdoldtian concept of the university

In the German states the eighteenth century had seen both decline and growth in the universities. McClelland sees two waves of reform during the century, with Halle, Breslau, Göttingen, and Erlangen being founded between 1694 and 1743, the foundation of Halle (in Prussia) in particular inspiring the House of

Hanover to establish Göttingen ('Europe's first modern university') as a rival institution.[18] It was the rise of these important new universities (while others were stagnating or approaching closure) that laid the foundations for the early nineteenth-century developments that sparked so much attraction to what would emerge as the German model of a university.

The creation of the University of Berlin in 1810 was an event of profound significance. Its origins lay in a combination of political crisis and intellectual fervour. When Halle was lost to Napoleon's Westphalia the distinguished philologist Friedrich August Wolf migrated to Berlin and sought the support of the Prussian King Friedrich Wilhelm III for the notion of establishing a new university there. The climate was propitious, given the urgings in Fichte's *Reden an die Deutsche Nation* of 1808 for Germany to look to the education of its people – and given Wilhelm von Humboldt's appointment as chief of the section of Cultus and Public Instruction in the Prussian Ministry of the Interior. Humboldt had been close to F. A. Wolf and sought later (unsuccessfully) to involve him in government.

Wolf (known to be 'eccentric, quarrelsome, despotic'[19]) 'contributed the lustre of his name, but no more', according to the eminent classicist Wilamowitz;[20] but others, especially Fichte himself (rector in 1811) and Friedrich Schleiermacher (1768–1834; rector in 1815) – both of whom had written papers proposing a new university – together with a large number of prominent academics who had been persuaded by Humboldt to move to Berlin, quickly established the university in its prime position in the Palace of Prince Heinrich on *Unter den Linden*. In founding the University of Berlin, Humboldt – in the view of a historian writing in 1878 – 'gave to Europe a new seat of learning, which has ever since stood on an equality with the very greatest of those of which Europe boasted before'.[21] And of course this modern university attracted the attention of British observers, one of whom could write in 1825 that 'there is not in Germany a better behaved, or more effective university than Berlin'.[22]

The Humboldtian 'idea' of the university consisted in two basic principles: *Einheit von Forschung und Lehre*, the vital 'unity', combination/interaction, of research and teaching; and *Lehr- und Lernfreiheit*, freedom to teach and to study. Essentially, then, the university teacher would be free to teach whatever he wished; the student would be free to attend lectures as he wanted, and to move between universities to sit at the feet of the most prominent professors; and the university teacher would embed his lectures in his research, thus bringing to his audience the latest thinking/discoveries in his subject. Underlying all of this would be a commitment to *Wissenschaft*, to 'science' as scholarship in both its broadest and deepest senses.

Humboldt, described by Matthew Arnold as 'one of the most beautiful souls that have ever existed'[23] spent twelve months in England in 1817/18 as the King of Prussia's resident in London. (He apparently showed no interest in Oxford and Cambridge, and the Elgin Marbles were seemingly more important to him than the condition of the country.)[24] Mark Schalenberg sees the Humboldtian principles (unity of research and teaching; freedom of research, teaching, study; promotion of the *Kulturstaat*; unity and priority of *Wissenschaft* for the work of the university) as scarcely important to the British universities, with their quite different traditions and priorities, and he points out that in any case these principles were not realised in Humboldt's day.[25] Humboldt, Schalenberg says, was known in Britain as a linguist and a philosopher rather than as a university reformer, despite his having been brought to the attention of an English-speaking audience by Sarah Austin in her 1854 book on Germany. And he quotes Lord Acton writing of

> Humboldt, the most central figure in Germany [. . .], who had forged the link between science and force by organising a university at Berlin, and who, until the murder of Kotzebue, had been the pride and the hope of intelligent Prussia, devoted the maturity of his powers to Malay roots. Those were the days in which the familiar type of the German scholar was generated, of the man who complained that the public library allowed him only thirteen hours a day to read, the man who spent thirty years on one volume, the man who wrote upon Homer in 1806 and who still wrote upon Homer in 1870, the man who discovered the 358 passages in which Dictys has imitated Sallust, the man who carried an electric telegraph from his house to the church and carried it no farther.[26]

German professors: caricature and politicisation

'German professors!' groaned out the Chancellor, as though his nervous system had received a shock which nothing but a week of Oxford air could cure.

Anthony Trollope, *Barchester Towers* (1857)

Lord Acton's was a not untypical view of German pedantic scholarship. The high ideals encapsulated in the Humboldtian principles could too easily translate into the narrow focus of the *Fachidiot*, the 'idiot specialist' (known too before Humboldt's day) who loses sight of the broader educative functions of a university. An observer in 1879 reported that the lecture of a German professor had been summarised as 'a heaping up of facts and ideas. A deluge of quotations, and an avalanche of bibliographic notes'.[27]

One of the best known caricatures of the German professor is the early gibe of Richard Porson (1759–1808), Cambridge Professor of Greek, who was offended by the criticism of his work by Gottfried Hermann (1772–1848) of Leipzig:

> The Germans in Greek
> Are sadly to seek;
> Not five in five score,
> But ninety-five more:
> All: save only HERMAN
> And HERMAN's a German.[28]

There is a remarkable contrast between the perception outside Germany of the giants of German scholarship and that of the plodding single-minded researcher lacking a wider view of his subject and its purpose.

In the middle of the century, as we have seen, the German model was attracting a great deal of attention. The Oxford theologian Edward Arthur Litton (1813–97) refers in his letter to Lord Russell on university reform:

> the practice of the continental universities, from which, if our insular pride will permit us, we shall do well to borrow a leaf. In Germany, for example,

there exist only, as amongst ourselves, learned professions, but, what does not exist in England, a profession of learning, which finds its sphere of exercise in the numerous universities of that country. To encourage young men of ability to devote themselves to this profession is one of the chief objects which the founder of a German university has in view. He therefore so constructs his system as to afford every opening that can be wished for to the rising talent of the country, both for probation and for display.[29]

He describes the 'licentiates (*privatim docentes*)', the extraordinary professors (*professores extraordinarii*), and the ordinary professors 'selected from the most eminent literary men of the age; they form the ruling body of the university, and are expected, not only to give lectures . . . but to promote by their works the advancement of learning in general',[30] and he talks of the advantages of this academic structure for the proper career of university teacher in contrast to the situation in England. This approach was supported later (1868) by Mark Pattison in his *Suggestions on Academical Organisation*:

> There remains but one possible pattern on which a university, as an establishment for science, can be constructed, and that is the graduated professoriate. This is sometimes called the German type, because Germany is the country in which the system has most recently borne the most signal fruits. The education given in German schools and universities is not superior, even if it be equal, to what is attainable in England or France. As teaching institutions, their universities have great merits and equally great defects. But as establishments for the cultivation and encouragement of the highest learning, the German universities have left everything of the kind at this moment existing in Europe behind them.
>
> [. . .]
>
> [I]t is not as schools, but as centres of mental activity in science, that these institutions command the attention of Europe, and have become the referees to whose verdict every product of mind must be unconditionally submitted.[31]

We have seen in the work of Howitt and Mayhew in particular a tendency to focus on the egregious customs of German students. But alongside that fascination with the student corporations and their practices there was a consistent admiration for the German university as a modern academic institution.

The Friedrich-Wilhelms-Universität opened its doors to students in 1810. Today renamed the Humboldt University (after both Wilhelm von Humboldt and his rather more famous scientist brother, Alexander), it has suffered its share of problems, including those of National Socialist hegemony, isolation in the Soviet sector of Berlin after the Second World War, and a subsequent forty-year period under the totalitarian government of the German Democratic Republic. It has now been restored to its former glory as the celebrated European research university it had become during the nineteenth century. It still displays over the staircase in the main entrance hall a text by Marx put there in 1953: *Die Philosophen haben die Welt nur verschieden interpretiert, es kommt aber darauf an, sie zu verändern* ('The philosophers have only interpreted the world in different ways, but what matters is to change it').[32]

A feature of German university life which was not so attractive to foreign observers was the tendency of the professoriate to become embroiled in politics. This ranged from an idealistic nationalism to support for extreme ideology of a racist and anti-intellectual tenor.

The Frankfurt National Assembly of 1848, the 'Parliament of Professors', counted 550 academics among its 585 members, 200 of whom were professors or judges. In 1870, at the time of the Franco-Prussian War, Emil Du Bois-Reymond (1818–96), *Rektor* of the University of Berlin, had described the university as the 'intellectual bodyguard of the house of Hohenzollern'.[33]

John Burnet quotes the extremist sentiments (in 1914) of the distinguished German chemist Professor Wilhelm Ostwald (1853–1932), 'not the ravings of a half educated Pangermanist, but the deliberate utterances of one of the foremost representatives of German Science' and those of the classicist Wilamowitz, to the effect that Germany should 'dictate peace to the rest of Europe'. 'I do not quote these utterances merely for their absurdity,' says Burnet,

> I for one would not choose to know as much Greek as Wilamowitz or as much Chemistry as Ostwald at the price of having my mind work like that.[34]

Wilamowitz, a signatory of the 1914 intellectuals' manifesto in support of German military action in the early stages of the First World War, was expelled from the Paris Academy as a result. Unrepentant, as *Rektor* of the University of Berlin he added to the Latin of the diplomas on which his name appeared *plerarumque in hoc orbe academiarum socius, e Parisina honoris causa eiectus* ('fellow of a great many of the world's academies, expelled, *honoris causa*, from the Paris Academy').[35]

During the Nazi era many German professors went into exile; others continued their academic work by reaching an accommodation with the regime; yet others prostituted their intellectual independence and judgement. The case of the philosopher Martin Heidegger has become especially notorious. He joined the National Socialist Party in 1933, shortly after his appointment as *Rektor* of the University of Freiburg, and he remained a member until the end of the war.[36] One Göttingen professor is quoted as declaring (in 1934) 'We renounce research for the sake of research. Sieg Heil!'.[37] Even a member of the university commission appointed by the Military Governor in the British Zone of Germany after the war, Friedrich Drenckhahn (1894–1977), had written Nazi mathematics papers of the most crude kind in the 1930s.[38]

After the Second World War the accusation made against the professoriate was that it had neglected its duty to truth. Robert Birley reported a discussion about the nature of the university commission with the Senate of the University of Göttingen during which the philosopher Professor Nicolai Hartmann (1882–1950) had said, 'You seem to think that all the Professors at Göttingen were Nazis':

> 'Not at all,' I answered. 'Of course they were not. The charge against the Professors at Göttingen is something quite different. It is that they were quite ready to accept a régime, the whole policy of which they know to be based on academic nonsense'. And to this I received the astonishingly generous reply, which I have never forgotten, 'To that charge, Mr Birley, we have no answer'.[39]

The Oxford classicist Professor E. R. Dodds (1893–1979), also involved in work
on the German universities during and after the war, visited Göttingen with a
delegation of the Association of University Teachers in 1947:

> When I called on the aged Max Pohlenz [1872–1962] at Göttingen he plunged
> at once into an eager discussion of Greek philosophy, exactly as if all that
> had happened since 1933 were an irrelevant and essentially unimportant
> interruption to our real business of scholarship.[40]

The implied widespread lack of moral or civil courage (*Zivilcourage*) diminishes
the scientific (*wissenschaftlich*) achievements. How culpable must we regard
scholars like Pohlenz? There is clearly an important distinction to be made
between those who remained *unpolitisch* and those who in one way or another
prostituted their learning in the service of an ideology they must have known
to be specious and absurd. Making that distinction was a difficult challenge for
those charged with the processes of denazification after the war.

With the reinstatement of professors who had left their posts, and the
denazification of the teaching force, it was possible to re-establish the universities of the western zones of occupation. Those in the eastern parts of Germany,
among them the University of Berlin (renamed the Humboldt University) and
the Universities of Halle, Jena, and Leipzig, were to suffer years of neglect,
with the teaching staff cut off from proper engagement with their peers in the
West. One 48-year-old lecturer, faced with reapplying for her post in an eastern
institution following Unification in 1990 said: 'Man kann nicht in einem Jahr
nachlesen, was man in 30 Jahren nicht lesen konnte' ('You can't catch up in
reading in one year what you haven't been able to read for 30 years').[41]

The eastern German universities, as they emerged from their forty years of
isolation from the West, provided many job opportunities for West German
academics who were able to outperform their eastern colleagues during the
selection processes for new or readvertised posts. Many students from the eastern
Länder migrated to the established western universities; those who had been
denied access to university by the GDR regime could at last embark on a higher
education. The system, already creaking, became even more overcrowded.

The modern period: no longer a model?

'The German University: A Heroic Ideal in Conflict with the Modern World'
Fallon, 1980 (book title)

The final school-leaving qualification, the *Abitur*, entitles access to university in
Germany, though in some subjects a *numerus clausus* exists which requires a certain minimum level of performance. For the most part, however, matriculation
is possible once the *Abitur* has been passed. The result is that the universities are
overcrowded and that the closeness of teacher to taught which characterises university teaching in England is rare except at the postgraduate level. Professors
are frequently overburdened with the routine of examining the large numbers
of more or less anonymous students who attend their lecture courses and need
to have their progress assessed. The 'mass university' of Germany is thus quite
different from its English counterpart. The readiness of German universities
to introduce BA and MA courses, along the lines of the recommendations in

the Bologna Accord, has not meant that they now operate in the same way as English universities. The German interpretation has been rather different, and it is seriously affected by the significantly larger numbers involved.

The German *Fachhochschule*, however, is now – and somewhat paradoxically – a model of interest to British observers. The *Fachhochschulen* provide shorter more vocationally oriented courses, much like the former British polytechnics, now developed into mostly minor universities. An HMI report on the *Fachhochschulen*, published in 1992, when the polytechnics still existed, looked specifically at how the German institutions coped with much larger numbers of students. (This was at a time when considerable expansion of the total number of students in higher education in England was identified as an ambition of government.)

Two important UK reports on university education included German provision as part of an investigation of the situation in a number of other countries.

Higher Education, the Robbins Committee's report of 1963, begins its coverage of the Federal Republic with a description of the past greatness of the German universities and the tensions arising from their continuing in a tradition rooted in the nineteenth century:

> In the Federal Republic the state of higher education at the present time and the problems to be faced present a sharp contrast with Great Britain. The tradition of academic freedom developed in German universities during the nineteenth century had world-wide influence. It enshrined the university as an institution of outstanding prestige devoted to the advancement of learning. The essential function of the university professor was the pursuit of knowledge, which involved the right to carry out research at will in congenial subjects. Teaching was clearly a subordinate task, and was primarily devoted to the training of future research workers. On the students' part, academic freedom involved the right to attend lectures in any combination of subjects, traveling from one university to another for the purpose – or indeed not to attend lectures at all; and the final examination was taken when the student was ready. Many aspects of this tradition are part of the common European heritage, but the fact that in Germany they were developed as a coherent philosophy at a time when German research was of outstanding and obvious quality was doubtless responsible for their great influence in other countries.
>
> In Germany the traditions have survived unchanged to a greater degree than elsewhere.[42]

The distrust of centralised control of education that had kept the *Land*-based structure in place and the importance attached to academic freedom in the German context are seen as being obstacles to the development of higher education 'in accordance with national requirements'. Germany had faced difficulties in expanding the system, in developing teaching as well as research, and in allocating research facilities on a rational basis.

The main report mentions a staff:student ratio of 35:1 for Germany in 1960, compared to 8:1 in Great Britain and associates this with 'quality of instruction'.[43] The longer period taken by students to complete their studies in Germany (typically five years) might indicate higher levels of attainment, but against the background of the perceived quality of instruction, the Robbins Committee felt that this was not necessarily the case. (German students, incidentally, were accustomed to argue that the British approach to higher education was too much like that of the school, compared to the more adult approach exemplified in the freedoms they enjoyed. With the move towards a BA/MA course structure, despite the problems involved, Germany now seems to be moving closer to something like the British model.)

The Robbins Report covers the German school system, the *Zweiter Bildungsweg* (the 'second pathway' to higher education), institutional patterns and student numbers, wastage and output, content and length of courses, postgraduate studies, staffing, research, administration and university and student finance, and student accommodation. For the most part the coverage is descriptive, with little critical commentary, apart from that provided at the outset to do with the restricting nature of a continuing tradition based on a glorious past.

Some forty-four years later the Dearing Report, *Higher Education in the Learning Society*, included routine accounts of higher education in other countries in an appendix. There is again mention of the importance of the historical inheritance:

> The German university system is in many ways consciously modelled on the ideas of Wilhelm von Humboldt when founding the University of Berlin in 1810 and a number of those whom the visiting team met referred explicitly to his influence. In particular
>
> - the importance of the combination of teaching and research;
> - the freedom of science;
> - university autonomy about the content and methods of teaching and research.
>
> The adherence to these principles of some of those met during the visit has consciously been strengthened by their perception of the dangers to higher education and to Germany when the principles are breached. This applies both to the First and Second World Wars and to experience in the former German Democratic Republic. In this context, the sense of history in German higher education is perhaps more obvious in colouring thinking than in the United Kingdom.[44]

The report, whose impact has been marginal compared to that of the Robbins Committee, goes on to cover access and participation, higher education and the economy, teaching and learning, quality and standards, research, funding and resources, governance, and – in a final section – the case for reform.

The reform issues are identified in detail:

- The 'unique nature' of the higher education system and its relation to international research and scholarship.
- The lack of will to limit access or to 'fully-fund entitlement'.
- The desirability of greater competition between institutions and the need to concentrate resources in 'centres of excellence'.
- The need for employers and industry to have some influence.
- The need for the development of key skills to be evident in the curriculum.
- The introduction of mechanisms to deal with weaknesses, including amongst academic staff.

- Plans to deal with the large number of professors who would reach retirement age early in the 21st century.
- More management responsibilities for Rectors and Deans. ✓
- The need to develop other forms of qualification, including a BA/MA structure.
- Younger graduates, sustained international competitiveness, institutional efficiency.[45]

In the case of both of these reports it is obvious that the German model could offer little in the way of stimulation for reform ideas in England. Rather, it served to show the limitations which had resulted from failure to develop the higher education system in ways more suited to an international context and the needs of a modern industrial nation. Reliance on the Humboldtian past was not deemed sufficient.

There was a growing sense that even that inheritance was no longer so obvious in the modern German university, that there was a 'Humboldtian myth' (*Mythos Humboldt*)[46], since the old ideals could not be realised in the modern mass university. Indeed, it was argued in the 1990s that the German university was rotten at the core (*im Kern verrottet*).[47]

It is clear, however, that the traditions of the German university had a profound influence on the way that the modern university emerged in England and the United States in the nineteenth century. In particular the university as a research institution owes much to the German model, not least in its adoption of the PhD.[48]

The next chapter resumes the narrative of developments in general education, starting with the situation at the end of the First World War.

Chapter 6

Developments in England and Germany, 1918–39

England is rubbing its eyes and gradually discovering the difference between teaching youth and advancing science. That difference no one needs to expound to Germany. And for this reason, its aberrations and inadequacies, deplorable, absurd, or unsound, are more rare and less significant than the aberrations and inadequacies which we have encountered elsewhere.

Abraham Flexner, 1930[1]

Until recently, German schools had the world's respect.

Erika Mann, 1939[2]

Education in Germany after the First World War

Germany has a long tradition of radical thinking about education, despite the inherent conservatism of the structure and content of educational provision. This is evidenced, for example, in the early embracing of Pestalozzi's ideas and in the later impact of the thinking of Herbart and Froebel and others. In the interwar period in particular, the *Reformpädagogik* movement (which dates from the 1880s in Germany, and lasted until the 1930s[3]) was innovative and radical in its approach to educational issues, and it attracted considerable attention – as 'the new education' – from other countries.[4]

As we have seen, Sadler had identified problems with the overburdened curriculum in German schools around the turn of the century.[5] The Table 8 gives a sense of the consistency of the curriculum followed by *humanistisches Gymnasium* pupils at periods from the early 19th century to the mid-1980s:

Critics argued that too much was being demanded of pupils, especially in the *Gymnasien* and the various *Realschulen*. The growth of *Realien*, coupled with an unwillingness to abandon classical subjects, meant that the curriculum was becoming overburdened. *Vielwisserei* (polymathy) became the main concern of the teaching and the soul-destroying burden of the pupil, if the *Abitur* examination was to be passed. 'The role of the teacher at all levels was to transmit knowledge in an authoritarian manner and the role of the pupil was to absorb it passively', as Arthur Hearnden puts it.[6]

Various types of secondary school (called at the time 'higher schools', *höhere Schulen*) had had equal status, *Gleichberechtigung*, in terms of the privileges attaching to their leaving qualifications since 1901. The curricula in these schools show progressive differences of emphasis, as the tables below (from 1918) demonstrate:

Table 8   Consistency of Curriculum in the German Gymnasium: Number of lessons in each subject

	Early 19th c.[1]	1889/90[2]	1927/8[3]	1986[4]
German	2	3	2	3
Latin	8	8	8	3
Greek	5	6	8	3
English	-	-	-	3
Mathematics	2	4	6	3
History/Geography	4	3	4	4
Sciences	1	2	-	5
Religion	1	2	-	2
Music/Art	1	-	-	2
Roman antiquities	2	-	-	-
Cultural history	1	-	-	-
Bibliography	1	-	-	-
Sport	-	-	-	3
Total	34	32	32	32

[1] Top class of Joachimsthal Senior Secondary School, Berlin. Source: Knoll & Siebert, *Wilhelm von Humboldt*, p. 38.

[2] Top class of Königliches Gymnasium zu Landsberg a.W. Source: *Programm des Königlichen Gymnasiums und Realgymnasiums zu Landsberg a.W.*, 1889/90, p. 27.

[3] Top class of Luisenstädtisches Gymnasium, Berlin. Source: *Jahresberichte der höheren Lehranstalten in Preußen*, Schuljahr 1927/28, Berlin (Union Deutsche Verlagsgesellschaft), 1930, p. 488.

[4] Tenth class (i.e. pre-*Oberstufe*) *Gymnasien* in Nordrhein-Westfalen. Source: *Gymnasium-Sekundarstufe I in Nordrhein-Westfalen*, Schriftenreihe des Kultusministers des Landes Nordrhein-Westfalen, Düsseldorf 1984, p. 82.

The curriculum of the *Oberrealschule* has escaped from that of the classical *Gymnasium* and shows a clear emphasis on the *realia studia*, on modern languages, mathematics, and science. The Emperor had said at the December 1890 conference, Wir sollen nationale junge Deutsche erziehen und nicht junge Griechen und Römer ('we should educate young German nationals and not young Greeks and Romans'.)[7]

Sadler had tempered his enthusiasm for the German system with some clear criticism:

> Over-organisation, excessive supervision from above, State control over the entrance to the professions, over-development of the civil service (governmental and municipal), the too linguistic character of the instruction, and a lack of variety of individual initiative are the evils from which German education is felt by many to be suffering at the present time.[8]

And he went on to point to the spirit of the English public school as a pattern which German educators might do well to emulate, since:

> Though many of our methods of instruction are not highly esteemed, our freedom from official uniformity is envied. It seems that it rarely happens for a German boy to be sorry to leave his school.[9]

The time was ripe for a reform movement that would concern itself with some of the fundamental questions regarding who should be taught what and how. Hearnden describes three aspects of the German *Reformpädagogik* movement: the new emphasis given to art teaching; the general importance attached to practical activities in the schools; and the 'creation of a school community that would simulate the social situation of the adult world'.[10]

Tables 9, 10, 11   Curriculum of Gymnasium, Realgymnasium, and Oberrealschule

A. Gymnasium

	VI	V	IV	U.III	O.III	U.II	O.II	U.I	O.I	Total
Religion	3	2	2	2	2	2	2	2	2	19
German and Historical Narrative	3 }4 1	2 }3 1	3	2	2	3	3	3	3	26
Latin	8	8	8	8	8	7	7	7	7	68
Greek	-	-	-	6	6	6	6	6	6	36
French	-	-	4	2	2	3	3	3	3	20
History	-	-	2	2	2	2	3	3	3	17
Geography	2	2	2	1	1	1				9
Arithmetic and Mathematics	4	4	4	3	3	4	4	4	4	34
Natural Science	2	2	2	2	2	2	2	2	2	18
Writing	2	2	-	-	-	-	-	-	-	4
Drawing	-	2	2	2	2	-	-	-	-	8
Total	25	25	29	30	30	30	30	30	30	259

B. Realgymnasium

	VI	V	IV	U.III	O.III	U.II	O.II	U.I	O.I	Total
Religion	3	2	2	2	2	2	2	2	2	19
German and Historical Narrative	3 }4 1	2 }3 1	3	3	3	3	3	3	3	28
Latin	8	8	7	5	5	4	4	4	4	49
French	-	-	5	4	4	4	4	4	4	29
English	-	-	-	3	3	3	3	3	3	18
History	-	-	2	2	2	2	3	3	3	17
Geography	2	2	2	2	2	1				11
Arithmetic and Mathematics	4	4	4	5	5	5	5	5	5	42
Natural Science	2	2	2	2	2	4	5	5	5	29
Writing	2	2	-	-	-	-	-	-	-	4
Drawing	-	2	2	2	2	2	2	2	2	16
Total	25	25	29	30	30	30	31	31	31	262

Tables 9, 10, 11   (Continued)

	VI	V	IV	U.III	O.III	U.II	O.II	U.I	O.I	Total
				C. Oberrealschule						
Religion	3	2	2	2	2	2	2	2	2	19
German and Historical Narrative	4 } 5 1	3 } 5 1	} 4 4	3	3	3	4	4	4	34
French	6	6	6	6	6	5 }	4 }	4 }	4 }	47
English	-	-	-	5	4	4 }	4 }	4 }	4 }	25
History	-	-	3	2	2	2	3	3	3	18
Geography	2	2	2	2	2	1	1	1	1	14
Mathematics	5	5	6	6	5	5	5	5	5	47
Natural Science	2	2	2	2	4	6	6	6	6	36
Writing	2	2	2	-	-	-	-	-	-	6
Drawing	-	2	2	2	2	2	2	2	2	16
Total	25	25	29	30	30	30	31	31	31	262

(Source: Burnet, Higher Education and the War, pp. 81–3 (Bracketed and grouped figures indicate latitude in the distribution of the hours available. The classes are numbered from VI, Sexta to U.I, Unterprima, and O.I, Oberprima)

The political turmoil of the Weimar Republic resulted in little of lasting effect being achieved, but there was an early decision that helped to give the education system an 'organic structure'.[11] The age of transfer from the elementary school to the *Gymnasium* was raised to ten (from nine) and private preparatory schools were abolished. This meant that there was effectively a common four-year elementary school for all, and that a primary stage was identified, with transfer to the *Gymnasium* forming the start of a secondary stage. Most children, however, still completed their school careers in the elementary school up to the school leaving age.

An important aspect of educational thinking during the Weimar years was the increasing emphasis placed on an awareness of Germany's cultural heritage. As with developments stimulated by victory and defeat in the nineteenth century, the defeat of 1918 and the Versailles Peace Treaty provided the stimulus for a resurgence of national and cultural pride. The curriculum of all types of secondary school[12] reflected a new emphasis on subjects associated with *Kulturkunde* (cultural studies) or *Deutschkunde* (German studies), and the *Deutsche Oberschule* was created, a new type of school, existing between 1923 and 1938 and specialising in the study of German language and literature. In addition the three main types of specialism (later to be reflected in the three main types of *Gymnasium*[13]) began to be developed – ancient culture in the *Gymnasium*, modern studies in the *Realgymnasium*, and mathematics and science in the *Oberrealschule*. Again the specialisation was intended to further awareness of a German, indeed a Germanic, heritage: as Hearnden puts it, 'through a close acquaintance with the soil in which [German culture] had its deepest roots'.[14]

Aside from the general political instability of the period, the failure of the Weimar Republic to achieve many of its reforms was due to the fact that initiative was left to the *Länder*: this inevitably led to a wide variety of experimentation – particularly noteworthy being that with the *Einheitsschule* (the 'unity' school, an early form of comprehensive school) – but to no overall cohesion of approach. In Thüringen a fully comprehensive system was attempted.

The *Gymnasium* largely escaped reform influence, except inasmuch as it was affected by the new curricular emphases, designed as a unifying measure in secondary schools, and the tendency to move away from the *Vielwisserei* approach to one that was more child centred. The *Gymnasium* was still essentially a *Lernschule*. It was to continue to provide a traditional subject-centred curriculum for the benefit of academic pupils after the twelve-year 'dead' period in German education when Hitler was in power. Lawson usefully sums up the lasting characteristics of the Weimar years:

> Before the 1930s . . . certain educational characteristics were established. Among these are the philosophical orientation toward life and school problems . . .; an authoritarian and nationalistic pattern, extending into the classroom methods and lessons and reinforced by an educational officialdom which included teachers; *Land* sovereignty in cultural affairs, with centralization within the *Land* structure of government; a selective spirit of secondary schooling – ranging from a terminal elementary school followed by apprentice training to the socially isolated *Gymnasium*, giving a formal, humanistic education – intended on the one hand to prepare the nation's leaders, and on the other, the mass of the people . . . It was rarely noted during or after the war that an active opposition to rigid instructional forms and controls, and to separate, unconnected, class-connotated school branches had grown during the first three decades of the century.[15]

The *Reformpädagogik* movement was inevitably linked both in fact and by association with social democratic or socialist/communist views: the *Bund entschiedener Schulreformer* (League of Radical School Reformers), for example, founded in 1919 by Paul Oestreich (1878–1959), a Berlin secondary school teacher, was to be 'a radical confession of faith in the idea of a free people's state and the spirit of social community'.[16] The league strongly supported the principle of the *Arbeitsschule* ('activity school'), designed to serve the individual, and the *Produktionsschule*, which was to serve the community and whose aim, as Oestreich put it, would be to achieve 'the totality of personality in the totality of society'.[17] At its conference in Mainz in 1923 the league attacked qualities encouraged in schools which it saw as reflecting a kind of inherent militarism: order, punctuality, discipline, and obedience.[18] It is not surprising that reform initiatives faced strong opposition when such highly regarded traditional values of the schools were under attack. Attempts to further the community schools (*Gemeinschaftsschulen*) met with criticism which insisted that they ran counter to the German heritage and were immoral in being co-educational.[19]

Firm attempts were made to minimise the influence of the church,[20] but because this became an issue that was politically extremely contentious little progress was made apart from the eventual recognition of the equality of status of denominational, inter-denominational, and secular schools.[21]

Experiments with 'life-related instruction' were very popular. Independent rural boarding schools, *Landerziehungsheime* (started by Hermann Lietz, 1868–1919), were developed, and the *Wandervogel* movement (founded in 1901) went from strength to strength. The practice of *Wandertage* (day walking excursions) was introduced into German schools. As one author has expressed it, before the 'social chaos' of the economic crisis 'the German school system was well on its way to becoming the most liberal and democratic in Europe'.[22]

With the coming to power of the National Socialist Party in 1933 this perception of German education was to be turned on its head, and the use of the German example was rather to warn against the corruptibility of education systems through autocracy, propaganda, and discrimination than to encourage any emulation of German practice. Even after 1933, however, there could still be admiration for aspects of educational provision in Germany.

A delegation of ten people, led by E. G. Savage, Senior Chief Inspector of Schools, visited Germany in November 1936 to report on physical training. A file in the Public Record Office is concerned with the production of the delegation's report, intended as a Board of Education pamphlet. Here is part of the concluding section of the draft report:

> Whatever one may think of such things as the so-called "Nürnberg Laws" and the New Militarism, and whatever doubts one may entertain about the Hitler jugend [sic] and even about the Labour Service, one cannot, in common fairness, withhold one's admiration for the excellent work that "Kraft durch Freude" is doing; it is far and away the most agreeable phenomenon of the Third Reich. If it is the task of Dr. Schacht and Dr. Darre [sic] to provide the necessary "panem" for the German masses, Dr. Ley is certainly seeing to it that, as far as he is concerned, they shall have something more and something better than mere "Circenses". There is no evidence whatever, to the unprejudiced observer, that the real object of "Kraft durch Freude" is the sinister one of merely ensuring that wage-slaves shall be kept physically fit for the daily grind at the mill and on the land. The spirit that informs the movement is manifestly far too generous for that. The idea is, of course, to teach the German worker sensible ways of occupying his leisure, and K.d.F. boldly faces the fact that the vast majority of people do not want to spend a great deal of time sitting at home and reading books: they want to get out into the open, exercise their bodies, play games and "do things", rather than "think things", with their fellows. It is constantly dinning into the worker's ears that a man's life is not all toil and labour, and points out that he has the right to demand of the State that it shall cater for his leisure in his manhood as it catered for his education in his childhood. National Socialism, he is told, recognises the justice of this demand, and is taking effective steps to see that he can every day look forward to a complete change of occupation – and a jolly one at that – after he has passed through the factory gates in the evening. "And so it is that the telephone-engineer can now look forward to spending a happy evening, say, in throwing the discus, the house-painter can look forward to boxing, the nursemaid to gymnastics, the warehouseman to jujitsu, the typist to ball games (to correct the tendency to round shoulders), the soldier to sailing, the housewife to swimming, the music-mistress to throwing the javelin – and all under the auspices of 'Kraft durch Freude'!"

One may perhaps conclude by quoting the following bit of doggerel from the end of a characteristic "Kraft durch Freude" advertisement:

> Und die Moral von der Geschicht'?
> Auch du darfst nicht beiseite bleiben!

Ob Leichtgewicht, ob Schwergewicht,
Auch du musst Leibesübung treiben.
Drum säume nicht, drum zögre nicht,
Bei K.d.F. dich einzuschreiben!

(What's the moral of this tale?
Don't you stay outside the pale!
Be you thin or [be] you fat,
"Jerks" are what you should be at!
So don't you dally, come on, boy,
Give in your name to "Strength through Joy"!)

Despite its caveats this appears in retrospect to be an embarrassing plaudit for a feature of National Socialist Germany which, though extraordinarily popular, might have aroused a certain degree of disquiet among foreign observers. Though it now seems remarkable that the movement could be seen as quite so praiseworthy, there was much general admiration of physical education in Germany right up to the outbreak of war, due in some measure to perceptions of German performance in the 1936 Berlin Olympics.[23]

In the published version the statement 'Whatever one may think of such things as the so-called "Nürnberg Laws" and the New Militarism, and whatever doubts one may entertain about the Hitler jugend and even about the Labour Service' is omitted, but elsewhere in the printed text there are still statements that create a sense of unease about the judgement of those conducting the investigation. It is remarked casually, for example, that *Kraft durch Freude* provides 'courses of all sorts [. . .] which any non-Jewish German may join for a nominal fee'[24] as if this was an understandable and acceptable condition.

On the so-called *Napolis* (*Nationalpolitische Erziehungsanstalten*, 'National Political Educational Establishments') there is nothing but praise:

These schools are as yet in their infancy, but they clearly have a future before them. They claim to be in a fair way towards producing a race of strong and sturdy men of directive and organisational ability and many-sided versatility, eager to assume responsibility and taste the sweets of leadership – not lawyers, engineers, poets, musicians, professors and "intellectuals". Large numbers of them will go into the army, which is at the present moment short of junior officers and where the training which they have received here will undoubtedly stand them in excellent stead.

[. . .]

The progress of these schools, combining as they do some features of the public schools of England and the military academies of the United States of America, together with much that is purely German, will be watched with interest not only in Germany but also by other countries.[25]

The comparison with the English public school is puzzling.

Only towards the end of the report is there a sign of doubt – unless the reader has been expected to read between the lines as, in other parts and without any further elucidation on the people involved, 'Herr Julius Streicher of Nuremberg' is mentioned as the founder of the Hitler-Jugend and we are told that 'the Führer himself' later took over the leadership and that 'Herr Baldur von Schirach', 'a young man in the early twenties, of great energy and vitality and passionately devoted to the Führer', became the *Reichsjugendführer* ('National Youth Leader'), or as the reader is guided through the rigid hierarchical structure of the organisation of the Reich as regards physical training.[26] There is almost a sense of awe in the text at such meticulous organisation.

In one of the final paragraphs of the report we can detect a note of reservation:

> Modern Germany, they say. has no use for a horde of young men and women carrying too much intellectual top-hamper, neurasthenics, pessimists, cranks and rainbow-chasers, a prey to "Weltschmerz" and defeatism.
>
> [. . .]
>
> German intellectualism, great as its services to learning and humanity have been in the past and strong and healthy as it probably is, in essence, at present, has certainly from time to time, for reasons that need not be elaborated here, shown a distinct tendency to "go bad in the bottle"; and of this none are more aware than the Germans themselves. It is quite within the bounds of possibility that some corrective to this tendency is necessary at the present moment – it is not desired to express any opinion on this point. But whether a corrective is necessary or not, there is no doubt that one is now being applied, and that drastically. Whether the present corrective, if it is necessary, is the right one in the circumstances, is certainly open to question. Whether the treatment is likely to go too far, it is as yet too soon to say. It may perhaps, however, be permitted to express the fear of the possibility of its going too far – in the case of a people with whom the Best has often tended to be the enemy of the Good. That physical education in itself is an excellent thing nobody can deny, but its continued prosecution to excess at the expense of the things of the mind and soul in a whole nation of the size and standing of Germany might lead to fearful consequence for her and to trouble for the whole world. "Corruptio optimi semper pessima!" ['Corruption of the best is always the worst'][27]

The report remains a curiously acquiescent account of developments in Germany which to more perceptive observers would have had a very sinister aspect.

* * * * *

A significant figure in the development of educational thought in Germany after the First World War whose ideas have had influence in other countries was the Austrian-born Rudolf Steiner (1861–1925). His educational philosophy found expression in the first 'Free Waldorf School', founded in 1919 and so named because it catered largely for children of the workers at the Stuttgart Waldorf-Astoria cigarette factory. Steiner schools still exist in many parts of the world, including most countries of Europe. The Steiner Waldorf Schools Fellowship describes the principles underlying the schools today:

> Steiner schools are always co-educational, fully comprehensive and take pupils from 3 to ideally eighteen. They welcome children of all abilities from all faiths and backgrounds.

The priority of the Steiner ethos is to provide an unhurried and creative learning environment where children can find the joy in learning and experience the richness of childhood rather than early specialisation or academic hot-housing. The curriculum itself is a flexible set of pedagogical guidelines, founded on Steiner's principles that take account of the whole child. It gives equal attention to the physical, emotional, intellectual, cultural and spiritual needs of each pupil and is designed to work in harmony with the different phases of the child's development. The core subjects of the curriculum are taught in thematic blocks and all lessons include a balance of artistic, practical and intellectual content. Whole class, mixed ability teaching is the norm.[28]

The continuing existence of schools run according to Steiner principles is testimony to the importance attached to alternative approaches to state provision. As with Montessori schools, the method and ethos of the schools provide a different style of education, and one that is not elitist and privilege bound, like most schools in the independent sector in England. Here too we can cite Kurt Hahn (1886–1974) who co-founded Salem School in 1920 and, after emigrating to Britain, started Gordonstoun School and the United World Colleges movement, which currently numbers thirteen institutions in five continents, teaching the curriculum of the International Baccalaureate.

* * * * *

Delegations from Liverpool Education Committee visited Germany in the period 1928–9. In 1928 they found school buildings and equipment in Berlin and Hanover to be especially admirable:

We are compelled to report that the latest Elementary, Secondary, and Trade Schools of such cities as Berlin and Hanover [. . .] are immeasurably superior in accommodation and equipment to the corresponding schools built by Municipal Authorities in England. The latest Elementary Schools of Berlin have cost nearly as much per place as any of the Liverpool Secondary Schools, and that notwithstanding lower costs of labour and building material. Spaciousness, convenience and comfort, beauty of decoration, lighting and furnishing, combine to place new German schools in an altogether different class to the corresponding schools built by Liverpool, and indeed, so far as we are aware, by any English city in recent years.[29]

There is recognition of the pre-war achievements in education in Germany, and an up-to-date account of the new structure, with admiration for provision in the continuation schools. The report concludes:

Even at the present stage in the evolution of the new educational systems an English visitor to the schools of Germany and Holland could hardly come away otherwise than profoundly convinced that except perhaps in the single domain of organised games the vast majority of the children of these countries are being provided with better opportunities for natural growth in beautiful and educative surroundings, more universal language training, and, above all, infinitely superior training in craft and art work than all but a very small proportion of the children of England.[30]

The 1929 report of a visit to schools of Austria and Germany could state that 'for spaciousness, comfort and convenience, the post-war, and in many cases the pre-war, schools of the leading German cities are vastly superior to the corresponding schools of Liverpool and, so far as we are aware, to those of many other English cities'.[31]

As we have seen with Davis's 1879 report for the Birmingham School Board, such local initiatives, in terms of reporting on education in Germany, served to disseminate information that would create a sense of contrast and highlight shortcomings in the home system.

Developments in England in the interwar period

In England, in the years following the end of the First World War, a situation had been reached where elementary education was free and universal. The majority of children completed their education in the elementary school, and left school at age 14. Access to secondary education on the other hand was limited and expensive. It was possible for children from poor families to gain scholarships, but they were often unable to take up awards since the income they would generate when they reached age 14 was needed by their families. It became increasingly clear that more would have to be done to produce a fair and equitable secondary education system. It would be important to recognise and reward potential as assessed by measured intelligence.

The notion of universal secondary education had much of its intellectual origin in the work of R. H. Tawney (1880–1962), whose book *Secondary Education for All* (1922), written in his capacity as a member of the Labour Party's Education Advisory Committee, envisaged there being different types of secondary school to which pupils would transfer at the age of 11+. Tawney had followed Sadler in promoting the work of the university extension movement, and he was to advise R. A. Butler as the 1944 Education Act was being put together.

In the 1920s and 1930s there was a growing acceptance of the psychological notion of there being three types of intelligence, and this idea was expressed in a number of official reports, the first of which was the Hadow Report on the education of the adolescent. Set up under the first Labour government (though reporting after the Conservative government under Stanley Baldwin had been elected), the Hadow Committee had the task of investigating the curriculum for children who would stay at school until age 15, taking into account their different 'tastes and abilities' and bearing in mind their future employment. In addition it was to report on appropriate examining at the end of their courses and on facilitating transfer to secondary schools at a point later than the normal age of entry to such schools.

The report begins with a remarkable statement which mixes a high-flown purple passage, alluding to Shakespeare's *Julius Caesar*, with stark 'bureaucratese':

There is a tide which begins to rise in the veins of youth at the age of eleven or twelve. It is called by the name of adolescence. If that tide can be taken at the flood, and a new voyage begun in the strength and along the flow of its current, we think that it will "move on to fortune." We therefore propose that all children should be transferred, at the age of eleven or twelve, from the junior or primary school either to schools of the type now called secondary, or to schools (whether selective or non-selective) of the type which is now called central, or to senior and separate departments of existing elementary schools.[32]

Here is the beginning of the structure later enshrined in the 1944 Education Act. There would be separate primary and secondary stages in a child's education, and transfer from the primary stage would take place at age 11. The school leaving age would be raised to 15 (which was not actually achieved until 1947.)

The report mentions Arnold's 1868 study of education in Germany, France, and Switzerland which, among others, helped to prepare the way for 'higher grade' schools in the final three decades of the nineteenth century.[33] And included among the appendices to the report are accounts of post-primary provision in other countries, including Prussia. The full text of the entry for Prussia is reproduced as Appendix 4 below. This particular summary is an excellent example of the thoroughness of reporting on educational provision in Germany to support policy discussion at a high level of importance in England. Again it is clear that progress in Germany had been way ahead of thinking in England about the post-primary stage of education.

The Spens Report of 1938, on secondary education with special reference to grammar and technical high schools, further progressed the notion of the three stages of education (primary, secondary, tertiary), recommending development of the technical school and of a tripartite structure of secondary education in terms of grammar, technical, and modern schools. It did not support the 'multilateral' or comprehensive school model. And it reinforced reliance on psychological evidence, especially in relation to intelligence testing. It recommended raising the school leaving age to 16 (not achieved until 1972).

Chapter I of the report is an 86-page detailed and scholarly 'historical sketch' of developments in secondary school provision in England since the Middle Ages, making use of Matthew Arnold's work and in particular that of the great nineteenth-century Royal Commissions. This comprises about one-fifth of the whole text. There is an appendix on secondary education by the distinguished comparativist, Isaac Kandel (1881–1965), who had written extensively on the organisation of this stage of education in England, France, Germany and the United States.[34] Kandel was naturally critical of the National Socialist policies, but made an important point about development in the Weimar Republic:

This important aspect of secondary education [certification based on the pupils' scholastic and general record and the teachers' estimates] need not be discussed further here. It is, however, pertinent in this connection to refer to the efforts made in Germany under the republican *régime*, first, to reorganise the curriculum from the point of view of the contribution which each subject can make to the total preparation of pupils for the world around them, and, second, to substitute for the traditional examinations a new form based upon the pupils' records, the teachers' estimates of ability, and exercises which seek to discover not so much what the pupils can at a given moment remember of their studies but what they can do with the materials which they have studied. In other words, all subjects were according to this scheme to develop living interests and the ultimate test of an education was to be not one of memory but of capacity. Even though this scheme in its full implications remained largely on paper, it suggests desirable lines of development, for it means that education can no longer be regarded merely as the mastery of a number of subjects but as the use of aspects of human activities to train individuals as human beings in mind and character, as citizens of a free country, with an understanding and appreciation of the world in which they live.[35]

As with the nineteenth-century texts, it is clear that the foreign example figured in the committee's efforts to be fully informed about the wider picture of secondary school provision in Europe and elsewhere, with Germany providing insight in terms of some possible good practice.

The Hadow and Spens reports had established that the principle of secondary education for all was achievable through a school structure that differentiated between children according to their measured intelligence. The Second World War interrupted progress towards this ambition, but unexpectedly provided an opportunity, through the existence of a coalition government, to introduce legislation that would finally make it a reality. The Norwood Report of 1941 confirmed what had been discussed in the 1930s and led eventually to the 1944 Education Act. This had taken fifty years or so to achieve, while Germany had had a well-structured system that had ensured that large numbers of children had been able to attend a secondary school of some kind since the late nineteenth century.

* * * * *

The interwar years in both countries saw the elementary school, the means by which 'national education' had been achieved, look like what the German term *Restschule* implies, a school for those 'left over', who for social or academic reasons would not be able to gain access to a secondary school and thence to a range of occupations with greater responsibility and to the professions. The *Volksschule* would eventually disappear, to be transformed into the *Hauptschule* (often today described as a *Restschule*. . .), and the elementary school in England would become in most instances the 'secondary modern school' as the policy of 'secondary education for all' was realised after the Second World War.

Attraction to the German model had to do with the climate of experiment and reform, as well as the high standards of buildings and equipment and the clarity of provision evident in a coordinated system, with checks and controls to ensure comparability between institutions. With the rise to power of the National Socialists in 1933 and the outbreak of war in 1939, the German model in education was to become attractive to outside observers only in terms of condemnation of developments at all levels, from the *Volksschule* to the university.

Chapter 7

From the Second World War to Post-War Reconstruction, Radical Reform, and Beyond in England: Lessons from Germany Since 1939

Many claims and counter-claims have been and are being made about the effectiveness of our system of education as compared with that of the Federal Republic and vice versa. At times some of these claims appear to say quite contradictory things about education in the Federal Republic and a number appear to be seriously ill-informed.

Her Majesty's Inspectorate, 1986[1]

The 1944 Education Act

The 1944 Education Act was an extraordinary achievement. Conceived in wartime, when greater priorities were occupying the minds of government ministers, it finally reached the goal argued for during the 1930s and earlier of 'secondary education for all' in England and Wales. As we have seen, the Spens Report had proposed a tripartite structure of modern schools, grammar schools, and technical high schools in 1938. The Norwood Report of 1941 described the basic structure that was again being recommended for secondary education:

At the age of 11+, or earlier in some cases, a child would pass into one of the three types of secondary education which we have postulated, secondary Grammar School, secondary Technical School, secondary Modern School. This first classification of pupils would necessarily be tentative in a number of cases, for the diagnosis of special interests and skills demanding a curriculum suited to them takes time. The next two years would be spent in what for convenience we call the 'Lower School' of one of the three types of school, and during these years a generally common curriculum would be pursued, though within limits there would be some variation. During these years the special interests of the child would be studied and, if desirable, transfer would be recommended. After two years a review of all pupils in the Lower School of all types of school would be made; promotion into the higher forms of the school in which a pupil found himself at 11+ would not be automatic, unless that were the right school for him. From the age of 13+ to 16+ a pupil would pursue a course of study suited to his abilities in the type of school which could offer it. This course would lead either to employment and to part-time continued education up to the age of 18+ or to whole-time continued education culminating in the University or in institutions offering opportunities for further study. We regard it as important that the doors to further study should be kept open along as many paths as possible, regard being had to the maintenance of the standard of such further study.[2]

There is – understandably for the time – no reference to the traditions in education in Germany built on this kind of tripartite structure. But there is a clear parallel with the German structure of basic (elementary) schools (*Volksschulen*), various kinds of intermediate/technical schools (*Mittelschulen* and *Realschulen*), and the academic *Gymnasien*. Later the German 'Framework Plan' (*Rahmenplan*) was to describe the rationale behind a tripartite secondary school structure:

This appears now as a too starkly differentiated – and in essence rather simplistic – way of dividing up pupils according to the three types of intelligence widely discussed in England in reports of the 1930s. But this was the reality of the tripartite structure envisaged for England in the 1944 Act and of the various education systems which prevail for the most part still in the *Länder* of the Federal Republic of today.

How were children to be selected?

We suggest . . . that differentiation for types of secondary education should depend upon the judgment of the teachers in the primary school, supplemented, if desired, by intelligence and other tests. On the basis of these combined verdicts a recommendation should be made that a pupil should continue his education at the type of school appropriate to him, due consideration having been given to the wish of the parent and the pupil. We recognise that this method of selection cannot become fully operative until there is sufficient provision of secondary education of various types.[4]

The flexible aspects of the Norwood Committee's recommendations are particularly interesting in retrospect: 'tentative' classification of pupils; two years of common curriculum; transfer between school types to be made possible in some cases; selection based on primary teachers' judgements of a child's ability and potential, and supplemented by intelligence tests; parity in terms of amenities and conditions.[5] These have been for the most part characteristics of the way the German tripartite system has worked, with some *Länder* (much later) operating

Table 12 German Secondary School Structure, derived from the *Rahmenplan für das deutsche Bildungswesen* (1959)[3]

Psychological type	School type	Occupational type
Theoretical (*theoretisch*)	*Gymnasium* ('*höhere Schule*')	'Intellectually leading' (*geistig führend*)
Theoretical/practical (*theoretisch-praktisch*)	*Realschule* ('*Mittelschule*')	'Practical with increased responsibility' (*praktische Berufe mit erhöhter Verantwortung*)
Practical (*praktisch*)	*Hauptschule* ('*Volksschule*')	'Carrying out instructions' (*ausführend*)

an orientation phase before final decisions are made between school type, and with the principle of 'permeability' (*Durchlässigkeit*) allowing – in theory at least – later lateral transfer between schools. An important difference in the German case is that the initial choice of school remains a right of parents, who are guided in their choice by the recommendations of primary school teachers.

The Education Act of 1944 did not actually name the three types of secondary school that the government had in mind:

> It shall be the duty of every local education authority to secure that there shall be available for their area sufficient schools:-
> [. . .]
> (b) for providing secondary education, that is to say, full-time education suitable to the requirements of senior pupils, other than such full-time education as may be provided for senior pupils in pursuance of a scheme made under the provisions of the Act relating to further education;
> and the schools available for an area shall not be deemed to be sufficient unless they are sufficient in number, character, and equipment to afford for all pupils opportunities for education offering such variety of instruction and training as may be desirable in view of their different ages, abilities, and aptitudes, and of the different periods for which they may be expected to remain at school, including practical instruction and training appropriate to their respective needs.[6]

Nor did it prescribe a curriculum for the various types of secondary school. The secular instruction in most types of school was to be 'under the control of the local education authority'.[7] In effect the control was simply devolved to schools, and it was not until the Education Reform Act of 1988 that a compulsory national curriculum was introduced, with, as we shall see, much consideration of the curriculum and assessment in German schools in the debate leading up to the legislation. The second post-war Labour Minister of Education George Tomlinson is credited with saying 'Minister knows nowt about curriculum' – a sentiment echoed much later by the Conservative Minister Sir David Eccles, who spoke of 'the secret garden of the curriculum'. What was taught was decidedly not seen as a matter for the central authority.

One effect of the Act was to accomplish the reverse of what its proposers had intended – a division on class lines:

> Instead of the three types of school enjoying parity of esteem, they had perpetuated in educational terms the British class divide between 'blue-collar' (secondary modern and technical schools) and 'white-collar' (grammar schools).[8]

The technical schools were not developed to the extent that they could achieve the status of the German *Realschulen*: they never constituted more than about ten per cent of the total number of secondary schools and were often housed in poor buildings. Failure to develop them has been seen as a now much regretted missed opportunity.[9] The secondary modern schools had low status, and even worse buildings and facilities, frequently simply those of the former elementary schools. What is more, pupils left school at 15 (without any proper qualifications) or at 16 or 18. Though the 1944 Act envisaged pupils staying on in education of some form until age 18 (as had the 1918 Act in its promotion of the continuation school concept), it has been only relatively recently (2007) that this ambition was converted to formal policy by the Labour government under Gordon Brown. Staying on in some form of education until age 18 has been a much admired feature of provision in education in Germany.

The most problematic outcome of the 1944 Act was the selection at 11+ on the basis of an IQ test and tests in English and arithmetic. It is reckoned that about 12 per cent of children were misplaced as a result of the 11+ examination,[10] and there was little chance of later transfer for those who were placed in a school type which did not suit their abilities. There was also considerable regional variation in the number of grammar school places available, with children in Wales having a better chance of getting into a grammar school, and with weightings in favour of boys. The starkness of the process is indicated in the way the results were reported to parents. The example below shows a letter from 1956 setting out the options available and indicating that children had in fact been put into four categories, ranging from an assessment that education until age 18 would be appropriate, to the dead end of a 'general' course to age 15.

SOUTHMEAD COUNTY PRIMARY SCHOOL
Princes Way, S.W.19

April, 1956
Dear **Mr Phillips,**

Your child **David**

As a result of the Junior School Leaving Examination has been recommended by the Selection Committee of the London County Council for a **H** Course in a Secondary School.

The secondary school courses available are:-

1. "H" course This is a six or seven year course leading to the Advanced level of the General Certificate of Education.

2. "5" – A five year course leading to the Ordinary Level of the G.C.E.

3. "5P" – A five year practical (technical) course.

4. "4" – A general four year course.

It will of course be possible at a later age to transfer a child from one course to another according to suitability.

Yours faithfully

E. B. Hart
Headmaster

Schools of the neighbourhood.

Secondary Schools. Courses offered.

Mayfield (Girls) 1. 2. 3. 4.
Wandsworth (Boys) 1. 2. 3. 4.
Elliott (Boys and Girls) 1. 2. 3. 4.
Battersea (Boys and Girls) 1. 2. 3. 4.
Southfields (Boys and Girls) 4 only

Congratulations on grammar category!

E. B. Hart

FIGURE 5   Example of 11+ results letter, 1956

An interesting feature of this particular letter, from the head of a London primary school, is that mostly the schools listed as options were comprehensive schools, with the nearest traditional grammar schools not included. London had some of the earliest comprehensive schools in the country, long before the changes of 1965 and after, and in this case it seems the head was keen to promote the interests of the new institutions in the locality. Once 'selected' for a particular type of school, however, there was very little opportunity to transfer up through the system: the headmaster's glib 'of course' in connection with the possibility of transfer from one course to another disguised the fact that movement between schools was most often in a downward direction.

The Central Advisory Council for Education published in 1959 an important report on the education of boys and girls aged 15 to 18. Known as the Crowther Report, it covered in particular the raising of the school leaving age, the nature of the 'sixth form', and further education. It mentions Germany in relation to the notion that the vocational content of the curriculum gives students 'a sense of reality and purpose' and it uses the German example to warn against one particular line of possible policy action:

> [The] process of vocational and quasi-vocational training has been associated in Germany with the regulation of entry to the occupations concerned. This may well not be an advantage in an age when flexibility is increasingly important. It certainly runs counter to English experience, which is that the lower the degree of skill, the more frequent the changes of job by young workers. There would be psychological as well as economic advantages and disadvantages in the setting up of specific, long-continued training programmes for a greatly increased range of less skilled jobs. This is a matter which lies outside our competence to judge, but it seems unlikely to us that extensions downwards on the German pattern will, or should, cover anything like the whole field of boys' employment.[11]

This assessment obscures an important point about German provision. It is precisely because particular occupations are linked with particular types of training that the workforce is so well equipped to perform efficiently and therefore to contribute to a strong economy. It is not possible, say, to train as a bookseller and then to switch to being a baker. Booksellers are properly trained, and if booksellers wish to be bakers they have to train as bakers. Flexibility of the kind defended in the Crowther Report would undermine the basic principles of German vocational training.

Appendix III of the report, by Hugh A. Warren, principal of the South-East London Technical College, covers technical and vocational education in Western Europe and includes a section on the Federal Republic of Germany. Two groups of members of the council visited Baden-Württemberg and the Ruhr district, and Holland and the Ruhr district respectively in June, 1958. The purpose of the study of foreign provision is commented on:

> The Council had no mission to provide a comprehensive review of [. . .] facilities in Europe. Rather was its interest restricted to the more limited task of gleaning from those countries information which might stimulate its deliberations in the education of the teenager in England. Recent changes and developments – such as the French "centre d'apprentissage", or the

German "second way" (der zweite Bildungsweg), or the Dutch intermediate technical school (uitgebreid technische school) – were thus of greater interest than stable time-honoured and well-known institutions such as the German Technische Hochschule, or the École Polytechnique of France.[12]

And it is pointed out that the council included several members with relevant experience of other countries: 'From the earliest days of its deliberations [. . .] the Council was kept informed of recent developments in our neighbouring countries'.[13] This part of the Report's apparatus comprises a full factual account of the German school system, with special detail on apprenticeships, types of *Berufsschule* (vocational school) and the so-called 'second pathway' (*zweiter Bildungsweg*) through the education system. The aspiration in the Report's recommendations that about half of the school population should continue in full-time education (including sandwich courses) until age 18 fell short of what was the case in Germany, but it was in line with the German principle of keeping children in education beyond the minimum school leaving age.

* * * * *

By the mid-1960s, under Harold Wilson's Labour government, it was clear that the comprehensive school offered the obvious solution to the problem of early selection and the potential cutting-off of opportunities for children who failed the 11+. Labour's Secretary of State for Education and Science from 1965 to 1967, Anthony Crosland (1918–77), issued a circular that requested LEAs to submit plans for the reorganisation of schools in their area along comprehensive lines. Circular 10/65 quoted a motion passed in the House of Commons on 21 January 1965:

> That this House, conscious of the need to raise educational standards at all levels, and regretting that the realisation of this objective is impeded by the separation of children into different types of secondary schools, notes with approval the efforts of local authorities to reorganise secondary education on comprehensive lines which will preserve all that is valuable in grammar school education for those children who now receive it and make it available to more children; recognises that the method and timing of such reorganisation should vary to meet local needs; and believes that the time is now ripe for a declaration of national policy.[14]

There are echoes here of the strange slogan adopted both by Wilson and his predecessor Hugh Gaitskell of a 'grammar school education for all'.[15] That this could only be achieved by abolishing the grammar schools was an interesting paradox: Crosland is reported as saying to his wife 'If it's the last thing I do, I'm going to destroy every fucking grammar school in England. And Wales. And Northern Ireland'.[16]

Progress was remarkably swift, to the extent that by the end of 1969 schemes had been approved for 129 out of a total of 163 LEAs.[17] And so England was moving away from a model which had much in common conceptually with that of Germany; Germany persisted in resisting the common secondary school (*Gesamtschule*), and where it was introduced it existed alongside other forms of secondary school and was favoured only in Social Democratic Party–controlled *Länder*.

Occupied Germany: the British Zone

As it became clear during the war that Germany would be defeated, there was considerable effort made to plan for the role of the Allies in overseeing the running of the country after the cessation of hostilities. For a while it had been anticipated that there would be some form of German administration in place, but the unconditional surrender changed the situation and the occupiers found themselves having supreme control over all aspects of German life.

Not surprisingly, during the war German education was viewed with widespread disapproval. The structure of the educational system was kept basically intact, but with the addition of party schools. The Hitler Youth movement pervaded the system, membership having become compulsory. The curriculum became politicised, with textbooks reflecting Nazi ideology. The universities experienced a period of great shame in terms of the prostitution of their commitment to independent scientific inquiry. New subjects like *Rassenkunde* horrified outside observers who saw the great institutions so admired in the nineteenth century now undergoing a crude transformation in line with Nazi ideology.

Memoranda produced during the war showed a thorough understanding of the historical development of education in Germany. The 'Geographical Handbook Series', for example, published in 1944 'for official purposes only', included in its four volumes on Germany a detailed account of education before 1933, together with an analysis of the nature of the National Socialist education system.[18] Such a text, together with many widely available non-official accounts of recent developments in education in Germany, provided the members of what was known as 'Education Branch of the Control Commission for Germany (British Element)' with essential background information as they faced the task of 'reconstructing' education in the British Zone. Among them we can cite *The German Universities and National Socialism* by the American Edward Yarnall Hartshorne (1937), *Education in Nazi Germany* 'by two English investigators' (1938), Erika Mann's *School for Barbarians: Education under the Nazis* (1939), E. R. Dodds's *Minds in the Making* (1941), Gregor Ziemer's *Education for Death: The Making of the Nazi* (1942), Peter F. Wiener's *German with Tears* (1942), Amy Buller's important book *Darkness Over Germany* (1943) which includes much coverage of education, Abraham Wolf's *Higher Education in Nazi Germany, or Education for World-Conquest* (1944), and other similar texts. In addition there were many unpublished background papers put together by experts charged during the war with writing internal policy briefs that might inform the work of the occupiers.

Let us take the work of E. R. Dodds as an example. Dodds, the Regius Professor of Greek at Oxford, had been involved since 1940 with an Oxford-based research department run by the Royal Institute of International Affairs and charged with the task of post-war international planning. Later this group transferred to London as the Foreign Office Research Department, where Dodds continued to work in the German section under the distinguished sociologist T. H. Marshall (1893–1981).[19]

Dodds investigated education in Germany, with a focus on the universities. In his 'Macmillan War Pamphlet' of 1941 entitled *Minds in the Making* he attempted to understand how education in Germany had come to be what it was under Nazi rule. Using 'official German sources' he examined five areas: the purpose of education, how it was controlled, what was taught, pupil selection, and the efficiency of the system. He saw four principal aims for the post-war period: making equality of educational opportunity a reality, adapting vocational education to the needs of a planned economy, education for responsible citizenship, and countering the 'virus of nationalism'.[20] Only the first of those ambitions had direct resonance with developing policy in England.

Dodds produced for internal use a long 'Memorandum on the German Universities in Relation to German Politics' in which he addressed the problem of 're-education':

> What the future of German education will be in the event of a British victory is much less obvious. But two things are clear: (a) no German Government can be acceptable to this country which is content to leave unaltered the existing German educational system; (b) on the other hand, no reform can be effectively introduced except by a German Government and with the willing support of some substantial section of the German people. Without such support, a foreign government can destroy education, but it cannot re-educate. It can impose new textbooks and new curricula, but whatever guarantee of 'political reliability' it demands from the teachers it cannot control the spirit of the teaching, still less the reactions of the taught.[21]

This view that only the Germans could manage the future reform of the educational system was one that was to prevail for the most part in the western zones. A joke of the time envisaged a British observer asking a German how long it would take to rebuild his country. The answer was 42 years. 'Why precisely 42?' 'Well, I suppose you intend to stay here for 40 years and it will take at least two to reconstruct everything after you've gone'. Imposition was in any case a problematic notion if the main aim during the occupation was to promote democratic processes: Michael Balfour put the problem in the form of a paradox:

> The British were very conscious of the fact that the faith which they wished to propagate involved a disbelief in the value of imposing faiths by order.[22]

The intention on the part of the British was then to encourage responsible German authorities – screened through the denazification process – to reconstruct educational provision along the democratic lines envisaged in the Potsdam Agreement:

> German education shall be so controlled as completely to eliminate Nazi and militarist doctrines and to make possible the successful development of democratic ideas.[23]

The guidance for how this was to be achieved is contained in Control Council Directive No. 54 on 'Basic Principles for Democratisation of Education in Germany' of June 1947. But the first Military Governor, Field Marshal Montgomery, had issued a 'Personal Message from the Commander in Chief to the Population of the British Zone in Germany') as early as August 1945, in which plans for education were outlined. It was couched in his own idiosyncratic brand of military terseness:

1. The Nazis debased your German education. They sought to pervert the minds of your children. They hid from them true things. They gave them

wrong values. They taught them to despise freedom and tolerance and to admire violence and oppression.

2. The Nazis were thwarted only by victorious battles fought by my troops and their great Allies.

3. I intend to have the wrong they did put right.

4. First, your schools and universities will be re-opened as soon as possible. It is no easy task. Nevertheless, schools in some parts are already re-opening and more will re-open in the next month or so. By 1st October all available schools (except Nazi ones) should be functioning again.

5. Three things are needed before the schools can re-open; adequate buildings, sufficient teaching materials, trustworthy teachers.

6. Schools which can be repaired will be repaired. Those which have had to house my troops, or displaced or homeless persons, or vital administrative services, will be cleared as circumstances make this possible.

7. The text books with which the Nazis poisoned the minds of your children will not be used again in schools. I am having reprinted as an emergency measure books formerly used in your schools. New books, written by Germans in Germany and reflecting a wholesome spirit, are coming along. They will be printed as fast as possible.

8. The teacher shortage will be serious. I shall tolerate no teacher in the schools whose record will not stand the most searching investigation. Teachers wrongfully dismissed will be re-instated. I shall release those teacher prisoners-of-war who are worthy to co-operate in the re-education of your sons and daughters.

9. Despite these steps, part-time schooling in many areas is likely to be inevitable for a long time. To remedy this, first priority will be given, once the children are back under healthy influence at school, to the training of new teachers and the re-training of old.

10. The reputation of your Universities fell low in the world's esteem under the Nazis. Their buildings suffered severe damage during the war. I shall allow no professor or lecturer to continue in office who prostituted his gifts in the service of Nazism. Buildings will be restored where possible.

11. I shall encourage Adult Education. The aim should be free discussion between German men and women of all conditions, faiths and ages.

12. My long-term aim is that, through a happy school life, German boys and girls should grow into worthy citizens of Germany and the world. Their independence of mind must make them secure against false doctrines of force and tyranny. You German men and women must learn your responsibilities, too, especially for what is done in the name of the community in which you live.

13. In all this we shall work with the Americans, the Russians and the French.

14. I shall impose on you no foreign principles of education nor methods of teaching. You will be free to experiment, to try out new ideas. My officers will help you. But I shall tolerate no return to Nazism, militarism, or aggression in any form.

15. You German fathers and mothers must do your part to win back your children to a saner way of life. I shall help you. You must help me. That is my order.

Field Marshal, Commander-in-Chief, British Zone[24]

Control Council Directive No. 54 is the most authoritative document of guidance for the future development of education in the western zones. It provided a potential blueprint for the German authorities in relation to all areas of education, and it echoed some of the preoccupations of the Allies in terms of educational reform in their own countries:

> The Control Council approves the following principles and transmits them to the Zone Commanders and to the Allied Kommandatura, Berlin, for their guidance:
>
> 1. There should be equal educational opportunity for all.
> 2. Tuition, textbooks and other necessary scholastic material should be provided free of charge in all educational institutions fully supported by public funds which cater mainly for pupils of compulsory school age; in addition, maintenance grants should be made to those who need aid. In all other educational institutions, including universities, tuition, textbooks, and necessary material should be provided free of charge together with maintenance grants for those in need of assistance.
> 3. Compulsory full-time school attendance should be required for all between the ages of six and at least fifteen – and thereafter, for those pupils not enrolled in full-time educational institutions, at least part-time compulsory attendance up to the completed age of eighteen years.
> 4. Schools for the compulsory periods should form a comprehensive educational system. The terms 'elementary education' and 'secondary education' should mean two consecutive levels of instruction, not two types or qualities of instruction which overlap.
> 5. All schools should lay emphasis upon education for civic responsibility and a democratic way of life, by means of the content of the curriculum, textbooks and materials of instruction, and by the organization of the school itself.
> 6. School curricula should aim to promote understanding of and respect for other nations and to this end attention should be given to the study of modern languages without prejudice to any.
> 7. Educational and vocational guidance should be provided for all pupils and students.
> 8. Health supervision and health education should be provided for all pupils and students. Instruction will also be given in Hygiene.
> 9. All teacher education should take place in a university or in a pedagogical institution of university rank.
> 10. Full provision should be made for effective participation of the people in the reform and organization as well as in the administration of the educational system.
>
> Done at Berlin on 25 June 1947[25]

'Equal educational opportunity for all', 'a comprehensive educational system', and 'health supervision' in particular resonate with the provisions of the 1944 Education Act.

Control over education, one of the 'dereserved' areas, was restored to German hands as early as 1 January 1947, once the immediate tasks of denazifying the teaching force and providing essential buildings and equipment were well under way. The problems were immense: at the end of the war – if we take Germany as a whole – some 92 per cent of the schools in Cologne had been destroyed or seriously damaged; Munich had only one-third of its pre-war classrooms; in Schleswig-Holstein there was one classroom for every 123 children; in Berlin there were only 162 schools available (149 had been destroyed and 36 heavily damaged; 221 needed serious repairs; 81 had been requisitioned for other purposes.) Of 32 higher education institutions in the western zones only six were relatively undamaged; six could use about 50 per cent of their buildings and eight about 25 to 30 per cent; twelve had been totally destroyed.[26] It used to be said – in terms of the destruction in the three western zones – that the Americans had the scenery, the French the wine, and the British the ruins. One distinguished German critic could acknowledge the difficulties of physical reconstruction and appreciate much that was accomplished in the British Zone, while still regretting that more was not achieved in terms of reform:

> No one can free the Germans from the responsibility for their own mistakes. An assessment of British policy during this time cannot, however, overlook the fact that although the education policy of the British Military Government was practical, helpful, tactful, not hasty or overbearing in taking decisions, it was apparently not able to help the Germans overcome their own basic failings and errors and open up new intellectual and social horizons for them.[27]

This was written in the aftermath of a critical report on education in Germany from the Organisation for Economic Co-operation and Development (OECD), in which the problems identified were traced back to missed opportunities in the past. It is difficult to accept, however, that there was an educational *tabula rasa* in Germany after the war, in which everything could be started afresh, with little or no consideration given to past traditions, and the British in particular were very conscious of this.

The OECD report had commented that

> The economic, social and political realities in Germany have changed fundamentally since the 1920s. Yet, in most important respects the education system has remained as it was recast after the Hitler period in the mould of those earlier times.[28]

We shall return to the 1972 OECD report below. There is validity in the criticism, but it seems unfair to put serious blame on policy making in the immediate post-war period, especially as far as the western Allies were concerned. In the Soviet Zone, of course, imposed policy was irresistible. In the western zones, despite an inclination in the US Zone to think that the American high school provided a model for reform; despite the tendency in the French Zone to see the task in Germany as a *mission civilisatrice*, despite a British sense – especially as far as higher education was concerned – that many British university practices were preferable to what was normal in Germany, the policy was to encourage the German authorities to devise their own plans for the recovery of education at all levels. And the German response could be characterised by the catchphrase 'On from Weimar!' How could it be otherwise? Head teachers were replaced and large numbers of staff suspended; emergency measures were in place to get sufficient numbers of teachers into the classrooms, including bringing people out of retirement.[29] The average age of teachers was high. In Nordrhein-Westfalen a mere 6.2 per cent of secondary school teachers were under 30; 55 per cent were 50 and over. In Berlin the average age of trained teachers was 57 in 1948.

Some serious suggestions for reform in higher education in the British Zone came too late to be more than a contribution to a continuing debate about possibilities. In 1947 – during one of the coldest winters on record – Professor Dodds led a delegation of the British Association of University Teachers (AUT) to Germany to report on conditions in the universities of the British Zone. The delegation produced a very critical report, later described by Robert Birley (1903–82), the charismatic Educational Adviser to the Military Government (later to be headmaster of Eton), as 'the biggest mistake we made in the educational field in Germany'.[30] The AUT report makes a damning indictment of the potential for reform:

We feel that we should place in the forefront of our Report our strong and unanimous impression that no radical and lasting reform of the universities which we have visited is likely to come about on the sole initiative of the universities themselves. This impression is not based merely on the fact that, apart from denazification and from some proposed changes in the relationship between universities and State, no radical measures have been introduced or seriously considered: their absence could well be explained by an unavoidable preoccupation with material needs. What convinces us that the universities cannot, unaided, reform themselves, is the consideration that:-

i. The German universities are at present controlled, as far as internal affairs are concerned, by groups of senior professors whose average age is high, whose academic ideals were formed under conditions very different from to-day's, and whose capacity for responding to new circumstances is therefore likely to be in general small;

ii. the social structure of the universities is bound up with that of the secondary schools, and both of them with the traditional structure of German society as a whole, so that reform of the educational system is unlikely to be brought about save in the context of a much wider movement of social reform.[31]

Later Birley was to set up a German commission which produced a much more detailed report on the possibilities for university reform.[32] But again its recommendations remained largely unimplemented.

With the founding of the Federal Republic in 1949 and the installation of Konrad Adenauer as chancellor there began a period of political stabilisation and stability during which the ground was laid for Germany's economic miracle, the *Wirtschaftswunder*. The slogan of Adenauer's Christian Democratic Union (CDU) in the election campaign of 1957 was *keine Experimente!* (no experiments!) – nothing was to be done to upset the political, economic, and social equilibrium that had been achieved by a country perched so dangerously between West and East during the Cold War.

The twenty-year period after the end of the war has been famously dubbed by Robinsohn and Kuhlmann 'two decades of non-reform' in education. They argue that:

In the early 1950s the characteristic features of the German school system had changed only slightly since the beginning of the century. There remained a vertical organization with its accompanying differentiated types of schools, pupils, and teachers, and, in particular, a dual system of general education and vocational training; highly centralized administration within each *Land*; and strict methods of grading and selection.[33]

Although the guidelines in Control Council Directive No. 54 had not, they admit, been followed in the education systems of the occupying powers, 'they were supposed to indicate the general current of progressive education from which Germany had been excluded for the previous twelve years':

> In the initial phase of the post-war period these principles were transformed into blueprints for reform in all *Länder*. They were, however, abandoned within the shortest span of time. Many points of the directive have never been implemented. Because of the unexpectedly speedy resumption of German independence and the quick realization of the futility of re-education dictated from outside, the allies stopped insisting on their implementation. The result was to discourage genuine German reform impulses. Cultural advisers contented themselves with the support of 'internal reform', which was quite acceptable to their German counterparts and of course open to any number of interpretations.[34]

The result was what Robinsohn and Kuhlmann call the 'low tide of educational engagement and scholarship' of the 1950s. Even the work of the *Deutscher Ausschuß für das Erziehungs- und Bildungswesen* (German Committee for Education), from its foundation in 1953 until the publication of its *Rahmenplan* in 1959, was

> done mainly in the setting of an older reform pedagogy and on the basis of personal experience and observation rather than on the much needed foundations of statistical survey, precise evidence, and systematic social analysis.

The *Rahmenplan* envisaged what was called a two-year *Förderstufe* ('promotion stage'), a concept later developed as the *Orientierungsstufe* ('orientation stage'), so that a final decision as to the most appropriate type of secondary school would be delayed.[35] The aim was to postpone the judgement about a child's future that would be of such great significance: an aim that was not lost on educationists in England who were arguing against early selection through the 11+ examination. The National Foundation for Educational Research produced a full checklist of arguments against selection at age 11:

a. the age of eleven is too early definitively to force what amounts to a pre-vocational choice; some 'rejected' children show that they are able to follow academic courses, while some 'accepted' children fail either to stay at school or to pass G.C.E. examinations;
b. the rhythms of physical and psychological development may be associated with intellectual growth; they differ widely in the pre-pubertal and pubertal period; there is some evidence that early developers, particularly girls, may have an advantage over late developers because of an accelerated mental growth, an advantage which disappears later;
c. the whole idea of a single decisive occasion is calculated to cause anxiety to parents, children and teachers; accidents of health, an 'off-day' and similar fortuitous chances out of all proportion to their real importance;

d. any examination or test provokes teachers and/or parents to attempt to prepare children for it; the 11+ procedures involving tests have a 'backwash' effect on the primary schools, and this is widely held to cramp educational initiative, by defining the syllabus in the fields tested and by giving them so prominent a place in the curriculum as to reduce the time given to other subjects not tested;

e. because of differences in the proportion of grammar school places, opportunities differ from locality to locality and between boys and girls;

f. there is also some evidence which suggests that present tests (and even more so, most other examining techniques) tend to favour 'convergent' (analytic or reproductive) thinking rather than 'divergent' (creative or productive) thinking.[36]

In the 1960s and early 1970s there were various other reform initiatives and much debate around the arguments of Georg Picht's polemic *Die Deutsche Bildungskatastrophe* ('The German Educational Catastrophe'), which anticipated serious economic consequences if deficiencies in the system were not addressed so that it could expand, and Ralf Dahrendorf's *Bildung ist Bürgerrecht* ('Education is a Civil Right'), which also argued for expansion and openness.

Why did Germany not develop the comprehensive school, the *Gesamtschule?* The answer may be found in the defences of the tripartite system:

- parents may choose which type of school their children attend;
- there is the possibility of lateral transfer from one type of school to another;
- leaving certificates of each type of school are not restrictive, but provide vertical access to other stages of education;
- some *Länder* in any case have an 'orientation stage' before a final decision is reached as to which type of school a child is best suited to attend.

To this may be added the argument of Benn and Chitty that although 'Germany was the odd country out in terms of ending academic selection . . . [this] was only possible because for 100 years it had developed a parallel technological elite'.[37]

In 1972 the OECD produced its critical report on Germany as part of its programme of 'Reviews of National Policies for Education'. The examiners introduced the section of their report describing shortcomings with a sharp critique:

In spirit and structure, schooling in Germany remains old-fashioned, as it does in several other European countries. In an age when mass secondary and higher education are being rapidly developed in the other advanced states, Germany has made do with a system that until now has effectively shut off some 90% of the children from the possibility of entering university-level education; that experiences great difficulty in remodelling curricula to suit modern conditions; in which teachers appear to follow authoritarian models in their classroom behaviour; and that is bureaucratically administered, lacking essential minimum elements of public, parental, and teacher and student participation in decision-making.[38]

Despite concerns about the slow pace of educational development in Germany, exemplified in particular by a reluctance to adopt the *Gesamtschule* as the 'normal' school in any of the *Länder* of the Federal Republic, there was still considerable attraction to the German example on the part of policy makers in England, especially as Margaret Thatcher's administrations moved inexorably towards far-reaching educational reforms in the 1980s.

Towards the 1988 Educational Reform Act in England

Towards the mid-1980s in England it was clear that substantial changes would be made in education. The agenda had been set in fact by the previous Labour government under the premiership of James Callaghan. Callaghan had made a remarkable speech in Oxford in 1976 which had sparked a 'Great Debate' on education, led by his Secretary of State for Education, Shirley Williams. Callaghan had wanted 'to begin a debate about existing educational trends and [to] ask some controversial questions'.[39] His speech at Ruskin College, Oxford, received wide and critical coverage. He spoke of complaints from industry about the lack of basic skills among employees, of an insufficiency of technological bias in science teaching, of girls abandoning science subjects, of the low standards of numeracy of school leavers, of informal teaching methods, and of reform of the examination system. And he made a statement, tempered with caveats, that indicated something of the way ahead:

> It is not my intention to become enmeshed in such problems as whether there should be a basic curriculum with universal standards – although I am inclined to think that there should be – nor about other issues on which there is a divided professional opinion such as the position and role of the Inspectorate.[40]

Against a background of increasing disquiet about standards – especially with regard to mixed-ability teaching and informal, child-centered teaching styles – the Great Debate facilitated the discussion of these and other issues. Its agenda covered four areas: the school curriculum 5–16, the assessment of standards, the education and training of teachers, and school and working life. The result was a green paper, *Education in Schools: a Consultative Document* (1977) and a wide-ranging curriculum review. Towards the end of the Callaghan administration plans were being made to require all local education authorities to introduce comprehensive schools.

In the election of 1979 Callaghan's government was defeated and the long Thatcher years began. After a slow start the pace towards radical reform quickened, and by the middle of the 1980s there was much comparison with education in Germany.

In 1983 S. J. Prais and Karin Wagner of the National Institute of Economic and Social Research published a discussion paper entitled 'Schooling Standards in Britain and Germany: Some Summary Comparisons Bearing on Economic Efficiency'.[41] This important paper, later reprinted with a slightly different title,[42] was widely reported and helped to establish in the minds of those concerned with policy issues the notion that British – specifically English – schoolchildren were lagging considerably behind German schoolchildren of similar age. Prais and Wagner were principally concerned with standards in mathematics, and in the course of a complex argument comparing what was required in the curricula of English and German schools, they concluded in particular that

> the German schooling system provides a broader curriculum, combined with significantly higher levels of attainment in core subjects, for a greater proportion of pupils than does the English system. Attainments in mathematics by those in the lower half of the ability-range in England appear to lag by the equivalent of about two years' schooling behind the corresponding section of pupils in Germany.[43]

This carefully worded finding, referring specifically to the 'lower half' of the ability range and to mathematics, was often interpreted as implying that all children in English schools were two years behind their German counterparts, as a graphic illustration of a few years later shows:

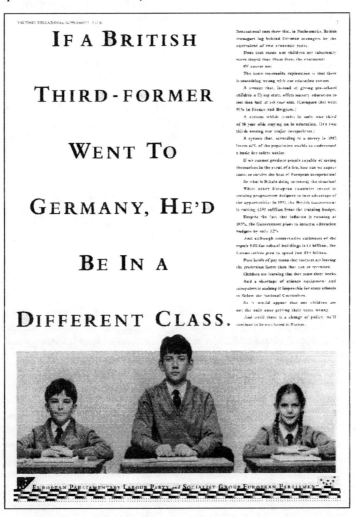

FIGURE 6   Two years behind? (Source: *Times Educational Supplement*, 7 December 1990, p. 7)[44]

Here we see a 'third-former' (aged 13 to 14) flanked on either side by German children two years younger. This powerful image of two years' difference encouraged much analysis of what German schools were doing to achieve their perceived higher standards.

In 1986 the first in a remarkable series of papers from the Inspectorate on aspects of education in other countries was published, the first such series since the reports issued by Michael Sadler's Office of Special Inquiries and Reports beginning in the mid-1890s. *Education in the Federal Republic of Germany: Aspects of Curriculum and Assessment* was followed at various intervals by seven further reports on education in Germany.

The 1986 report dealt with a range of matters germane to government thinking in anticipation of the far-reaching legislation to be proposed in the Education Reform Bill of 1987. It was based on a two-week visit in June 1985 to schools in Bavaria and Nordrhein-Westfalen by a team of six inspectors. Though the inspectors were cautious about the conclusions that might be drawn from studies of education in other countries – they talk, in Sadlerian terms, of the mistaken belief that attractive features can be '[unravelled] from the seamless robe of the system of which they are an integral part and [woven] into the very different warp and woof of our own'[45] – they nevertheless set about their task in terms of the lessons that might be learnt for education in England, 'to comment on those aspects which it seems to us hold out most promise of leading to constructive comparisons, debate and action'.[46]

At the start of the report the inspectors summarise the main attractions of the German system, before analysing those 'features and characteristics' which 'strike informed English observers as having important messages for us':

The Federal Republic's system sets out to provide qualifications for all its pupils. It is not wholly successful in this, but its achievements are impressive. Within its differentiated system of education and training it appears more successful than we are in retaining a large proportion of pupils in general education or in education and training until 17 or 18 years of age; in providing attainable goals for them to work towards; and in not hiving off different groups of pupils in ways that cut them off from the mainstream of general education.

These arrangements in general education, linked as they are with a training system in which industry plays a leading and responsible part, combine to give a broad range of pupils a range of qualifications to aim for; the possibility of threading their way through an interrelated system; and a sense of hope in that they are not dropped out of the system early on.

It is this framework that has an important and cumulative influence upon the expectations of teachers, pupils, parents, employers and the nation at large. Because there is understanding of and broad agreement about what education is seeking to achieve in respect of pupils' needs, parental aspirations, employers' general requirements and the nation's social and economic intentions, the standing of education, of its teachers and its institutions, is relatively high. At all levels these conditions have largely beneficial effects upon pupils' attitudes toward education and consequently upon the standards they achieve.[47]

There are echoes here of the points made in Callaghan's speech of ten years earlier. Later in the report we can isolate some of the features of educational provision in Germany that provide further evidence of its attractiveness to those working towards the changes that were to come with the 1988 Act:

- The most important fact to bear in mind about the Federal Republic's system of assessment generally and about the *Abitur* in particular is that for the Federal Republic it works. Many teachers and officials put much effort and money into developing curricula and subject- and assessment-guide-lines and to overcoming local inconsistencies. Ultimately, however, the system works because virtually everybody involved seems determined that it should do so. [. . .] It is, as much as anything else, an article of faith. This wide agreement about education and its assessment is in itself an important message for English education where such agreement, undertaking and trust are lacking.
- The curriculum is in the lead and has public confidence and clarity; teacher training in all its practical aspects . . . is well-tried and effective.
- The educational system in the Federal Republic is efficient at achieving quickly a broad consensus about which subjects to teach, in which years and for how many pupils.
- There can . . . be a greater confidence that pupils' work in each year and ability group bears a clear relationship to subsequent work than is often the case in England.
- There is a degree of openness and general accountability about the assessment system in the Federal Republic which would be much appreciated by pupils, parents and employers in England.[48]

The assessment system in place in German schools had also attracted attention at a more local level. In 1984 John Pearce and two colleagues produced a report on schools in Hessen, with a focus on the nature and use of the *Notenskala*, the six-point assessment scale on which pupils' work is assessed in German schools:

Our inquiry started from the intuition that a system where marking habits were not freely idiosyncratic might have some lessons for British practice. We were surprised by the way in which a system open to abuse as formalistic had been seized upon to make assessment both an inseparable part of the teacher's daily work and a vital element in his self-respect. [. . .] [Answers to our questions] all pointed to an assessment system that engaged the firm commitment of teachers.[49]

The authors of this report could not identify an immediate possibility of adopting marking procedures like those of the *Notenskala* in any national context (at a time when examining in England was moving towards the introduction of the GCSE in 1988), but used their favourable impression of it to argue at least for a clarification and definition of the assessment practices in use in English schools. Like previous studies we have noted, this account is interesting as an example of a local effort to investigate an aspect of education in Germany in order to inform discussions 'at home'.

Writing in 1989, Detlef Glowka summarised in five categories those aspects of the German education system which had been singled out for particular attention by Her Majesty's Inspectors and others:

  i. The continuous assessment of pupil performance;
  ii. The compulsory nature and breadth of the curriculum;
  iii. The wide distribution of school-leaving qualifications and the systematic correlations between them;
  iv. The developed and systematic paths towards accredited vocational education;
  v. The regulating force of central guiding and controlling authorities.[50]

'It appears', Glowka concludes, 'that in these five areas something could be learnt from the Germans'. At the same time he notes that they constitute central features of the 1988 Act.

The main perceived advantages of the generalised German education system were closely allied to the general thrust of reforms in England and Wales under Conservative governments since 1979. Those advantages had to do with accountability at all levels, with greater centralised control coupled with responsible, regulated autonomy, with government-controlled authority in the curriculum and in assessment, with high standards, and with increased respect for education generally. Though it was clear that there was much in educational provision in the Federal Republic that would not lend itself to the uncritical adulation of educationists in the United Kingdom, its general coherence at home, its acceptability to most people involved with it, and its acknowledged high standards continued to provide a challenge to policy makers in the United Kingdom.

Not all observers were convinced. Correspondence in the *Times Educational Supplement* in 1977 mentioned 'grubbing for marks' in German schools and resultant cheating ('universal, systematic, continuous, mutual, and brazen'). Marking in German schools was said to be characterised by 'narrow rigidity'; continuous assessment put pupils 'in an almost chronic state of exam panic'; grade promotion arrangements could mean repeating a whole school year on the basis of bad marks in one subject.[51]

I participated in an internal seminar at the Department of Education and Science in November 1986, when there was at the same time discussion of aspects of education in France and Japan (also the subject of DES reports.) My task was to speak specifically on secondary schools in Germany at a point when the Prais and Wagner paper was being widely discussed and when the DES report on the curriculum and assessment was made available. I recall a special interest on the part of the DES on *Arbeitslehre*, on school-based preparation for the world of work, but the discussion was wide-ranging. I concluded:

> The German system appears to work well when judged by certain criteria: parental choice operates; there is comparability of parental expectation of and actual provision in the various types of school; teachers have attained a high degree of professional status: vocational training is excellent and measurable standards generally are high. Judged by other criteria, however, there are some obvious problems: competition between the various types of secondary school is now rife, to the considerable disadvantage of the *Hauptschule*; curriculum development tends to lag behind other countries and to be restricted by ministerial guidelines; the propaedeutic function of the *Gymnasium* limits scope at the upper secondary level; the rigid assessment procedures create

considerable unhappiness and stress; comprehensive schools develop at a snail's pace because they are always in competition with what the *Gymnasien* and *Realschulen* can offer.

How we in Britain might benefit from studying the German experience is difficult to determine, but I suspect that it is from the successful *Realschulen* and from the highly developed vocational training arrangements that the best lessons are to be learnt. The German approach to control of the curriculum and to assessment procedures might all too often serve as warnings of potential problems to those wishing to propose similar styles for our own system. They are embedded in the nation's culture and history to an extent that makes them appear wholly natural in the German context.

[. . .]

In reaching a conclusion about the nature of secondary school provision in Germany we are left with the paradox of, on the one hand, admiration for a system which appears properly co-ordinated and well defined – and one which produces impressive measurable outcomes – and, on the other hand, apprehension that these positive features are achieved through means which are not so easily sanctioned. Consider this assessment:

> Over-organisation, excessive supervision from above, State control over entrance to the professions . . ., the too linguistic character of the instruction, and a lack of variety of individual initiative are the evils from which German education is felt by many to be suffering at the present time.

That harsh judgement, familiar to those who know the German system, leaves us with a checklist of concerns. It was written by Michael Sadler in 1903.[52]

And another part of the text echoed the point made in the DES report about the consensus on which the system was built:

> One main advantage [of the German system] should be borne in mind: the Germans have decided what it is their school system offers; it is clearly stated and known to all who have a part in the system. For better or worse this incontestably clear approach does mean that parents know what precisely they can expect for their children from a particular school and they are able, through well-established procedures, to make sure that it is provided.[53]

This implies of course uniformity of provision, a 'sameness' in the system that enables expectations of it to be met.[54] Matthew Arnold's criticism of the 'chapter of accidents' that had produced the educational provision in England of his day continued to hold true to a large extent and still in the 21st century shapes much local provision, where uniformity is shunned in favour of 'choice and diversity', with multiple school types creating a bewildering array of choice for those actually able to exercise it. We shall return to the choice and diversity policy later.

Sir Keith Joseph, the Secretary of State for Education closest to Mrs Thatcher, used often to refer to German models when making speeches about education. His successor, Kenneth Baker, the architect of the 1988 Act, continued to do so, making an extraordinary comment in a television interview in 1986:

> . . . there will have to be much greater influence from the centre, more direction from the centre as far as the curriculum is concerned. And I think

many teachers will welcome this. At the same time . . . I don't want to chill and destroy the inventiveness and creativity of the teachers [. . .] I don't want to go down the completely regimented German way, because . . . it took all those years from Bismarck onwards to get it agreed. But I do want to have more bench marks, more central control of the curriculum.[55]

Against the background of serious discussion of provision in education in Germany this comment is puzzling: What evidence was there that education in Germany was 'regimented'? And Baker appeared to associate the 'central control' in Germany with an adverse effect on 'inventiveness and creativity'. There was also the curious implication that there was one German 'system' and not the eleven (at that time) regional systems that Germany's federal structure allowed, since of course the *Länder* have cultural autonomy (*Kulturhoheit*). As to 'all those years since Bismarck' needed to reach agreement on the curriculum: even if that was an accurate historical statement it would be as nothing compared to the long historical route that 'control' in education in England had taken, without many periods of consensus, since the first vote of government funding to education in 1833. (As we have previously noted, civil servants were enjoined to remember always to speak of 'maintained' rather than 'state' schools, in order to make it clear that the state was supportive and not controlling.)

In his memoirs Baker laments the abandoning of the tripartite structure of secondary education, arguing that the English education system had lost its way in the 1960s:

I had been amazed that Britain had decided to abandon the structure of its education system in this way, and as each year passed it became clearer that the high hopes of the comprehensive movement had not been fulfilled. We began to make comparisons with other countries, particularly Germany and France. In West Germany, nine out of ten sixteen-year-olds got a Hauptschule certificate covering Maths, German, a foreign language and two other subjects. The equivalent in England was the Certificate of Secondary Education Grade 4, and only four out of ten English school leavers achieved this standard.[56]

He describes how he produced a 'blueprint for education reform' in 1986 in which he identified what he felt to be wrong:

1. Widespread dissatisfaction with the *standards* of education.
2. The quality of teaching is not what it should be.
3. Too many children in the 4th and 5th year in our towns and cities absent themselves since they are bored.
4. A disciplined framework is all too rare.
5. There is a stark choice between the state sector 93% with private sector 7% – there are not enough halfway houses to allow the effective exercise of parental choice.
6. Too many LEAs are imposing their own political prejudices upon the system in their charge.
7. Their administration at the local level is frequently inefficient, over-bureaucratic and costly.
8. There is too much local variety in what is still regarded as a national system.[57]

It might be thought that the German example could provide a stimulus for reform in these areas. Standards, teaching quality, 'a disciplined framework', administrative inefficiency, and the opposite of 'too much local variety' at least constituted aspects of educational provision in which Germany had not been unsuccessful, and there are clear examples of consideration of education in Germany being brought into the debate, as we have seen.

The contrasts in important aspects of approaches to education can be summarised as shown in Figure 7.

The 1988 Education Reform Act '[redesigned] the educational chessboard'.[58] Its main provisions had been set out in the Conservative Party manifesto of 1987 in terms of four major reforms: a national core curriculum, all secondary schools and many primary schools to have control over their budgets, an increase of parental choice, and the possibility for schools to opt out of LEA control.[59]

The Act provided for a national curriculum, national tests, 'open' enrolment, local financial management of schools, and the establishment of city technology colleges and 'grant-maintained schools'; it abolished the Inner London Education Authority and increased the powers of the Secretary of State for Education. Some of its measures were centralising, some decentralising or 'delocalising', as described in Figure 8 below.

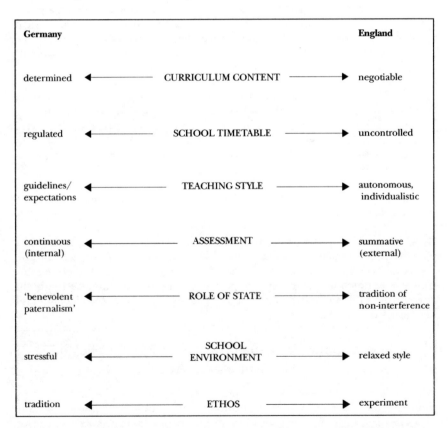

FIGURE 7 Contrasts: Germany and England (Source: Phillips, *Four Periods of Educational Reform in England*, p. 124)

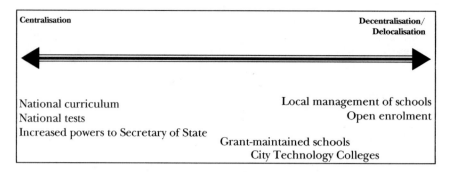

FIGURE 8   1988 Education Reform Act: Centralising and Decentralising Measures (Source: Phillips, *Four Periods of Educational Reform in England*, p. 129)

There is not much here that corresponds to the German example, except in relation to the principle of control over the curriculum; but what emerged from the Act was quite different. Teachers were overwhelmed by a hugely over-prescriptive national curriculum which has had to pass through a whole series of revisions over the past two decades and more to make it manageable and realistic. National tests have also been highly contentious, and are a world removed from the regular teacher assessment which is embedded in the German approach. Thatcher, whose only ministerial experience prior to becoming prime minister was as Secretary of State for Education in the Heath government, 1970–4, was apparently not too pleased with how things turned out:

> The national curriculum – the most important centralizing measure – soon ran into difficulties. I never envisaged that we would end up with the bureaucracy and the thicket of prescriptive measures which eventually emerged. I wanted the DES to concentrate on establishing a basic syllabus for English, Mathematics and Science with simple tests to show what pupils knew. It always seemed to me that a small committee of good teachers ought to be able to pool their experience and write down a list of topics and sources to be covered without too much difficulty. [. . .] I had no wish to put good teachers in a straitjacket.[60]

What is particularly interesting in the Thatcher reforms, however, is that they effectively took forward the ideas sparked by Callaghan's 1976 speech and the 'Great Debate' that followed it. The Blair government of 1997 was content to continue in much the same vein, tampering with grant-maintained schools but keeping the fundamental direction of the policies pursued under Thatcher and her successor John Major.

Education in the German Democratic Republic and German Unification

While in the western zones of occupation after the war there was an inclination from the outset to move swiftly to a position in which the Germans would be able to resume responsibility for education and to reconstruct the systems in place in the *Länder* along democratic lines that would meet the general requirements of the Potsdam Agreement, in the Soviet Zone the system, once the German Democratic Republic (GDR) came into being, was to be developed according to Marxist-Leninist principles and in line with the expectations of the Communist Party, in the case of the GDR the Socialist Unity Party (*Sozialistische Einheitspartei*). The traditional structure of *Volksschule*, *Realschule*, and *Gymnasium* was to be replaced by a common school, and classes were to be of mixed ability. From 1959, after a long period of evolution, the ten-year general polytechnical school (*zehnjährige allgemeinbildende polytechnische Oberschule*) became the normal school of the German Democratic Republic. This was in essence the 'purest' form of comprehensive school: there were no rival private or denominational institutions which would cream off or otherwise extract pupils from the state system, and the inner structure of the school did not permit a formal differentiation between them. Later, in the so-called *erweiterte Oberschule* ('extended upper school') there was the possibility for pupils – provided they or their parents were not in disfavour with the party – to pursue an academic curriculum that would lead to forms of higher education.[61]

The main attractiveness of the model to some observers lay in its simplicity: one type of school for all pupils aged 6 to 16 with no selection by ability. The integration of work experience and vocational training, though not as developed as what was in operation in the Federal Republic, was also a feature of the system that deserved attention. As with other eastern bloc countries, what happened in the schools was 'normal' in the sense that classroom teaching was for the most part efficient and professional. But with the political changes of 1989 and after the GDR system was soon to be of historical interest only.

The events of 1989 which saw the fall of the Berlin Wall and the gradual collapse of communism took most politicians by surprise. Margaret Thatcher in particular was anxious about a too strong Germany emerging from a unification of the Federal Republic and the German Democratic Republic. But unification proved inevitable and had been achieved by October 1990. In March 1990 Thatcher had called a meeting at Chequers with Douglas Hurd, the foreign secretary, and a very distinguished group of historians and authorities on Germany in order to try to understand the Germans. The specialists declined to support her fears; Hurd recorded in his diary: 'They none of them shared her extravagant suspicions of Germany, but this just makes her flail about more. All good humoured, but they are half amused, half depressed by her prejudices'.[62] A memorandum of the meeting recorded part of the discussion that referred to the very different Germany of the day compared to the pre-war era:

It was argued that our basic perception of Germans related to a period of German history running from Bismarck until 1945. This was the phase of imperial Germany, characterised by neurotic self-assertiveness, a high birth-rate, a closed economy, a chauvinist culture. It had not been greatly affected by defeat in 1918, which had been regarded in Germany as unfair. German attitudes, German teaching, German historiography all continued virtually unchanged after 1918, together with a sense of Germany's historic mission. [. . .] But 1945 was quite different and marked a sea-change. There was no longer a sense of historic mission, no ambitions for physical conquest, no more militarism. Education and the writing of history had changed. There was an innocence on the part of the new generation of Germans. We should have no real worries about them.[63]

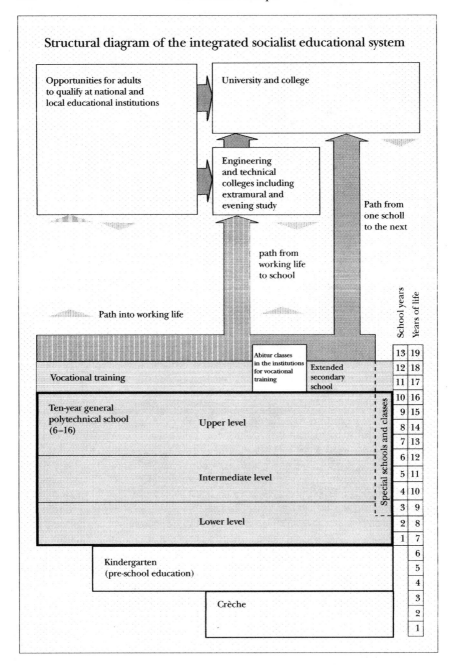

Structural diagram of the integrated socialist educational system

					School years	Years of life

Opportunities for adults to qualify at national and local educational institutions

University and college

Engineering and technical colleges including extramural and evening study

Path from one scholl to the next

path from working life to school

Path into working life

			School years	Years of life
	Abitur classes in the institutions for vocational training		13	19
Vocational training		Extended secondary school	12	18
			11	17
Ten-year general polytechnic school (6–16)	Upper level		10	16
			9	15
			8	14
			7	13
	Intermediate level		6	12
			5	11
			4	10
			3	9
	Lower level		2	8
			1	7
Kindergarten (pre-school education)				6
				5
				4
Crèche				3
				2
				1

Special schools and classes

FIGURE 9   Structure of the Education System of the GDR

The references to teaching here ignore the long period of 'non-reform' in education following the war, when the pre-war system was effectively resurrected, but show an appreciation on the part of those present of the considerable advances in style in post-war Germany. Following unification the challenge for education was to be to integrate the two very different systems and to change the embedded curriculum and teaching styles which had prevailed in the GDR since the end of the war.

It seemed to some observers that there was an opportunity in unified Germany to experiment with a proper comprehensive system in the five new *Länder* which had constituted the territory of the GDR. As we have seen, the ten-year poly-technical school was in effect the purest form of comprehensive school, with no differentiation among pupils and no rival school types available to affect the pupil intake. And the teachers were trained to cope with pupils of all abilities. But all five of the new *Länder* decided quickly to move towards a West German structure for secondary schools, with all of them introducing the *Gymnasium*, alongside the *Hauptschule* and *Realschule* (Brandenburg), the *Hauptschule, Realschule,* and *Gesamtschule* (Mecklenburg-Vorpommern), or a common school with pathways towards the *Hauptschule* or *Realschule* leaving qualifications (Sachsen, Sachsen-Anhalt, and Thüringen).[64] This further reinforced the traditional tripartite structure, but with variations in the case of three of the *Länder* that softened the dividing line between *Hauptschule* and *Realschule*.

The importance of vocational education and training

Nigel Lawson, Conservative Chancellor of the Exchequer (1983–9) under Margaret Thatcher, describes the importance of company-based training:

> I always argued strongly that, to the greatest extent possible, the employer, rather than the taxpayer, should pay for training. This is far more likely to lead to the sort of training the market requires. As industry became more profitable, larger companies found it was far more sensible to invest in train-ing, even if they lost some of their trained staff to other and often smaller companies, than to bid up the wages of an ever-decreasing pool of skilled labour. Company-based training is the norm in Germany, for example, which is often cited as a model in this field.[65]

The German 'dual system' of vocational education and training (VET) has attracted significant attention from educationists and politicians for a very long time and in many countries. Based as it is on a unique compact between the state and employers it provides young people with an assured continuation of their general education up to age 18 in conjunction with varieties of on-the-job training funded by enterprises. This provision has been in stark contrast to that in Britain. Here is a view of the situation in 1990:

> Although Britain and Germany are both industrial societies, they have differed fundamentally in training youths. Germany has a well-developed system of vocational education and training (VET) and Britain does not. British and German school-leavers differ in their chances of finding a job, in the training that goes with the job, and in the wages that they can expect to earn as adults. A British youth has a greater chance of becoming unemployed. German firms today reap the benefit of past investment in training: they have a highly-skilled workforce, and master workmen who can train the next generation of apprentices to a high standard.
>
> Generalisations about nations refer to differences of degree, not kind. There are millions of well-trained British workers, and each year more than a

hundred thousand British youths achieve vocational qualifications. But these figures are insignificant by comparison with Germany. In labour forces of similar size there are more than 15 million trained German workers, about treble the number in Britain, and half a million youths annually achieve vocational qualifications, five times the British figure. Thus, the average level of skill in the German labour force is higher than the average in Britain.[66]

Given this kind of comparison, to the detriment of Britain, it is small wonder that there was renewed interest in VET provision in Germany. Her Majesty's Inspectors produced a further report on education in Germany in 1991. This second report in the series, *Aspects of Vocational Education and Training in the Federal Republic of Germany,* was based on a visit to four *Länder* in the summer of 1990. The inspectors looked principally at vocational education and training for apprentices under the dual system in off-the-job training in vocational schools and on-the-job training in industry.

The German VET model (see figure 9 below) incorporates the principle of 'permeability' (*Durchlässigkeit*) which allows transfer within the pathways of the education system at multiple stages. From this outline model it can be seen, for example, that access to the university, or to forms of further education, or to the workforce can be achieved by a 'normal' secondary school leaver attaining sufficient qualifications via VET routes in the Dual System. There is an elegant balance in the system that policy makers elsewhere regard with great envy, and it is small wonder that attempts are made to replicate aspects of it in reform proposals for less well-developed provision.

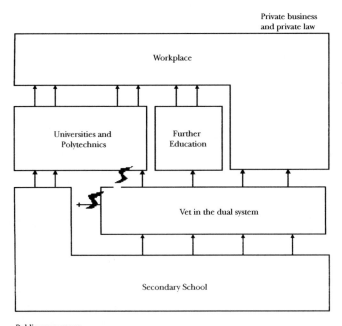

FIGURE 10   Vocational Training in Germany: The Dual System

At the beginning of their report the inspectors highlighted the strengths of the vocational education and training system of Germany as they perceived them:

The vocational qualification system in the FRG appears to be well understood by employers, parents and students. The frameworks for vocational curricula and regulations for training are set down at Federal level, interpreted and translated into courses by the individual *Länder* which, in turn, are implemented, in the light of individual needs, by the Chambers. There are no national examining and validating bodies. The current debate in the United Kingdom about the need for a clear and coherent system of vocational qualifications is not echoed in the FRG.[67]

The report speaks of 'the greater parity of esteem in the FRG than in the United Kingdom between academic and vocational courses and their respective qualifications' – an advantage which reminds us of Michael Sadler's judgement in his 1916 Guildford speech – and it associates the respect accorded to apprenticeship qualifications with that given to the master craftsman (*Meister*) qualification, the *Meister* being 'regarded as an exemplar of craftsmanship of the highest quality'. The advantages of the German system are perceived to consist in:

- the high commitment of employers to training;
- the willingness of employers to pay for training;
- the readiness of some employers to train more apprentices than they need;
- the high participation rates in training which are secured by the legal basis which training has in the FRG;
- a simple and readily understood system of vocational qualifications;
- the regulating role of the Chambers in accrediting training companies and examining and assessing trainees;
- the partnership between the vocational schools and industry and commerce;
- the partnership between employers and the trade unions.[68]

Publication of the report coincided with the discussions that followed the issuing of a government white paper on further education,[69] for which the German system had provided a model, and so the HMI investigation can be seen as an integrated part of the policy-making process,

Four further reports between 1992 and 1995 were also concerned with vocational education and training in Germany. They are: *Aspects of Education in Germany: Design, Technology and Engineering, 14–19* (1993)[70], *Aspects of Full-time Vocational Education in the Federal Republic of Germany* (1993), *The Development of Double Qualification Courses in Secondary Schools in North Rhine Westphalia* (1994), and *Post-16 Vocational Education and Training in Germany* (1995).[71] Together with the 1991 report this constitutes an extraordinary concentration of attention on German VET models.

The first 1993 report, based on a visit to Bavaria, identified strengths in school provision, among them high levels of achievement in mathematics and science as required subjects for all pupils; centrally approved curriculum guidelines; curricular breadth, including foreign language study, and breadth that is sustained post-16; and the fact that careers in engineering are held in high regard. In their overall conclusions the inspectors anticipated a weakness that was to become very apparent in Germany's results in the OECD's PISA surveys:

> In general the educational system in Bavaria for the 14–19 age group prepares young people in large numbers for careers in German engineering industry. Great attention is paid to accuracy and quality of manufacture, but there is not as much attention, as there is in England, to developing competence in devising solutions to problems which do not have predetermined answers. There is considerably less emphasis than there is in England on preparing young people for careers in design, and those who reach higher education in this field do so with much greater difficulty.[72]

The second 1993 report, on full-time vocational education, was mostly enthusiastic. It lists in summary form the strengths and relative weaknesses of what was observed in Hessen and Niedersachsen during the summer of 1992:

Range

Young people in Germany who leave school at 16 are offered a range of opportunities for vocational education and training.

Framework

All vocational courses are part of a clear and established framework of progression to higher education and employment.

General education

By comparison with many vocational courses in England and Wales, and National Vocational Qualifications (NVQs) in particular, vocational courses in Germany have a greater emphasis on general education, particularly mathematics and language, as a means of facilitating progression and personal and social development.

Second chance and progression

The *Berufsfachschulen* (full-time vocational schools) provide students with the opportunity to improve their secondary school qualification either with a view to progressing to higher education and/or to obtain vocational qualifications relevant to future employment.

Exemption

Students who successfully complete certain courses at a *Berufsfachschule* may be exempt from the first year of an apprenticeship under the Dual System or may obtain a recognised vocational qualification.

Resources

The *Berufsfachschulen* are well equipped and excellently maintained. By comparison with further education colleges in the United Kingdom, however, their libraries are small and limited in scope and there are fewer facilities for private and individual study.

Timetable

Students on vocational courses in Germany are taught for significantly more hours per week than their counterparts in the United Kingdom.

Assessment

By comparison with many vocational courses in the United Kingdom, the full-time vocational courses in Germany place less emphasis on course work. Assessment for certification is by examinations which are locally marked but not moderated to the same extent as comparable examinations in England and Wales.

Pastoral care

Systems of pastoral care for full-time students in Germany are less structured than in the United Kingdom and some teachers express diffidence about taking on a counselling role for which they are not trained.

Work experience

Students on full-time vocational courses in Germany have less work experience, as part of their course, than their counterparts in the United Kingdom.

Income

By comparison with further education colleges in the United Kingdom, the *Berufsfachschulen* do not normally generate income through sales and services to the general public.

Quality control

Examination results are the main performance indicators in *Berufsfachschulen* and there are few procedures for quality assurance and control by the institution.[73]

The strengths identified here are unsurprising: the range of opportunities available; clear pathways; continuing general education; possibilities to build on and improve existing school qualifications; impressive buildings and equipment; and longer time devoted to education and training. Some of the less positive conclusions are by comparison insignificant and are not necessarily weaknesses: the part played by course work has been a much contested topic in England; and German teachers, like teachers in France and elsewhere, are not expected to have a pastoral role but to concentrate on their teaching specialisms.

The report on 'double qualification courses' in North Rhine Westphalia was specifically undertaken in the context of qualification routes being developed for post-16 students in the UK. The report mentions in particular the wide range of subjects, including a modern foreign language, studied by pupils working towards both the *Abitur* and a vocational qualification, and it concludes its main findings, curiously, with a statement about mutual lessons to be learnt:

GNVQs are being introduced in England and Wales as part of the reformed system of national qualifications. Germany has yet to make a decision on a change of this scale in relation to its changing economic needs. Each country may wish to draw further lessons from these important initiatives.[74]

Quite what the authorities in North Rhein Westphalia might learn from the example of GNVQs was not explained. (GNVQs were to be phased out between 2005 and 2007.) The 1995 report on post-16 vocational education and training in Germany made a stark contrast between what had been achieved in Germany and the targets for the UK:

> In Germany, initial vocational qualifications obtained through the dual system are approximately equivalent to the NVQ at level 3 on offer in the United Kingdom. About 80 per cent of the German workforce hold vocational or professional qualifications. By the year 2010 it is expected to be 90 per cent. The national learning targets for the United Kingdom envisage that 60 per cent of the workforce will be qualified to NVQ level 3 or equivalent by the year 2000. In 1994 the figure was about 40 per cent. In the United Kingdom, we are aiming to have 60 per cent of young people by the age of 21 achieving NVQ level 3 or equivalent by the year 2000. In Germany, this has already been achieved.[75]

(In 2010 in England, '53.1 per cent of 21 year old men had a qualification at, or qualifications equivalent to Level 3 or above compared with 54.3 per cent of 21 year old women'.)[76]

There is not much evidence that the changes in vocational education and training in England have been shaped to any great extent by investigation of the German example, unless in the spirit of continuing general education as part of vocational training and the recent (2007) policy to keep young people in some form of education until age 18 ('raising the participation age').[77] But what the German model has consistently provided – especially in respect to the compact between the state and the employers which underpins it – is an aspiration, an ideal that is effectively unattainable outside of the conditions over time which have created it in Germany.

* * * * *

Over this long period it is clear that the waves of reform in England were considerably far reaching, at times effectively rewriting the educational agenda (as with the 1944 and 1988 Acts), while in Germany – despite the flurry of activity from the late 1950s to the mid-1970s – the traditional structure of the system was upheld and only seriously threatened in the aftermath of the results from PISA. Certainly there has been no very serious attempt to promote the comprehensive principle, even given the theoretical chance of developing the East German model after Unification.

The British interest in education in Germany started with a serious and sustained engagement with reconstruction and policy development in the British Zone of Occupation after the war, when the way was eased for German policy makers to pick up the threads from the pre-war system. Observing the remarkable economic recovery of Germany – the *Wirtschaftswunder* – it was natural for British and other observers to equate economic success with educational provision, and specifically with the highly developed dual system of vocational training. This has proved to be the aspect of provision in Germany that has attracted most attention. At the same time, as faith in the comprehensive school as the solution to the endemic problems of a differentiated secondary school system began to diminish, observers wondered what could be learnt from the determination of the Germans to adhere to a policy which seemed – and still seems – so out-of-step with other Western countries, most of which have moved towards a common system of secondary schooling. Lessons might be learnt from the curriculum and from assessment processes in German schools, and from the controls that the *Land* ministries exercise, but there was no taste for a wholesale dismantling of the common system of schooling – instead there was a flirtation with grant-maintained schools and their successors, with city technology colleges, and most recently with Labour's city academies (seen by critics as grammar schools under a different guise.)

As the century drew to a close there was evidence of renewed interest in the United States in education in Germany. The US Department of Education issued a dense 255-page report on the subject whose aim was to complement the Trends in International Mathematics and Science Study (TIMSS) data. Its rationale was to investigate four policy areas 'of key interest to US policy makers': 'national standards in education, teachers' preparation and working lives, the role of school in adolescents' lives, and how students' differences in ability are managed by the school system'.[78] The focus here is more on content than on form; on the curriculum and teaching rather than on administration.

* * * * *

If you set up a school and it becomes a good school, the great danger is that everyone wants to go there.

John Prescott, 2005[79]

Prime Minister Tony Blair would talk of the 'post-comprehensive era'[80], but the models were the US charter schools and aspects of educational provision in Sweden and The Netherlands rather than Germany. The 2010 Conservative Party manifesto mentioned the United States and Sweden specifically:

Since the free schools programme was established in Sweden, over 1,000 new schools have opened. They have been founded by foundations, charities and others – and they have attracted pupils by offering better discipline and higher standards. Because any parent can take the money the Swedish government spends on their child's education and choose the school they want, standards have risen across the board as every school does its best to satisfy parents.

Drawing on the experience of the Swedish school reforms and the charter school movement in the United States, we will break down barriers to entry so that any good education provider can set up a new academy school. Our schools revolution will create a new generation of good small schools with smaller class sizes and high standards of discipline.

Our school reform programme is a major part of our anti-poverty strategy, which is why our first task will be to establish new Academy schools in the most deprived areas of the country. They will be beacons of excellence in areas where school standards are unacceptably low.

We want every child to benefit from our reforms. So all existing schools will have the chance to achieve academy status, with 'outstanding' schools pre-approved, and we will extend the Academy programme to primary schools.[81]

Choice and diversity are the watchwords espoused by both Conservative and Labour governments, and their popularity has had to do with a rejection of any policies supporting what is perceived as an old-style socialist uniformity. The role of local education authorities has diminished progressively from the time of the premiership of Margaret Thatcher to the extent that 'local authority' control now seems anomalous.

In May 2010 the Conservative/Liberal Democratic Coalition Government in England announced that all schools would be invited to apply for 'academy' status. The Secretary of State for Education wrote to all head teachers promising greater freedom and independence and to make the process of becoming an academy quicker and less bureaucratic. Schools judged by Ofsted to be outstanding would be fast-tracked through the application process. The first new academies would start in September 2010 and apart from receiving some 10 to 12 per cent additional funding they would benefit from:

- freedom from local authority control
- the ability to set their own pay and conditions for staff
- freedom from following the National Curriculum
- greater control of their budget
- greater opportunities for formal collaboration with other public and private organisations
- freedom to change the length of terms and school days
- freedom to spend the money the local authority currently spends on their behalf

This 'would shift power from central and local government back to heads and schools'. The Secretary of State, Michael Gove, said:

> The Government is genuinely committed to giving schools greater freedoms. We trust teachers and headteachers to run their schools. We think headteachers know how to run their schools better than bureaucrats or politicians.[82]

The initiative was in line with the so-called 'free school' movement espoused by the Conservatives, the models, as we have noted, being the charter schools of Sweden and the United States. In the context of any comparison with the way the education systems of the sixteen *Länder* of Germany are managed, this is a very strange situation, but it is one that has been under discussion in one form or another since the 1988 Education Reform Act. Conservative Prime Minister John Major had sought to enable all schools to opt out of any local authority control. But the result of the kind of independence proposed by Michael Gove would be that the country would return to a system in which the 'chapter of accidents' of which Matthew Arnold had spoken in 1868 would be evident in what might be available in any given locality. Far from following the patterns evident in the German example, in which in the simplest terms it is possible to say that 'a school is a school is a school', so clear are the expectations of provision within the *Länder*, the diversity would be baffling to parents.

A one-time leader of the Labour Party, Neil Kinnock, had disagreed strongly with Tony Blair on the question of diversity of provision: he is quoted as believing that 'the multiplicity of types of schools was a false objective that was bound to come to grief',[83] but such 'multiplicity' had remained on the agenda beyond

Blair's premiership and into the Brown government. The 2010 Labour Party election manifesto promised a 'choice of good schools in every area – and, where parents are not satisfied – the power to bring in new school leadership teams, through mergers and take-overs, with up to 1,000 secondary schools part of an accredited schools group by 2015'.[84] So much for Baker's criticism of 'too much local variety in what is still regarded as a national system'.

There is no reference to Germany.

The new century saw the German example come under considerable scrutiny and much criticism from within and without. German schoolchildren had usually performed well in the studies of educational attainment undertaken by the International Association for the Evaluation of Educational Achievement (IEA). When the OECD started its PISA surveys, however, the results turned out to be quite different – to the extent that the German language acquired a new coinage: *PISA-Schock*.

> The strongest shock waves of PISA 2000 resulted from the fact that in the overall ranking Germany had only achieved a position below the OECD average. To attain only rank 21 in the reading skills assessment and rank 20 in mathematics and science, out of 31 participating countries, was totally at odds with the German and international expectations of a nation with a high standard of living and a school system which had enjoyed a high international reputation since the nineteenth century. Alarmingly, the proportion of young Germans who did not even attain level 1 in literacy (considered the minimum competence for participating in the labour market and in responsible citizenship) was almost 10%.[85]

These were very unexpected results, seen to be even worse when the details were looked at more closely. There were considerable regional variations, and although *Gymnasium* pupils scored above the OECD average in reading, those in the *Hauptschule* scored way below the average (394; OECD average 500). The *Hauptschule* did indeed appear to be a *Restschule*. Those seeking to understand the reasons for the disappointing performance of German schools saw a need for a common system of schooling – in the form of the comprehensive school, the *Gesamtschule* in some form – as is the case in other European states.

Since the *Pisa-Schock* Germany has subjected its provision in education to close scrutiny. There has been much evaluation of practice, including the setting-up of agencies to monitor quality and standards. But the system remains structured in a way out of line with most European preferences; its vocational education provision, especially in the eastern *Länder*, has suffered from under-resourcing; and the universities are overcrowded and struggling to modernise and to conform to the expectations of the Bologna Accord. There has been a considerable slackening of foreign attraction to the German model, with the exception of vocational education and training, which still serves as an ideal aspiration for policy makers in other countries.

Chapter 8

Evaluating the German Example

These things are made in Germany,translated in America and misunderstood in Great Britain

Henry Holman[1]

In their 1974 study *A Mythology of British Education*, Bell and Grant write of the disappearance of the image of the Prussian schoolmaster as drill-sergeant and of the then general view that the German education system could be characterised in terms of 'cool efficiency and modernisation'. Not true, they argue: the structure of the West German system was 'one of the most old-fashioned and backward-looking in Europe', with high drop-out rates from secondary education and a resistance to the reforms proposed in the 1950s and 1960s.[2] Is there then a mythology of German education, a general notion of exceptionally advanced provision in Germany which has persisted over the past two hundred years or so but with a tenuous relation to reality? Has the main attraction on the part of British observers consisted in the fascination with the *contrast* between the two systems, with its more 'exotic' features, at the expense of an understanding of substance? Have there indeed been any lessons to learn from the German example? Has the perception been stronger than the reality? (Armytage argues that 'invocation of another country is based not so much on what exists, but what people want to think exists in that country'.[3]) The evidence shows, however, that since 1800 there has been much that has been admired in the nature of educational provision at all levels in Germany.

The twentieth century had seen interest in the German example in education veer from a mixture of fascination and horror, through admiration (in particular for what Germany had achieved in vocational education and training and its association with a remarkably strong economy), temptation to emulate German approaches to the prescribed curriculum, and attraction to German styles of assessment, to scepticism and a cooling-off of interest in the light of surprise results in the PISA surveys. In general too, following the introduction of comprehensive schooling in England from the mid-1960s, there was a degree of nostalgic hankering after the traditional structure of secondary education still so much in evidence in Germany. The nineteenth-century tradition of commissioning reports on educational provision in other countries, in connection with official inquiries into educational issues, continued to be a feature of the processes of decision making, from Sadler's reports at the turn of the century to the important series of HMI reports in the 1980s and 1990s, from the Bryce Report of 1895 to the Dearing Report of 1997.

Like many other education systems, among them those of France and Japan, and despite developments that have relaxed the control mechanisms of central authorities, that of Germany is predicated on a level of uniformity in provision that has not been the case in England. The term 'uniformity' is often used in the context of education in a pejorative sense: it is frequently preceded by the adjective 'dull' and is taken to involve restriction and lack of imagination. This need not of course be the case. A 1993 study of French and English primary schools showed, for example, that within the central measures in place in France, French teachers appeared to have rather more freedom than their English counterparts.[4] The strengths inherent in uniformity have to do with its resulting from the establishing of clear rights and expectations: the state – in a central or regional or local manifestation – decides what it is that the system consists in, and this is made transparent, through legislation and official regulations and guidelines, for teachers, parents, and pupils. In this regard there have been many points at which English policy makers have sought to learn lessons from German experience: in the nineteenth century in terms of compulsory school attendance and forms of systemic structure; in the twentieth century in terms particularly of the agreed curriculum. But in England there has not been a will to interpret legislation in ways that create the kind of uniformity which is evident in the structure of education in the German *Länder*, to decide in effect that 'a school is a school is a school'.

In the early 1800s there was little attention paid to education in Germany, partly through indifference to the question of responsibility for provision, partly because of relative lack of contact with the Continent. But once it had been agreed, in 1833, that the government would provide funds to support the voluntary societies, the search for models could begin in earnest, and the German example proved to be the most obvious among them. This was not surprising, since the eighteenth-century advances in Germany were quite exceptional in comparison to the situation in other parts of Europe. There were of course difficulties in praising or seeking to emulate state efforts in education when the state in question was perceived to be illiberal, but the voices of those who could point to the results (in terms of literacy in particular and the sheer numbers of children being educated) were loud and clear. If Germany could provide for the education of its children, why could not Britain?

With the investigations of Victor Cousin and others, information became available which was more authoritative than the exhortations of individuals with less well-informed direct or indirect experience of German schools. And it is clear that such reports – Cousin's in particular – were very influential and served, even if they were inaccurate in some regards, to bolster the arguments of policy makers seeking a greater role for the state in the education of its people. Precisely in what way this might be achieved preoccupied the thoughts of those concerned with policy for several decades. There were many obstacles, not least among them the concerns of the churches about religious education, concerns that have always bedevilled educational reform in the United Kingdom and that continue to do so.

The efforts of Matthew Arnold to highlight educational provision in Germany and elsewhere in the 1860s were of great significance. Not only did he inform the work of the commissions to whose investigations he contributed, but he also published his findings in book form so that they were able to reach a wider audience. He was no naïve believer in 'policy borrowing'; rather, he saw the foreign example as informing discussion in England, as helping to remedy what he saw as a result of his experience as a school inspector – a situation in education in England that was to a large extent unsatisfactory. And it was not only elementary education that could profit from his analyses. Moves to establish secondary education on a firm footing, and to develop a modern concept of the university, also owe much to his advocacy.

Michael Sadler was 27 when Arnold died, and he can be seen in many regards as his heir. His huge contribution to the debate about educational provision in England covered the whole range of possible topics, from eurhythmics to examinations, and he demonstrated a profound knowledge of Germany and the Germans. His many writings on education in Germany over a long period of engagement with the subject provided a continuation of Arnold's endeavours well into the twentieth century. In particular he continued the efforts to create a climate for the proper development of secondary education in the early years of the century, and through his pioneering work in the Office of Special Inquiries and Reports he established an expectation (begun with the work of the nineteenth-century commissions) that the foreign example should be investigated as part of any reform discussion. As we have seen, the twentieth-century official commissions routinely included allusion to education abroad, with Germany figuring prominently. And so, by the time of the 1986 report from Her Majesty's Inspectors on curriculum and assessment in German schools and the remarkable series of reports on education in other countries which followed it, it was to seem natural that, as Almut Sprigade puts it, 'where there is reform, there is comparison'.

Sadler too wrote cautiously about learning from the foreign example. His address to a meeting in Guildford in 1900 ('How Far Can We Learn Anything of Practical Value From the Study of Foreign Systems of Education?') is frequently quoted in the literature of comparative education. In it he argues that proper study of education in other countries will result in better fitness to understand the 'home' system.[5]

In relation to the spectrum of educational transfer (Figure 1), discussed in Chapter 1, ideas from Germany clearly belong in the category 'introduced through influence'. Any suggestion of 'direct importation' of policy and practice is a chimera, but during the nineteenth-century discussions about what a national system of education in England might look like it is clear that the German example – in terms particularly of compulsory school attendance and how to ensure that it happens, on the place of religious education, and on the role of the state – played a significant part in the background of decision making. There was no doubt that Germany had a supremely efficient education system which was attracting widespread attention. If Germany could make such progress why indeed could England not do likewise? In general, the German example was used to encourage rather than resist reform, to 'scandalise' the shortcomings in England, to recall Steiner-Khamsi's term.

In the post-war twentieth century the main impetus for attraction to education in Germany was of course the country's extraordinary economic success, the 'economic miracle' which surely, it was argued, had something to do with educational provision. And the obvious feature that might account for such economic prosperity was the unique 'dual system' of vocational education. The dual system has attracted world-wide attention, but it remains an unobtainable ideal, a distant aspiration, for most countries contemplating development in VET provision, and any imitative arrangements are mostly mere shadows of what Germany has managed.

Table 13 Categorisation of Legislation, etc., in Terms of Use of the German Example

Legislation, reports, etc.	Factors in cross-national attraction
Select Committee Report, 1834	Strategies, enabling structures, processes
Newcastle Report, 1858	Enabling structures
Cross Report, 1888	Strategies, enabling structures, processes
1902 Education Act (Balfour Act)	Strategies, enabling structures, processes
1918 Education Act (Fisher Act)	Strategies, enabling structures, processes
Robbins Report, 1963	Strategies, enabling structures
HMI Report, 1986	Enabling structures, processes

(Source: Adapted from Ochs & Phillips, Comparative Studies and 'Cross-National Attraction', p. 336).

In a study of 2002 an attempt was made to use the model described in Figure 2 (Chapter 1 above) to analyse the potential usefulness of the German example at key moments in educational policy making in England. Among the moments selected were: 1834 (Select Committee Report); 1858 (Newcastle Report); 1888 (Cross Report); 1902 (Balfour Act); 1918 (Fisher Act); 1963 (Robbins Report); 1986 (HMI Report on Education in the Federal Republic of Germany). In each case an attempt was made to identify the main aims of the investigation or legislation in question and to examine outcomes in the light of aspects of educational provision in Germany that had been discussed or that were commonly known at the time. The results were summarised as shown in Table 13.

The analysis tended to show an inclination to focus on 'enabling structures' and 'processes' in terms of the model – which would indicate a general use of the foreign example precisely to 'learn lessons' and to contribute to the solution of problems by providing practical examples of what might be possible. There is, not surprisingly, no evidence of direct 'borrowing' – the purposeful transfer of educational policy – though there have been times when it was fervently wished that the German example could in some measure be 'imported', despite the strictures of significant commentators like Matthew Arnold or Mark Pattison or Michael Sadler. Rather some German ideas at significant moments have been taken into account as reform was contemplated in England, and there has also of course been influence of a more general kind through the work of educational thinkers in Germany from the early nineteenth century onwards.

* * * * *

The German example in education is of particular interest to comparativists precisely because it has been over the past two hundred years and more a model to be taken into account when evidence has been needed of what might be possible in terms of educational change. At various times it has served both to encourage and to dissuade. But it is clear that whatever the climate in the reform debate in England, learning something from the German experience has been a perennial factor. There has been a slackening off of attention to Germany in recent years, especially since the OECD's PISA results have been used to rank education systems, but there is every reason to suppose that the German system, still so idiosyncratically different from that of many other European nations, will continue both to attract and repel as policy makers struggle to make decisions for the twenty-first century.

Appendices

(1) Educational Provision in Germany, 1886

Source: R. Laishley: *Report Upon State Education in Great Britain, France, Switzerland, Italy, Germany, Belgium, and the United States of America; including a Special Report Upon Deaf-Mute Instruction*, Auckland, New Zealand (New Zealand General Assembly), 1886. (Reprinted in Fraser & Brickman, *A History of International and Comparative Education*, pp. 386–7 & pp. 392–3.)

GERMANY

Religious instruction – (a) Consideration shown (b) Basis of education	(a) Not only is religious liberty carefully protected, but great consideration is shown towards (virtually) all. (b) Religion universally the basis of education, occupying the first place on elementary programmes. Religious instruction also included in normal school course.
Gratuitous primary education	Primary education not, as a rule, gratuitous. For instance, gratuitous in Berlin, although not, as a rule, in Saxony or Bavaria, or indeed even throughout Prussia. Where primary schools not free, free schools usually provided for poor children. But available for all unable to pay. Instruction in infant schools is not, as a rule, free. In supplementary schools the law varies according to the State. Books are not generally free, except in cases of poverty.
Compulsory attendance	Period 6–14 at primary school. In some places further attendance is obligatory. For instance, in Saxony those children who at the expiration of the 8 years have not satisfactorily progressed must attend one year longer. And, in some places, boys after the 8-course, if they are not being elsewhere educated, must attend a continuation school for three years longer. Attendance good – "a habit of the country."
Protection of children against injurious employment	Children are protected. Terms vary in different States. In Prussia, for instance, industrial work for wages prohibited under the age of 9; in Baden 11, and so forth.
School age	No limit, but there are certain ages, as elsewhere, when it is considered that pupils should attend certain grades of schools, and learn certain subjects. Gradation of tuition considered excellent.

Local government, by locally elected authorities	State supremely controls; but there are large powers of local government, including powers to

(a) Regulate religious instruction (subject to protection of minorities);
(b) Levy direct taxes;
(c) Control expenditure, and
(d) Manage administrative details.

Under Minister in each State is State Board. There are also Boards for provinces and districts and school committees in each parish.
Exceptional division of nation into sovereignties a cause of excellence.

Sources of support	Primary and (generally) secondary schools, mainly supported by local taxation, levied by communes and municipalities, and by fees, with aid from States in case of need. But universities and polytechnics are maintained by the States, and by fees.

Teachers	(a) No pupil teachers.

(b) Must possess diploma.
(c) Normal schools – Admission only after passing examination; not gratuitous; except for those not able to pay; course 3 to 6 years – some for training masters and some for training mistresses; although latter not so numerous.
(d) Salaries small, but fixed.
(e) Pensions granted. Proportions of pension to salary varies in different States. Usually, however, the amount depends upon duration of service.

Female teaching not favoured, especially for higher classes. Co-operation of teachers in inspection. Thorough training of teachers. Better trained than in England.

Infant schools	Attendance not compulsory, but children usually frequent them from 2 to 6.

They are to be found in most places; but they are not universally public institutions; nor are they favoured in Germany, medical opinion being against school training before 6. [1] All, however, are subject to State inspection. Kindergarten exercises are not formally recognized as a necessary step in State education.

Classes of state schools	Generally-

(a) Infant (not everywhere public schools);
(b) Primary;
(c) Supplementary (attendance in some places compulsory, when education not pursued at secondary school);
(d) Preparatory secondary (this frequently 6–9 1st stage);
(e) Modern;
(f) Upper modern;
(g) Classical;
(h) Polytechnic;
(i) Universities.

Subjects of study in primary schools	Taking Saxony as an instance – Religion and morals. The German language, including reading and writing. Arithmetic. Geometry. History – geography and geology – natural history – physics. Singing. Drawing. Needlework (for girls). No standards. Horticulture in Baden compulsory. Class numbers regulated by law. Home lessons usual. Over-pressure, as evidenced by defective eyesight, &c.
Physical training	Marked recognition of importance of drill and gymnastic exercises. Liberal expenditure upon it. Recognized that without such physical training the severe examinations could not be undertaken. Widely admitted that even more than at present is desirable.
Inspection and examination	In addition to ordinary inspection, each primary school every third or fourth year is carefully inspected by an expert member of a Board of Education. The Inspectors confer and co-operate with the teachers.
Continuation schools and half-time scholars	Continuation schools important feature in Germany. Attendance compulsory in some places, where pupils on leaving primary do not join secondary school. Some preparation for industrial pursuits. Instruction is not universally gratuitous, although when fees are charged they are small. Half-time system exists, but to no great extent.
Secondary and higher schools	Instruction not, as a rule, gratuitous, except when scholars have distinguished themselves and are not able to pay; then free tuition generally available. In certain schools certain number of free places, and sometimes dinners or suppers and dinners, available for poor scholars. Generally day schools. No state secondary schools, as a rule, for girls. But there are some excellent ones.
Technical instruction	In addition to supplementary schools, science and art everywhere fostered, especially science. Thus: (a) Apprenticeship schools, (b) Trade schools and women's work schools, (c) Real schools, (d) Higher technical schools, and (e) Polytechnics. There are also art schools. Workshops in primary schools not yet introduced: but drawing well taught. Special teaching of horticulture in Baden; and there are some domestic-economy schools for girls. Most adult schools in Germany, France, and Belgium are Sunday schools; and the technical schools on the Continent are said to be mainly founded by manufacturers.
Scholarships	No State scholarships; but there are some scholarships in universities available from Royal or private legacies. They are, however, only awarded to scholars. (a) Who have distinguished themselves, and (b) Are too poor to otherwise continue studies. They are generally small.

State supervision respecting private schools	Private schools are under Government inspection and supervision. Teachers must be thoroughly qualified and possess diploma.
	Comparatively few private schools, and little private tuition.

(2) German Influence on Education in England

Source: Michael Sadler: 'Germany in the Nineteenth Century', in: *Germany in the Nineteenth Century. Five Lectures*, Manchester University Press, 1912, pp. 122–5).

From the time of the Reformation English educational ideas and policy have at intervals been strongly influenced by German thought and by the results of action taken by various German governments for the improvement and regulation of schools and universities. To Luther and Melanchthon, to the Pietists and the Moravians, to Fichte and Wilhelm von Humboldt we can trace in succession a considerable number of the movements which, during the last three centuries and a half, have produced great changes in English education. In the earlier part of the nineteenth century a great wave of German influence came into English educational thought through S .T. Coleridge, who, in 1830, in his essay *On the Constitution of Church and State according to the Idea of Each*, echoed the teaching of Fichte and maintained that the aim of statesmen should be 'to form and train up the people of the country to obedient, free, useful and organisable subjects, citizens and patriots, living to the benefit of the State and prepared to die in its defence'. Thomas Carlyle did even more than Coleridge to familiarise the English public with German ideas of State-organised education, especially in *Past and Present* (1843) and in *Latter-Day Pamphlets* (1850). At an earlier time, throughout the great speeches on education made in Parliament by Brougham, Roebuck and others during the years 1833–5, German precedent for compulsory education was quoted as a proof of the practicability of making elementary instruction obligatory by law. But it was through the Prince Consort that enlightened German ideas as to the action of the State in public education were most widely extended in political and official circles in England. During the twenty-one years of his residence in England, Prince Albert succeeded, with the help of Lyon Playfair and others, in developing the State Department of Art and Science and in promoting wise extensions of State activity in elementary and technical education.

The success of the Prussian army in the war with Austria in 1866 drew attention to the military value of the intelligence and discipline which had been diffused throughout the German people by the elaborate organisation of State-aided schools. The impression thus produced upon the public mind was one factor which led to the carrying of the Elementary Education Act in 1870 and to the subsequent adoption in 1876 of the principle of compulsory education.

Of all recent writers, Matthew Arnold was the most successful in drawing the attention of responsible English administrators to the importance of German methods of educational organisation. He showed that a study of German achievements in the sphere of educational policy was indispensable to British statesmen. His reports are classical. And they were the forerunners of a long series by other hands. It would be just to say that he slurred over the great political difficulties which would at once confront any statesman who attempted to set up in England the administrative machinery of German education. He said with very little qualification what may be said in praise of the German system, and with as little qualification what may be said in dispraise of the English. But he impressed on his fellow-countrymen a higher ideal of what the State may aim at in the diffusion of culture, and, directly or indirectly, the more recent trend of English policy in higher and secondary education is due in considerable measure to the influence of what he wrote.

Of all foreign influences upon English educational thought during the last forty years the German has been with the exception of the American, the most formative and penetrating. It has touched every grade of our education from the Kindergarten to the University. To Froebel and his followers has been mainly due the more spontaneous training of little children. The official definition of the purpose of the public elementary school, now printed in the code of the English Board of Education, bears the impress of the ideas of Fichte and of Herbart. School hygiene and the medical inspection of school children owe much to German precedent and research. Many of the improvements in the methods of teaching modern languages may be traced to the work of Professor Viëtor of Marburg and his associates. The new conception of the continuation school, at once technical and humane, organised in direct relation to industry but with a broad civic purpose, has been mainly derived from German sources and especially from the work of Dr. Kerschensteiner of Munich. Nor will any historian of English education during the nineteenth century fail to record the far-reaching influence of many of our citizens (men and women) of German birth and stock, who furthered the progress of new educational ideas and institutions in their own districts or in the nation at large. Every educational student in England owes a debt to what he has learnt from German writings and from German example. Berlin, Jena, Marburg, Frankfort-on-Main and Munich have each, in a remarkable degree, influenced the recent educational thought of this country.

In three respects German influence has been especially strong in English education during the last seventy years. It has supported the idea that the State should bear an effective part in the regulation of all grades of national education. It has stimulated in the highest degree the scientific study of the philosophy of education and of methods of teaching. And it has helped in securing a more general acceptance of the view that the State can increase the economic welfare of the nation by the systematic encouragement of liberal and technical education and of systematic scientific research.

(3) Imitating German Education, 1916

Source: Michael Sadler: 'Need We Imitate German Education?' *(The Times,* 14 January 1916).

A correspondent wrote to a newspaper the other day:- "If German education is as perfect as some would have us believe, how can we explain the savagery and lawlessness which we have found permeating all ranks of the German armies? If German education produces the people we are fighting, how can any enlightened Englishman write of its excellence?" This puts concisely an argument which will have to be reckoned with in any attempt at social reconstruction in England after the war.

I

The answer is that no one whose words have weight has ever said that German education is perfect. It has great faults as well as great excellence. It makes good use of all second-grade ability, which in England is far too much of a waste product. But something in the atmosphere of it makes the Germans too ready to obey. How to get more all-round intellectual keenness into English life, without draining off the reserves of energy which are needed to keep up moral pluck and independence of character, is the main question which the reformer of English education, whoever he may be, will have to tackle. Nor is it true that savagery and lawlessness permeate all ranks of the German armies. There is, I admit, a very significant and deep-seated difference between what we and the Germans think honourable in war. The Germans, as we say, are not "sportsmen." But the evidence at present available seems to show that a very large proportion of the unspeakable brutalities which have disgraced the German name in this war have been done to order. They seem to have been due as a rule to a habit of excessive obedience.

The war has proved the enormous power of education over the minds and souls of men. Applied with persistence and pedantic pertinacity, it is the most formidable engine in the modern world for controlling conduct and swaying purpose. England has shrunk from using this power in a masterful way. We have fumbled with it and been frightened of it. Our reasons for not putting the power of education to its full and most effective use have been partly sound and partly stupid; stupid, in so far as we have failed to realize how powerful a dynamo education may become; sound, in so far as, for fear of its being misapplied by the State, we have deliberately foregone the advantages of using an instrument which can be set to cut deep into moral freedom and into private judgment on fundamental questions of right and wrong. But whatever we may feel about its capital defect – its idol-worship of the State and its subordination of conscience to system and success – German education has high merits. These have been made clearer than ever by the experience of the war. German education has made the nation alert to science. It has made systematic cooperation a habit. It has taught patriotic duty. It has kept a whole people industrious. Combined with military training, it has given them the strength of discipline. It has made profitable use of second-rate intelligence. It has not neglected the mind.

Great Britain is finding that better education has become one of the most urgent of her necessities. Our social welfare, the effectiveness of our industries, the elasticity of our commerce, and, above all, the future quality of our national life, will depend upon education in a very great degree. No one can predict at present the economic state in which we shall find ourselves after the war. It would, therefore, be premature at this stage to attempt any precise statement of the changes in our educational system which may have to be made. No one knows how much we shall be able to afford. And cost will be a determining factor. We shall have to cut our coat according to our cloth. But it is not too soon to try to see the whole question in perspective, or to analyse the factors which English education must strengthen or preserve.

II

In modern education, which for the last twenty years has been everywhere in a state of tension and painful hesitating readjustment to the new conditions of thought and life, there are many great representative forces – Germany, the United States, and the British Empire. Each is typical of a different point of view; each contributes a different experience; and each can testify to the amazing power of educational influences when effectively applied. Germany stands for unity based on the State. The United States stand for variety based on the individual. The British Empire stands for an attempt at moral unity, based, partly, on individual experience, partly on the inherited tradition of various social groups, partly on administrative organization. Germany and America have worked on simpler theories and have had the advantage of greater simplicity of aim. The British is the more complex view, the least easy to define, and the most liable to ineffective compromise. But the facts themselves are complex. The British tradition at its best seems, to me at least, to have got nearer to the truth than either the German or the American. But British education, when it falls below the best, as is too often the case, is far less effective in accomplishing its aim than are the German and the American in accomplishing theirs.

British education, and especially English education at its best, is stronger than any other in the development of personal character. The same care which the Germans have lavished on ways of securing intellectual attainment, and which the Americans have spent on methods of fusing together the diverse elements in their heterogeneous population, has been given in Britain, and particularly in the best English schools, to questions of personal conduct and character. British education has also been at least as effective as the German or the American in fostering the will to make that supreme sacrifice of life or limb which is claimed from a man in the hour of national peril. But it has been less successful than the German in producing a reasoned conviction that daily sacrifice must be made by the individual for the welfare of the local community to which he belongs. And on the intellectual side British education, with brilliant exceptions, is, as compared with the German (though not with the American), feeble – but markedly less so in Scotland than in other parts of the British Empire.

III

The gravest defects of English education are (1) The absence of an exacting standard in the training of the mind (as contrasted with training in conduct), with a resulting disparagement of the importance of general knowledge and a failure to realize the value of pure science as the fruitful source of new applications of scientific knowledge to the needs of life and industry; (2) uninstructedness of parental opinion in matters of education, showing itself in indifference to the quality of teaching and in capricious and casual choice of schools; (3) failure to stimulate the intellectual interests of boys and girls of average capacity, with resulting wastefulness in the husbanding of the mental powers of the nation; (4) inertness of mind towards science, alike in industry, in public administration, and in domestic management; and (5) neglect in many homes and schools of proper pride in perfect cleanliness of the person, in grace of bearing and of manner, and in neatness of attire – a neglect which is accompanied by the serious evils of ignorance of the proper care of infant life, of uneconomical allocation of expenditure in the household budget, and of neglect of the remedial physical defects of children.

It is incumbent upon us to cure these defects for three reasons. First, the remediable defects in our English education are an obstacle to the growth of a fine social quality in our national life. They lessen the buoyancy, the adaptability, and therefore the happiness of the English people. Secondly, they gravely impair the future prospects in our industrial enterprise, increase the cost of our administration. Thirdly, the weaknesses in our education will hamper us in fulfilling the great mission which has been entrusted to the British Empire, and to Great Britain more than to any other part of the Empire, in upholding the principle of disciplined freedom and in maintaining the conviction that conscience and international morality, and not the authority of the State, are sovereign in human affairs.

But we shall be called upon to find a remedy for these educational defects at a time of poverty, when, moreover, the hard question of the right education of girls and women will have become more than ever urgent, and when there will be many other envious claims upon the thought of the nation – claims which will require us to deal with a variety of connected social problems at one and the same time and on a consistent plan. It is some consolation to know that there is evidence that, given the right discipline and training, the British are among nations one of the most responsive to the influence of education. But great educational changes cannot be lightly improvised or easily carried through. And their full benefits (as Bacon said of planting woods and colonies) are not realized until after an interval of nearly 30 years. Nor can great educational improvements be enacted by administration or by Parliamentary order alone. Education derives its power not from Acts of Parliament or administrative machinery, but from a spiritual movement of the national life. It needs organization and far-seeing direction, but it can easily be cramped by excess of administrative control. Confusion in educational standards is a bad thing, but over-organization a worse.

Our fundamental need in English education is for leadership by a great statesman, strong through support from a great weight of public opinion and resolved to kindle in England a purposeful zeal for educational reform. Granted this, the national will would effectively focus itself on this question and produce such a change in our customary standpoint as to get far more than hitherto out of the devoted labours of our teachers and educational administrators. A world-famous thinker once said, "*Whatever we wish to see introduced into the life of a nation must first be introduced through its schools and universities.*" This is true, but the nation must be determined to get it thus introduced and must itself cooperate in diffusing its influence through all the channels of home life and industrial activity. And in order to further the British idea of civilization, British schools must essay a double task, endeavouring to impart both the love of knowledge and the care for conduct; love of adventure and readiness to endure routine; capacity for individual initiative and patience in the work of scientific cooperation.

(4) Post-Primary Education in Prussia

Source: Hadow Report, 1927, Appendix IVB, pp. 305–308, accessed from Derek Gillard's valuable digitalised version of the Report. See 'The History of Education in England', http://www.educationengland.org.uk/documents/hadow1926/2616.html).

The *Mittelschule* in Prussia occupies much the same position in the educational system as the *École Primaire Supérieure* in France, but its history, despite certain resemblances, shows many contrasts. Elementary schools were fostered by the Prussian government almost continuously from the Reformation. Frederick the Great tried to establish compulsory attendance in the rural districts, but the curriculum was very limited. After the disaster of Jena in 1806 Stein realised that a free state made larger demands upon the intelligence and character of its citizens. The reorganisation of the elementary schools was a national necessity, and to accomplish this a reformed corps of teachers was required. A number of young teachers were sent to study Pestolozzi's work in Switzerland and training colleges which were to propagate his ideas were established in various parts of Prussia. At the same time the higher or secondary schools were reorganised by von Humboldt. At that date there were a number of schools – especially in the smaller towns, offering a course of instruction superior to that of the elementary schools, but not reaching the level of the higher schools. No attempt was made to give these schools a definite organisation, they were deliberately left out of the scheme in order to secure the establishment of a sufficient number of higher schools.

It is true that the establishment at Berlin of a training college for urban teachers (*Stadtschullehrer*) seemed to indicate a desire to provide these intermediate schools with teachers of wider qualifications, but the attempt did not last long. The generous impulses of the revolutionary era were gradually weakened; the Berlin college trained teachers only for the ordinary elementary schools and the ministerial rescripts of 1854 reduced this training to a mere mechanical preparation for imparting a limited amount of information.

With the establishment of the Empire the period of restraint ended. In 1872 Falk, the Prussian Minister for Education, produced a new code for the conduct of elementary schools in Prussia which reduced the amount of mechanical repetition and allowed the teacher to develop his instruction on more liberal lines. He also published a separate course of study for *Mittelschulen*, recognising the need for a type of school which went beyond the limits possible in a school bound to accept all those children liable to compulsory attendance, and at the same time offered a curriculum better adapted to the needs of commerce, trade and industry than the higher school (i.e. secondary) school.

The *Mittelschule* was only one type of the many intermediate schools which lay between the *Volksschule* and the higher schools. It was differentiated from the ordinary elementary school by its curriculum, and the length of its course. The normal type had nine classes – each of a year's duration – and so retained its pupils till the age of 15, while the statutory obligation to attend the elementary school ceased at the age of 14. It also included at least one foreign language in its course and a larger measure of elementary science and mathematics.

No special encouragement was given by the state to the development of these schools. After 1878 a period of social legislation was begun in Germany. The elementary schools benefited. State funds were provided to assist the poorer communities and the salaries and pensions of the elementary school teachers were regulated by law. None of these benefits reached the *Mittelschulen*, which were wholly supported by the communes.

In 1910 the State intervened to establish new curricula and to define more closely the function of these schools. There are really three distinct groups of schools. First the *Mittelschule* proper, then the other boys' schools, which are really preparatory for the higher (i.e. secondary) schools, and lastly a large number of girls' schools which give a course of a secondary school type, but not sufficiently advanced to be regarded as a full secondary school.

The regulations of 1910 were more precise than the instructions of 1872. They provided for alternative courses of studies, whereas in 1872 only one course was suggested of a general character amplifying the curriculum of the elementary schools by the introduction of a modern foreign language and a certain measure of science.

There is no convenient detailed description of the various forms which these intermediate schools assumed, but they were very diverse in organisation and content. Some had a ten years' course; a very few had only a single year; some taught one modern language, some two; some taught only Latin. Most of the larger towns preferred to establish *Realschulen* which were recognised as secondary schools and offered a six years' course from the age of 9. In Berlin a special type of *Realschulen* was created in which the beginning of the modern language instruction was deferred till the third school year, with a view to facilitating the transfer of boys from the elementary schools at about the age of 12. Berlin being mainly a commercial city was able to dispense with the *Mittelschule*, and there was the further inducement that the Leaving Certificate of the *Realschulen* carried with it the right to serve for one year as a volunteer instead of the three years required of the ordinary recruit. This was a social privilege highly esteemed in Germany, and explains the lack of interest in the *Mittelschule*.

Under the Regulations of 1910 there were five different types of curriculum prescribed. The first type was a general curriculum for boys, the second was devised to meet the needs of boys entering commerce and industry, the third was a curriculum for girls which had no bias towards practical ends, the fourth was for those schools preparing for the higher schools except the *Gymnasium* (the fully classical school), and the last provided a course for those schools which prepared for the *Gymnasium*.

After the revolution of 1918 the position of the *Mittelschulen* was called again into question. Their continued existence was opposed by the advocates of the elementary schools, who objected to the withdrawal of the better pupils from those schools, as this rendered more difficult the improvement of the elementary schools themselves. At the same time there was an expansion of the secondary school system and new types of schools were created, one of which was based on the completed elementary school course; between the two it was felt by some no place was left for the *Mittelschule*, but Herr Boelitz, a former Minister of Education, strongly urged their retention on the ground that in the interest of trade and industry and of the lower placed officials some more practical course than that provided by the secondary school was required.

It was felt that the academic teacher was not well suited to give the kind of instruction desired and as a matter of fact the bulk of the teachers in *Mittelschulen* are those holding the *Mittellschullehrer* diploma. The diploma is obtained under Regulations framed in 1901. No course of training has been established, but the qualification is acquired by passing an examination to which fully qualified elementary school teachers, candidates for secondary school teachers' certificate or for the certificate of theology are admissible. The bulk of the candidates are elementary school teachers. Elementary school teachers may be employed in the *Mittelschule* but must acquire the additional qualification or give up the work. Of the assistant staff in 1921 8.11 per cent had academic qualifications, 62.53 per cent held the *Mittelschule* diploma and 23.2 per cent were elementary teachers not fully qualified for *Mittelschulen*. The rest (6.16 per cent) were assistant teachers without academic training. Of the head teachers 67.82 per cent had the qualification of the Headship of an elementary school, 25.3 per cent were qualified secondary school teachers.

In 1924 new programmes were issued by the Ministry for the *Mittelschule*. The changes since 1910 have all been in the direction of laying greater emphasis on the practical side of the instruction.

Notes

Notes to Chapter 1: Policy 'Borrowing' in Education and the German Example:
Historical and Theoretical Perspectives

1   Murray, *Life of Matthew Arnold*, p. 240.
2   Cousin, *Report on the State of Public Instruction in Prussia*, p. 292.
3   Haines uses the term 'the German example' in a paper of 1958, 'German Influence upon Scientific Instruction in England, 1867–1887'.
4   'Programme for International Student Assessment'.
5   Ashton, *The German Idea: Four English Writers and the Reception of German Thought 1800–1860.*
6   Albert was installed as Chancellor of the University of Cambridge in 1847, a role which he fulfilled with great enthusiasm (see Chadwick, *Prince Albert and the University*).
7   Cogan, *The Rhine*, vol. I, p. 2.
8   Ibid., pp. 4–5.
9   *The Times*, 22 November 1833, cited in Sprigade, *Where there is Reform there is Comparison*, p. 215.
10 Thomas, *The Ends of Life*, pp. 5–6.
11 The following text is taken largely from Phillips, *Reflections on British Interest in Education in Germany in the Nineteenth Century*, pp. 9–11.
12 De Staël, *Germany*, vol. I, p. 17.
13 Hickson, *Dutch and German Schools*, p. 1.
14 Phillips, 'Periodisation in Historical Approaches to Comparative Education'; 'Comparative Historical Studies in Education'.
15 Paulsen, *German Education. Past and Present.*
16 Sadler, 'The History of Education', p. 103.
17 Phillips, 'Learning from Elsewhere in Education', p. 301.
18 Sadler, 'Progress of Education in England, 1823–1923', pp. 67–8.
19 Unpublished D.Phil thesis, University of Oxford.
20 *English-German Relations in Adult Education, 1875–1955. A Commentary and Select Bibliography.*
21 For a survey of Sadler's writings on Germany see Higginson, 'Sadler's German Studies' and 'Ein englischer Pionier der Studien ausländischer Schulsysteme'; for a list of Sadler's publications see Pickering, *Sir Michael Sadler. A Bibliography of His Published Works*. Three studies of Sadler's work by Sislian are also useful.
22 Among modern historical studies of aspects of education in Germany several stand out as being of exceptional importance: *Schooling and Society: the Politics of Education in Prussia and Bavaria, 1750–1900*, by Schleunes; *Prussian Schoolteachers: Profession and Office, 1763–1848*, by La Vopa; *Secondary School Reform in Imperial Germany*, by Albisetti; *State, Society, and the Elementary School in Imperial Germany*, by Lamberti; *Absolutism and the Eighteenth-Century Origins of Compulsory Schooling in Prussia and Austria* by Melton; *Students, Society, and Politics in Imperial Germany*, by Jarausch, and *State, Society, and University in Germany 1700–1914*, by McClelland. The Max Planck Institute's *Between Elite and Mass Education* contains a historical account of US-German 'interactions' in education (pp. 1–65).

Notes to Chapter 2: Testing the Ground: The Beginnings of British Interest in Education in Germany

1. Trollope, *Belgium and Western Germany in 1833,* vol. II, p. 170.
2. Arnold, *Schools and Universities on the Continent,* p. 165.
3. Sir Joshua Fitch, quoted in Welton, 'Education', p. 971.
4. Morrish, *Education Since 1800,* p. 7. Laqueur shows that enrolment in Sunday schools grew steadily from 1800 to 1850 and estimates that 'very few working-class children after 1830 could have escaped at least a few years in Sunday school' (*Religion and Respectability,* p. 45.). In 1788 under 60,000 pupils were enrolled in Sunday schools; by 1821 the figure was nearly 750,000; in 1851 it was more than two million (Hilton, *A Mad, Bad, and Dangerous People?* p. 534).
5. The dame schools were often only schools by name, 'consisting of a damp, dark cellar where an ancient female or disabled male gained a precarious and mean livelihood by collecting together a number of children' (Smith, *Life and Work of Sir James Kay-Shuttleworth,* p. 72).
6. The nine institutions in the early decades of the nineteenth century called 'public' schools in the Royal Commission of 1864 were St Paul's, Merchant Taylors', Westminster, Eton, Winchester, Charterhouse, Harrow, Rugby, and Shrewsbury. For the early history of the grammar schools see Watson, *The Old Grammar Schools.*
7. Stephens, *Education in Britain, 1750–1914,* pp. 21–2. A House of Commons Select Committee on the Education of the Lower Orders in the Metropolis estimated that about 7 per cent of the population (one in fourteen or fifteen) were attending day schools in 1816.
8. Birchenough, *History of Elementary Education in England and Wales,* p. 60. For a detailed discussion of problems with the early statistics of education see West, *Education and the Industrial Revolution,* pp. 8–30.
9. Schweizer & Osborne, *Cobbett,* p. 81.
10. Hibbert, *George III,* p. 211. Lancaster's system was criticised by the popular writer and educationist Mrs Trimmer (Sarah Trimmer) in *A Comparative View of the New Plan of Education promulgated by Mr Joseph Lancaster* (1805), and she in turn was subjected to a vitriolic piece (apparently by the Rev Sydney Smith) defending Lancaster in the *Edinburgh Review,* vol. IX, no.17, 1806, pp. 177–84.
11. Mann, *Report of an Educational Tour,* p. 43. Bell had written in 1808: 'It is [this system's] distinguishing characteristic that the school, how numerous so ever, is taught solely by the pupils of the institution under a single master, who, if able and diligent, could, without difficulty, conduct ten contiguous schools, each consisting of a thousand scholars' (Gosden, *How They Were Taught,* p. 2).
12. Seaborne, *Education,* p. 50.
13. Silver & Silver, *Education of the Poor,* pp. 12–13.
14. *Dictionary of National Biography.*
15. Cruickshank, *Church and State in English Education,* p. 3.
16. Caruso, 'Locating Educational Authority: Teaching Monitors, Educational Meanings and the Import of Pedagogical Models. Spain and the German States in the 19th Century'.
17. *The Times,* 10 May 1819, quoted in Sprigade, *Where there is Reform,* p. 159.
18. Mann, op. cit., p. 58.
19. *The State of Popular Education in England* (Newcastle Report), vol. 1, p. 98.
20. Silver, *English Education and the Radicals,* p. 33.
21. Silver & Silver, op. cit., p. 12. Cole & Postgate, among the critics of the Bell and Lancaster systems, say they 'annihilated any possibility of education' (*The Common People,* p. 308).
22. Simond, *An American in Regency England,* pp. 131–2.
23. Birchenough, op. cit., pp. 28ff.
24. Welton, op. cit., p. 971.
25. Albert Venn Dicey, quoted in Smith, *History of English Elementary Education,* p. 103.
26. MacDonagh, *Early Victorian Government,* pp. 23–4.
27. Birchenough, op. cit., p. 58.

28 Halévy, *The Liberal Awakening*, p. 107.

29 *Education et Croissance Economique*, p. 45. Abigail Green in her comparative study of Hanover, Saxony, and Württemberg, *Fatherlands*, reminds us that it is 'clearly right to realise that Prussian history is not German history' (p. 8).

30 Melton, *Absolutism and the Eighteenth-Century Origins of Compulsory Schooling in Prussia and Austria*, p. 46.

31 Tews, *Ein Jahrhundert preußischer Schulgeschichte*, pp. 13–15. The American Henry Barnard saw the importance of the *Principia* in their being issued 'at a time when the government of scarcely any state of Europe had as yet given impulse to the awakening of an interest in public schools' (Cubberley, *Readings in the History of Education*, p. 457.)

32 Melton, op. cit., p. 174. See also Paulsen (1908), p. 138.

33 Maynes, *Schooling for the People*, p. 52.

34 Schleunes, *Schooling and Society*, p. 15; Melton, op. cit., p. 115. The German text is in Paulsen, *Geschichte des gelehrten Unterrichts*, vol. II, p. 70: 'Auf dem platten Lande ist es genug, wenn sie ein bißchen lesen und schreiben lernen; wissen sie aber zu viel, so laufen sie in die Städte und wollen Sekretärs und so was werden'. Zedlitz, incidentally, is credited with establishing in the *Oberschulkollegium* the precursor of a centralised ministry of education for Prussia (see Alexander, *The Prussian Elementary Schools*, p. 22).

35 Schleunes, op.cit., p. 16.

36 Paulsen, *Geschichte des gelehrten Unterrichts*, vol. II, p. 70.

37 Alexander, *The Prussian Elementary School*, pp. 24–6.

38 *German Education*, p. 178.

39 Turnbull, *Educational Theory of J. G. Fichte*, p. 281.

40 Sadler, 'The Strength and Weakness of German Education', pp. 307–8.

41 Paulsen, *German Education*, p. 240. Original text: 'Alle Zweige der Haushaltung werden ohne viele Mühe in kurzer Zeit einen Flor gewinnen, den auch noch keine Zeit gesehen hat, und dem Staate wird, wenn er ja rechnen will und wenn er etwa bis dahin nebenbei auch noch den wahren Gundwert der Dinge kennen lernen sollte, seine erste Auslage tausendfältige Zinsen tragen', Fichte, *Reden an die Deutsche Nation*, p. 352.

42 Seeley, *Life and Times of Stein*, vol. II, p. 288. Seeley identifies Fichte's influence on Stein's plans for reform: 'In the educational schemes which were discussed in the later months of the Ministry and in the more elevated tone which the Reformers began to take Fichte's influence is traceable; it seems to have dictated the closing paragraph of [Stein's] Political Testament', ibid., p. 29.

43 Gordon & White, *Philosophers as Educational Reformers*, pp. 48–50.

44 'A Country of Schools', Nipperdey, *Deutsche Geschichte, 1800–1866*, p. 451.

45 Sweet, *Wilhelm von Humboldt*, Vol.II, p. 23. For the criticism in Humboldt's letter to Goethe, see Freese, *Wilhelm von Humboldt*, p. 522.

46 [D]er gemeinste Tagelöhner, und der am feinsten Ausgebildete muss in seinem Gemüth ursprünglich gleich gestimmt werden, wenn jener nicht unter der Menschenwürde roh, und dieser nicht unter der Menschenkraft sentimental, chimärisch, und verschroben werden soll'; Humboldt, Litauischer Schulplan, *Werke*, vol. IV, p. 189.

47 Theodor Litt, quoted in Knoll & Siebert, *Wilhelm von Humboldt: Politician and Educationist*, p. 47.

48 Knoll & Siebert, ibid., p. 37.

49 *Schools and Universities on the Continent*, p. 232.

50 Eduard Spranger, cited in Knoll & Siebert, p. 36.

51 Weinstock, *Wilhelm von Humboldt*, p. 17.

52 *German Education*, p. 241.

53 Kandel, *The Training of Elementary School Teachers in Germany*, pp. 10ff.

54 Paulsen, *German Education*, p. 243. Original German text: '. . . daß des Königs Majestät "den regen Sinn, welcher sich für das Elementarschulwesen betätige, nicht anders als beifällig anerkannten, zugleich aber darauf aufmerksam machten, daß solches in seinen Grenzen gehalten werden müsse, damit nicht aus dem gemeinen Mann

verbildete Halbwisser, ganz ihrer künftigen Bestimmung entgegen, hervorgingen"'
(Paulsen, *Das deutsche Bildungswesen*, p. 153.)

55 Figures from Friederich, *Das niedere Schulwesen*, p. 127 and Herrlitz et al., *Deutsche Schulgeschichte*, p. 52.

56 Brock, 'The Oxford of Peel and Gladstone', p. 38.

57 Dodd, *An Autumn Near the Rhine*, p. 382. See also Phillips, 'Problems with an Alien Tongue'.

58 Morgan, *Critical Bibliography*, p. 8. The fluctuations evident in Morgan's graph correspond to trends in German book production during the period, which show similar peaks in the 1840s and 1880s, with troughs in 1810–20 and the 1850s, probably as the result of some of the factors Morgan identifies (see Sagarra: *An Introduction to Nineteenth Century Germany*, p. 282.) British publishers recognised the importance of familiarity with German: Walter Graham Blackie, son of the Glasgow publishing house, went to Leipzig in 1839–40, aged 23, in order to learn German and gain knowledge of bookselling in Germany (see Blackie, *A Scottish Student in Leipzig*).

59 Buzard, *The Beaten Track*, p. 19.

60 Cf. Richter, *Bibliotheca Geographica Germaniae*, for listings of books on all aspects of Germany up to the 1890s.

61 Mullen & Munson: '*The Smell of the Continent*', p. 69.

62 Ibid.

63 Adams, *Letters on Silesia, Written During a Tour Through that Country in the Years 1800, 1801.*

64 *Recent Measures for the Promotion of Education in England*, pp. 21–2.

65 *Letters on Silesia*, p. 362.

66 Ibid., pp. 366–7. Felbiger was largely responsible for the regeneration of the *Volksschule* under Frederick; later he was summoned to Vienna, where he drafted Maria Theresia's *Allgemeine Schulordnung* of 1774.

67 Ibid., pp.367–8.

68 One American scholar saw the American edition (1814) of De Staël's book as marking the beginning of the influence of German thought on 'American life and education', Walz, *German Influence in American Education and Culture*, p. 8.

69 See Herold, *Mistress to an Age*, p. 382.

70 De Staël, *Germany*, vol. I, p. 194.

71 *DNB: Missing Persons*, p. 319.

72 *Notes and Reflections During a Ramble in Germany*, pp. 83–5.

73 Halévy, *Thomas Hodgskin*, p. 40.

74 Hodgskin: *Travels in the North of Germany*, vol. 2, pp. 218–19.

75 Ibid., p. 217.

76 Ibid., p. 215.

77 Ibid., pp. 239–40.

78 Ibid., p. 242.

79 Ibid., p. 261.

80 Boyle, *The Tyranny of Numbers*, p. 29.

81 Biber, *Henry Pestalozzi*, p. iii.

82 Biber, *Beitrag zur Biographie Heinrich Pestalozzi's.*

83 Hickson, *Dutch and German Schools*, pp. 1–2.

84 By 1903 it could be reported in England that in the past twenty years there had been 'a steady increase in the influence of the Herbartian system' (Hayward, *The Critics of Herbartianism*, p. 1). Johann and Bertha Ronge had established a Kindergarten along Froebelian lines in 1851, first in their home in Hampstead and from 1853 in Tavistock Place, London (Lawrence, *Friedrich Froebel and English Education*, p. 36). Frederic Hill's children attended the school. The number of German emigrés in London following the failed revolutions of 1848 had created propitious conditions for such an innovation. The Ronges published *A Practical Guide to the English kinder garten* in 1855 and it was frequently republished. Although the Kindergarten had been banned in Prussia in 1851, this English manifestation was given 'financial as well as moral support' from the British government (Ashton, *Little Germany*, p. 180.) The Shirreff sisters, Emily (1814–97) and Maria (1816–1906), prominent educationists supporting

the cause of women's education, were particularly active in promoting Froebelian principles and served respectively as President and Vice-President of the Froebel Society. They had considerable influence on public policy (Ellsworth, *Liberators of the Female Mind*, p. 261.)

85 Dodd, *An Autumn near the Rhine*, p. 172.
86 Ibid., p. 174. The view underlying such a warning was to be clearly expressed in popular and enduring fashion in the hymn 'All Things Bright and Beautiful' of 1848:

The rich man in his castle,
The poor man at his gate,
God made them, high or lowly,
And ordered their estate.

87 Ibid., pp. 329–30.
88 Russell, *Tour in Germany*, vol. II, p. 80.
89 Ibid, vol. I, p. 131.
90 Ibid., p. 136.
91 Ibid., p. 156.
92 Ibid., p. 134.
93 Sherer, *Notes and Reflections*, pp. 83–5.
94 Strang, *Germany in MDCCCXXXI*, vol. I, pp. 331–2.
95 Ibid, pp. 333–5.
96 Smith, *Notes Made During a Tour*, pp. 52–3.
97 Goodrich, *Universal Traveller*, pp. 424–5.
98 *Cabinet Gazetteer*, 1853, p. 690. Another, later, example would be the entries on Prussia and Wurtemberg in Beeton's popular *Dictionary of Geography* of 1868: '[In Prussia] the most complete system of national education has been established on an excellent system, and attendance at school is compulsory' (p. 649); education in 'Wurtemberg' is 'Good. There is a school in every commune or parish under the control of government, and every child above six and under fourteen years of age is compelled to attend' (p. 864).
99 From 1842 until 1894 Mudie's circulating library, about one third of whose stock was devoted to non-fiction, would make publications like these available to a large readership.

Notes to Chapter 3: Establishing State Involvement in Education: The German Example in England, 1833–70

1 Bache, *Report on Education in Europe*, p. 174.
2 Hickson, *Dutch and German Schools*, p. 8.
3 Brown, *The Church's Part in Education*, p. 4.
4 Bulwer Lytton, *England and the English*, vol. 1, p. 282.
5 Fränzl, *Statistik*, vol. 3, p. 92.
6 *Edinburgh Review*, 58:117, pp. 9–10.
7 See Sutherland, *Elementary Education in the Nineteenth Century*, p. 11.
8 Quoted in the *Edinburgh Review*, 58:117, p. 7.
9 Hansard, 17 April 1850, vol. 110, col. 462–3.
10 Goodman, 'A Historiography of Founding Fathers?'
11 Austin, 'Cousin's Report on the Prussian System of Education: Necessity and Practicability of a National System of Education'. The review is anonymous, but Austin is listed as the author in the *Wellesley Index* (vol. II, p. 149).
12 Bulwer Lytton, op. cit., p. 291.
13 *DNB*. For a full account of Sarah Austin's life, see Hamburger & Hamburger, *Troubled Lives*.
14 Cousin, *Report on the State of Public Instruction in Prussia*. A summary account of Cousin's report, together with a description of the New York common school system by John A. Dix, Superintendent of Common Schools, was put together by J. Orville Taylor and published in the United States in 1836 as *A Digest of M. Victor Cousin's Report on the*

State of Public Instruction in Prussia. Cousin described Austin's translation as 'excellent' (Ulich, *A Sequence of Educational Influences*, p. 47).

15 [Mrs Austin], *Germany, from 1760 to 1814, or Sketches of German Life from the Decay of the Empire to the Expulsion of the French* (1854).

16 Froude, *Thomas Carlyle*, vol. II, p. 189.

17 Oxford DNB entry for Sarah Austin.

18 Austin, 'Cousin's Report', p. 284.

19 Vol. XXXIV, no.1. Cousin's report on Holland (*On the State of Education in Holland, as Regards Schools for the Working Classes and for the Poor*) was published in English translation in 1838.

20 Brewer, *Victor Cousin*, p. 54.

21 Pattison, *Report*, p. 167.

22 Ibid., pp. 84–5.

23 Bulwer Lytton, op. cit., pp. 274–5. Bulwer Lytton's account of education in Prussia and the contrast he makes with provision in England is drawn upon in an American publication of 1838 by E. C. Wines, addressed in part to the Chairman of the Committee on Education in the legislature of New Jersey (*Hints on a System of Popular Education*).

24 Ibid., p. 287.

25 Ibid., p. 289.

26 Ibid., p. 358.

27 Murphy, *Church, State and Schools in Britain*, p. 16, quoting a source of 1882.

28 Schweizer & Osborne, *Cobbett*, p. 84.

29 Montmorency, *The Progress of Education in England*, p. 74.

30 Simon, *The Two Nations and the Educational Structure*, p. 164. For Roebuck's speech see *Hansard*, vol. 20, cols 139–66. The full text is reproduced in Montmorency, *State Intervention in English Education*, pp. 325–51.

31 Smith, *History of English Elementary Education*, p. 138.

32 Montmorency, *State Intervention in English Education*, pp. 327–8.

33 Ibid., p. 329.

34 Ibid., p. 333.

35 Ibid.

36 Hansard, 17 August 1833, vol. 20, col. 735.

37 Roberts, *Salisbury*, p. 817.

38 Ibid., pp. 818–19.

39 Trollope, *Belgium and Western Germany in 1833*, vol. II, pp. 169–70. The village was St Goar.

40 Ibid., pp. 172–3.

41 Ibid., p. 170.

42 Ashton, 'A Machine for Progress'.

43 Introduction, *Quarterly Journal of Education*, vol. I, January-April 1831, p. 2.

44 *Penny Cyclopaedia*, vol. XIX, p. 72.

45 Ibid., vol. XXI, p. 53.

46 Ibid.

47 Ibid., p. 54.

48 Smith, op. cit., p. 148.

49 House of Commons: *Report from Select Committee on the State of Education*, 1834.

50 Ibid., pp. 37–8.

51 Ibid., p. 129.

52 Ibid., p. 221.

53 Ibid., p. 215.

54 Nipperdey, 'Mass Education and Modernization', p. 157.

55 'The School Education of Prussia', pp. 205–6.

56 Barron, *A Few Notes on the Public Schools and Universities of Holland and Germany*, p. 28.

57 Ibid., pp. 26–7.

58 Ibid., pp. 50–2.

59 Ibid., pp. 66–8.

60 Central Society of Education, *First Publication, Second Publication,* and *Third Publication,* 1837, 1838 & 1839 respectively.

61 Wyse, 'On the Present State of Prussian Education', p. 376.

62 Ibid., p. 390.

63 Ibid., pp. 378–9.

64 Ibid., p. 380.

65 *Oxford DNB* entry on Thomas Wyse.

66 Letter of 4 February 1839, quoted in Maclure, *Educational Documents,* p. 42.

67 Selby-Bigge, *Board of Education,* p. 4. Distrust of state involvement and defence of voluntary effort persisted, with the example of Prussia being used negatively. During the second reading of the Industrial Schools Bill in March 1857, for example, George Hadfield MP (Liberal member for Sheffield, prominent in the anti-Corn Law League, and a Congregationalist) argued for the advantages of voluntary effort over the 'evils' of compulsion:

It was a great mistake to look to the House or to the Exchequer for the education of the people. Let them look to the result of compulsory education in Prussia. He was of opinion that the advocates of compulsory education were producing evils of the most serious character; while it was his conviction that great advantages were already secured in the matter of education by the voluntary efforts of benevolent people. (*Hansard,* 4 March 1857, vol. 144 col. 1853).

68 Walpole, *Life of Lord John Russell,* vol. 1 p. 329.

69 They were Rev John Allen (educated at Westminster and Trinity College, Cambridge), who had been a schoolmaster and chaplain to a bishop, and Hugh Seymour Tremenheere (educated at Winchester and New College, Oxford, where he was a Fellow), who was a barrister (Dunford, *Her Majesty's Inspectorate of Schools,* p. 3).

70 Wilson, *Views and Prospects,* p. 63.

71 Ibid., p. 63.

72 Their 'stature' was not always to be so obvious. Sir George Kekewich, Secretary of the Education Department (1890–1900) and of the Board of Education (1900–3), recounts an amusing incident:

Inspectors were not always of distinguished mien. Tradition has it that one of them, of lofty attainments but of lowly stature and common features, was examining a school when the great lady of the neighbourhood walked in. 'Where is Her Majesty's Inspector?' Humbly the teacher indicated the little man sitting at the desk. 'That Her Majesty's Inspector!' said the lady; 'I don't believe a word of it,' and flung out of the school. (Kekewich, *The Education Department and After,* pp. 129–30).

73 *Educational Documents,* p. 48.

74 Wilson, *Views and Prospects,* p. 70.

75 Pile, *The Department of Education and Science,* p. 31. The early history of the Inspectorate is fully documented in Lawton & Gordon, *HMI.*

76 Kay, *Recent Measures,* p. 20.

77 The National Archives: PRO: ED9/12. Letter of 13 September 1847, J. P. Shuttleworth to Lord Palmerston.

78 Dyce, *Schools of Design,* p. 1.

79 Ibid., pp. 36–7.

80 Hickson, *Dutch and German Schools.* Hickson was editor and proprietor of the *Westminster Review* from 1840 to 1852: a part of the text had appeared earlier in that journal.

81 *Dutch and German Schools,* pp. 20–1.

82 Ibid., p. 21.

83 Ibid., p. 31.

84 Ibid., p. 32.

85 Ibid., p. 33.

86 Ibid., p. 38.

87 Ibid., p. 43

88 Lee, *Laurels & Rosemary,* pp. 123–50; Margaret Howitt (ed.): *Mary Howitt: An Autobiography,* pp. 293–326.

89 *DNB* entry on William Howitt.

90 Howitt, *Life in Germany,* p. 465.

91 Dodd, *An Autumn Near the Rhine*, p. 380.
92 Howitt, *Life in Germany*, p. 279
93 Howitt, *German Experiences*, p. 306.
94 Laing, *Notes of a Traveller*, p. 231; Howitt, *German Experiences*, pp. 309–10.
95 Vaughan, *The Age of Great Cities*, p. 189.
96 *German Experiences*, p. 332.
97 Ibid., p. 301.
98 Ibid., p. 303.
99 Ibid., p. 310.
100 Ibid., p. 337.
101 Engels, *The Condition of the Working-Class in England*, p. 111.
102 *German Experiences*, p. 328.
103 Sadler, 'Need We Imitate German Education?', *The Times*, 14 January 1916.
104 *German Experiences*, p. 305.
105 Mayhew, *The Upper Rhine*, pp. 318–19.
106 Roach, 'Education and the Press', p. 109; Geitz, Heideking & Herbst, *German Influences on Education in the United States*.
107 Mayhew, *German Life and Manners*, vol. I, p. 562.
108 Ibid., p. 565.
109 Ibid., pp. 583–4.
110 Ibid., vol. II, pp. 70–1.
111 Ibid., pp. 78–9.
112 Lawn (ed.), *Modelling the Future*, p. 13. See also Bennett, *Science at the Great Exhibition*. For a history of the world exhibitions, see Kretschmer, *Geschichte der Weltausstellungen*.
113 Davis, *The Great Exhibition*, pp. 201–3. The 'German' exhibits were under the aegis of the Zollverein and accredited to the individual states.
114 *Newcastle Report*, vol. I, pp. 1–2.
115 Pattison, 'Popular Education in Prussia', p. 169.
116 Ibid., p. 170. Pattison knew Germany well. He served as the Berlin correspondent of *The Times* and was highly regarded by the paper for his mastery of the detail of Prussian politics (Jones, *Intellect and Character in Victorian England*, p. 47.) As a scholar he was especially well informed about the development of theological scholarship in Germany.
117 *Newcastle Report*, vol. I, p. 300.
118 V. H. H. Green, *Oxford Common Room*, p. 198. In 1856 Lake (1817–97) had been a member of a commission reporting on military education on the Continent.
119 *Newcastle Report*, vol. IV, p. 168.
120 Ibid., p. 165.
121 Ibid., p. 241.
122 The National Archives: PRO FO83/297.
123 TNA: PRO FO83/295.
124 *Clarendon Report*, vol. I, pp. 36–7.
125 Vol. II, p. 51.
126 Ibid.
127 Ibid., pp. 53–4.
128 'Mit der Jungfrau von Orleans beschäftigte die Klasse sich seit Ostern, seit dreiviertel Jahren. Den Sitzengebliebenen war sie sogar schon aus dem Vorjahr geläufig. Man hatte sie vor- und rückwärts gelesen, Szenen auswendig gelernt, geschichtliche Erläuterungen geliefert, Poetik an ihr getrieben und Grammatik, ihre Verse in Prosa übertragen und die Prosa zurück in Verse'. Mann, *Professor Unrat*, p. 9.
129 *Clarendon Report*, vol. II, p. 59.
130 Shrosbee, *Public Schools and Private Education*, p. 61.
131 *Taunton Report*, vol. I, p. 72.
132 Ibid., vol. VI, pp. 444–5.
133 McCrum, *Thomas Arnold, Headmaster*, p. 62.
134 Armytage, *The German Influence on English Education*, p. 23. On Arnold and 'muscular Christianity' see Newsome, *Godliness and Good Learning*, p. 207.
135 Rowse, *Matthew Arnold*, p. 86.

[136] Arnold, *Schools and Universities on the Continent*, p. 155.

[137] Ibid., p. 163.

[138] Ibid., p. 165.

[139] 'It is not a matter of schools and universities remaining in a sluggish and feeble state of habit, but that through them the education of the nation should be raised to an ever higher level'. Ibid., p. 177.

[140] Ibid., p. 185.

[141] Ibid., p. 197.

[142] Ibid., p. 231.

[143] Ibid., p. 232.

[144] Ibid., p. 256.

[145] Ibid., p. 267.

[146] Ibid., p. 281.

[147] *Journal of Education*, vol. X, 1 May 1888, p. 242.

[148] Ibid., vol. VIII, 1 December 1886, p. 483.

[149] Ibid., vol. IX, 1 January 1887, p. 10.

[150] Connell, *Educational Thought and Influence of Matthew Arnold*, p. 280.

[151] *Journal of Education*, vol. VIII, 1 December 1886, p. 483.

[152] Murray, *Life of Matthew Arnold*, p. 240.

[153] Archer, *Secondary Education in the Nineteenth Century*, p. 186.

[154] Armytage, op. cit., p. 58.

[155] Barker, *Modern Germany*, p. 360.

[156] Hill, *National Education*, vol. II, p. 70.

[157] Ibid., pp. 71–2.

[158] Hawkins, *Germany*, p. 205.

[159] Ibid. Hawkins goes on to say that 'the most informed peasant in Europe has appeared to me to be the Scotch, while the Austrian rustic is perhaps the happiest'.

[160] Laing, *Notes of a Traveller*, p. 218.

[161] Kay, *Social Condition and Education of the People*, vol. II, pp. 1–2.

[162] Ibid., p. 18.

[163] Ibid., pp. 39–40.

[164] Ibid., p. 275.

[165] Ibid., p. 276.

[166] Ibid., p. 277.

[167] Green, *Education and State Formation*, p. 4.

Notes to Chapter 4: Towards a National System of Education in England, 1870–1918

[1] Arnold, *Reports on Elementary Schools*, p. 117.

[2] Brereton, *Studies in Foreign Education*, p. 253.

[3] Thomson, *England in the Nineteenth Century*, p. 135.

[4] Leathes, pp. 24–5.

[5] Kolb, *The Condition of Nations*, pp. 372–3.

[6] Holland, 'Germany', p. 823.

[7] Morley, *Life of Gladstone*, vol. II, p. 305.

[8] Matthew, *Gladstone*, p. 203. Gladstone's anonymous article, 'Germany, France, and England', was published in the *Edinburgh Review* of October 1870 (132).

[9] Hansard, vol. 199, col. 441, 17 February 1870.

[10] Ibid.

[11] Ibid., col. 439.

[12] Ibid., col. 461–2.

[13] Morley, *The Struggle for National Education*, p. 25.

[14] Murphy, *The Education Act 1870*, p. 79.

[15] Musgrave, *Society and Education in England Since 1800*, p. 45.

[16] Seaborne, *Education*, p. 61.

[17] Payne, *A Visit to German Schools*, p. vi.

[18] Ibid., p. 255.

19 Ibid., p. 271.
20 Davis, *Report on Schools in Germany and Switzerland*, p. 12.
21 Ibid., p. 14.
22 Ibid., p. 23.
23 Ibid., p. 27.
24 Ibid., p. 49.
25 Ibid., p. 53.
26 Ibid.
27 Ibid., p. 54.
28 Ibid., p. 56.
29 Ibid., p. 58.
30 Ibid., p. 59.
31 Ibid, p. 17. Cf. Karl Heinz Gruber's description of 1977, in connection with 'continental' or specifically Austro-German norms: 'The standard teaching unit is the year group of 30 children, and often more, with one teacher in a rectangular classroom that has a blackboard to the front, windows on the left (so that the right, writing hand does not overshadow the writing) and a door on the right that is always closed during lessons'. Gruber, 'Backwards to Europe'.
32 Samuelson Report, Second Report, 1884, vol. I, p. 15.
33 Ibid., p. 8.
34 Ibid., p. 511.
35 See Kretschmer, *Geschichte der Weltausstellungen*; Rooper, *School and Home Life*; Hart, *The International Health Exhibition*.
36 Bird, *Higher Education in Germany and England*.
37 Ibid., p. 2.
38 Ibid., p. 5.
39 Ibid., p. 8.
40 Ibid., p. 92.
41 Gautrey, *Lux Mihi Laus*, p. 23.
42 The National Archives: TNA: PRO Ed 14/30.
43 Ibid.
44 TNA: PRO Ed 36/1, letter of 26 October 1885 from Education Department to Secretary of the Treasury, approved by the Lord President on 24 October.
45 TNA: PRO Ed 36/1. Letter to Matthew Arnold dated 3 November 1885.
46 Letter of 2 April 1886.
47 Arnold's *Special Report*, p. 25.
48 Laishley, *Report Upon State Education*, pp. 51–2.
49 TNA: PRO FO 83/978. Circular of 14 March 1887.
50 TNA: PRO FO 83/978. Initial capitalisation of individual words as in original.
51 TNA: PRO FO 83/978. Letter of 7 May 1887, from Sir Edward Malet.
52 Letter of 6 May 1887. Original German: 'Nach der jetzt vorliegenden Rückäußerung des Herrn von Goßler [Prussian Minister of Education] würde die Erfüllung des Wunsches der Königlich Großbritannischen Regierung erheblichen Schwierigkeiten begegnen, da die Verhältnisse, welche bei der Fragestellung maßgebend gewesen zu sein scheinen, wesentlich andere sind, als diejenigen, welche in Preußen, – und ebenso in den übrigen deutschen Bundesstaaten – obwalten. Die Schwierigkeiten würden sich noch steigern wenn, wie aus der Beifügung eines besonderen Fragebogens für Frankfurt fest geschlossen werden könnte, Britischer Seits erwartet wird, daß die sehr ins Einzelne gehenden Fragen für jeden Bezirk und jede große Stadt in Preußen beziehungsweise Deutschland beantwortet werden. Der Königl: Großbrit: Regierung, beziehungsweise der König: Kommission für Unterricht und Erziehungswesen wird es aber leicht sein, sich über das Preußische Volksschulwesen aus folgenden hier beigefügten Druckwerken die gewünschte Auskunft zu verschaffen'.
53 Letter of 28 March 1887.
54 Adapted from *Final Report of the Commissioners* (1888), pp. 439–45.
55 Ibid. (adapted), pp. 440–1.
56 Ibid., pp. 128–32.
57 *Foreign Returns*, (1888).

⁵⁸ *Journal of Education*, vol. XV, 1 May 1893, p. 295.

⁵⁹ The discussions in question considered the pros and cons of instituting a new series, with an ultimate decision not to do so, despite a memo of 29 November 1949 by W. R. Richardson in response to a proposal from Toby Weaver: 'The idea of reviving the S.I.R. series of publications attracts me: it would be a suitable series for those volumes which we are always talking about and which we shall one day want to produce – on education overseas', TNA: PRO: Ed121/386. The Board of Education had, however, continued to publish a pamphlet series on educational topics which included coverage of aspects of education in other countries, including Germany.

⁶⁰ Bashford, *Elementary Education in Saxony*, pp. 21–2.

⁶¹ Ibid., p. 23.

⁶² The term 'secondary education' was an invention of Matthew Arnold, originating in the French. (Banks, *Parity and Prestige in English Secondary Education*, p. 1.) The *Oxford English Dictionary* cites his *Popular Education of France* (1861) as including its first use.

⁶³ Phillips, 'Michael Sadler and Comparative Education', p. 43.

⁶⁴ *Who Was Who*, vol. III.

⁶⁵ Bryce Report, vol. V, pp. 27–33.

⁶⁶ Ibid., returns for the German Empire, pp. 607–33.

⁶⁷ Ibid., p. 590.

⁶⁸ Ibid., 613.

⁶⁹ 'Report of the Education Committee of the London County Council Submitting a Report of the Council's Officers on Bathing Arrangements in Schools in Germany and Holland', TNA: PRO: Ed 14/19, apparently written by James Kerr, Medical Officer (Education).

⁷⁰ Robson, *School Architecture*, p. 70.

⁷¹ *Wilhelm von Humboldt*, ed. Heinrich Weinstock, p. 17.

⁷² Here Humboldt was basically misunderstood, with serious consequences for the development of the *Gymnasium* as *akademische Leistungschule* (academic 'achievement/ performance' school). Hearnden summarises the misinterpretation thus: 'The demand that pupils should become at home in all branches of knowledge came to be more significant than the requirement that they should be fired by a spontaneous enthusiasm', *Education, Culture and Politics in West Germany*, p. 22.

⁷³ Georg Kerschensteiner, *Begriff der Arbeitsschule*, quoted in Diane Simons, *Georg Kerschensteiner: His Thought and Its Relevance Today*, p. 32.

⁷⁴ Armytage, *The German Influence on English Education*, p. 34.

⁷⁵ The *realia studia*: sciences, mathematics, geography, history, modern languages, among others; as opposed to the *humaniora studia*. The classics maintained their grip on the *Gymnasium* curriculum, however, and the *Realschulen* tended to give added importance to Latin in order to increase their status. In 1897 Wilhelm Rein summed up the importance of modern studies thus: 'This school [Abbotsholme] is able to open men's eyes to the folly of the excessive attention and recognition usually bestowed on the memory of mere words and phrases; to the folly of the so-called "classical' education, namely, the doctrine that the training of the mind is best attained through "formal' studies, such as Latin grammar and Greek verses. These in reality employ precisely the same powers as are used in the study of French or physics, but the latter subjects have in addition an intrinsic value not possessed by Latin or Greek'. (Preface to Hermann Lietz, 'Emlohstobba: Fiction or Fact' (1896), in Reddie, *Abbotsholme* pp. 264–5.

⁷⁶ 'Emlohstobba' in Reddie, *Abbotsholme*, p. 383. Herbart was effectively discovered by educationists in England some fifty years after his death, with the translation in 1892 of his *Allgemeine Pädagogik aus dem Zweck der Erziehung abgeleitet* ('General Padagogy derived from the Aim of Education') as *The Science of Education; its General Principles Derived from its Aim*. (Adamson, *English Education, 1798–1902*, p. 492.) One late 19th-century British academic described Herbart as 'the first strictly scientific educationist' (Holman, *English National Education*, p. 48), in the context of a discussion of the 'wealth of sound theory' in education emanating from Germany (ibid., p. 49.)

⁷⁷ The development of education in Germany from 1870 to 1914 was described by Sadler as 'one of the intellectual wonders of the world, a great piece of administrative

engineering, deliberately planned, adequately financed, untiringly carried forward to its aim', 'The Strength and Weakness of German Education', p. 305.

78 Paulsen, *German Education, Past and Present*, pp. 207–8.

79 *Deutsche Schulkonferenzen*, vol. 1: *Verhandlungen über Fragen des höheren Unterrichts*, pp. 4–5.

80 Landes, *The Unbound Prometheus*, p. 348.

81 Dresden (1828), Nürnberg (1829), Stuttgart (1829), Cassel (1830), Hannover (1831), Augsburg (1833), Braunschweig (1835).

82 Landes, *The Unbound Prometheus*, pp. 346–7. See also Argles, *South Kensington to Robbins*, Roderick & Stephens, *Scientific and Technical Education in Nineteenth-Century England*, and James, 'The German Experience and the Myth of British Cultural Exceptionalism'. For an early account, with considerable coverage of Germany, see Fabian Ware, *Educational Foundations of Trade and Industry* (1901).

83 Simons, *Georg Kerschensteiner*, p. 39.

84 Ibid., p. 33.

85 Bertram, 'The Continuation Schools in Berlin', *Board of Education Special Reports on Educational Subjects*, vol. 9, *Education in Germany*, p. 452. Bertram reports that the schools had 'maintained till now such flexibility that curriculum and standard of instruction are not determined by State regulations, but by the needs of the students attending the classes', p. 457.

86 Quoted in Alter, *The Reluctant Patron*, p. 135.

87 As cited in Sanderson, *Education and Economic Decline in Britain, 1870 to the 1990s*, p. 19.

88 Hawkins, *Modern Languages in the Curriculum*, p. 123.

89 Brebner, 'The Teaching of Modern Languages in Germany', p. 483.

90 Ware, 'The Teacher of Modern Languages in Prussian Secondary Schools', p. 521.

91 Arnold, *Schools and Universities on the Continent*, pp. 267–8.

92 Firth, *Modern Languages at Oxford, 1724–1929*, p. 75.

93 Truscott, *Red Brick University*, p. 33.

94 Lyster, 'Higher Schools for Girls in Germany', pp. 207–85.

95 Lange, *Higher Education of Women in Europe*, p. 98.

96 Rhys, *The Education of Girls in Switzerland and Bavaria*, pp. 61–2.

97 Ibid., p. 55.

98 Ibid., pp. 69–70.

99 Johnson, *The German Mind*, pp. 67–8.

100 Kandel, *The Training of Elementary School Teachers in Germany*, pp. 111–19.

101 Kamm, *Hope Deferred*, p. 214.

102 For a succinct history of the *höhere Mädchenschule*, see Küpper, 'Die höheren Mädchenschulen'; for a full account of the history of girls' education in Germany, see the two volumes of Kleinau & Opitz (eds): *Geschichte der Mädchen- und Frauenbildung*.

103 Beale, 'Modern Languages', in Beale, Soulsby, & Dove, *Work and Play in Girls' Schools*, p. 94.

104 Paulsen, *The German Universities: Their Character and Historical Development; The German Universities and University Study*.

105 Bode, *German Universities. A Review of Prof. Paulsen's Work on the German University System*.

106 Burnet, *Higher Education and the War*, p. 69.

107 Williams, *"Made in Germany"*, pp. 151–2.

108 Sadler, 'The Ferment in Education on the Continent and in America', pp. 4–5.

109 Birch, *Our Victorian Education*, p. 1.

110 Hobsbawm, *Industry and Empire*, pp. 159–60.

111 Holman, *English National Education*, p. 199. Holman had been Professor of Education at the University College of Wales, Aberystwyth; 'Germany is our rival in trade because she is our superior in schools', he writes towards the start of his account of educational developments in England (ibid., p. v.).

112 Arnold, *Schools and Universities on the Continent*, p. xxii.

113 *Higher Education and the War*, p. 3.

114 Roach, 'Education and the Press', p. 107.

[115] Rowse, *Matthew Arnold: Poet and Prophet,* p. 81.
[116] The National Archives: PRO Ed 24/1880. Part of the text is reproduced in Phillips, *Reflections on British Interest in Education in Germany in the Nineteenth Century,* pp. 42–4. The archives of the Office of Special Inquiries and Reports have not survived in discrete form.
[117] Hansard, House of Commons, 24 March 1902, col. 854. Balfour's biographer, Kenneth Young, argues that 'the general drift of the Bill was to bring education in England up to the standard long since achieved in most German states' (*Arthur James Balfour,* p. 203.)
[118] Ibid., col. 867–8.
[119] Ibid., col. 901.
[120] Ibid., col. 903–4.
[121] Ibid., col. 915.
[122] Sadler, 'The History of Education', in *Germany in the Nineteenth Century. Five Lectures,* pp. 103–27.
[123] Edited by W. P. Patterson.
[124] 14 January 1916. See Appendix 3 below for the full text. In 1914 a scholarly study of the German *Oberlehrer* (secondary school teacher), by William Setchel Learned, had appeared in the United States, in which the teaching profession in Germany was described as having 'a professional structure of great perfection' (p. 101). In 1915 the US Bureau of Education issued a bulletin, prepared by George E. Myers, on vocational education in Germany, reporting that Prussia had made more progress in the 'thorough and practical character' of its vocational education than any other country.
[125] Sadler, 'The History of Education', p. 127.
[126] Sadler, 'The Strength and Weaknesses of German Education', p. 301.
[127] Ibid., p. 312.
[128] Ibid., p. 313.
[129] Originally published as *Pédagogie de Guerre Allemande,* Paris (Librairie Fischbacher) 1917.
[130] For the attitudes of British academics to the German universities during the war, see Wallace, *War and the Image of Germany.*
[131] Maclure, *Educational Documents,* p. 167.
[132] *Final Report of the Departmental Committee on Juvenile Education in Relation to Employment after the War,* vol. I, *Report,* p. 16.
[133] Ibid., p. 12.
[134] Fisher, *Educational Reform: Speeches,* p. 48.
[135] See Doherty: 'Compulsory Day Continuation Education. An Examination of the 1918 Experiment'. In the opposition to the 1918 Act it was noted that the continuation school was a German notion: 'We are fighting this War against Prussianism,' said one Conservative Member of Parliament, 'and I do not think that the people when they understand this Bill will be willing to set up a latter day Star Chamber in respect of those young persons [. . .] and their parents', Andrews, *The Education Act, 1918,* p. 48.
[136] Clay, *Compulsory Continuation Schools in Germany,* p. ii.
[137] Ibid., p. 2.
[138] Ibid., p. 5.
[139] Ibid., p. 6.
[140] Roderick & Stephens, *Scientific and Technical Education in 19th Century England,* p. 87.
[141] There was so much discussion of *Kultur* that the concept lent itself easily to satire and parody in England. A 1914 spoof version of Lewis Carroll's *Alice in Wonderland,* for example, had the Dodo say 'You see, so many words have lost all their original meaning. "Treaty", for example, or "culture"!' (Wyatt, *Malice in Kulturland,* p. 8.)

Notes to Chapter 5: Excursus: Aspects of the German University

[1]   Trollope, *Barchester Towers,* ch. XI.

2   A. H. Sayce, *The Times*, 22 December 1914. Sayce was Professor of Assyriology at Oxford.
3   Mitchell, *History of the University of Oxford: The Eighteenth Century*, p. 1.
4   Negley Harte, *The University of London, 1836–1986*, p. 64.
5   Holmes, *Coleridge: Early Visions*, p. 219.
6   Ibid., p. 221.
7   Edith Morley assigns high importance to Crabb Robinson's enthusiasm for German culture: 'To him, more than to any one else, is due the influence of German thought and German literature on England in the first quarter of the nineteenth century', *Henry Crabb Robinson in Germany*, p. 3.
8   Robinson, *Diary Reminiscences, and Correspondence*, vol. 1, pp. 220–1.
9   Brockliss, 'The European University in the Age of Revolution', p. 109.
10 Röhrs, *The Classical German Concept of the University*, p. 24.
11 Vizetelly, *Berlin*, vol. II, p. 83.
12 Ibid., p. 107.
13 Haldane, *Autobiography*, p. 23.
14 Ashby & Anderson, *Portrait of Haldane*, p. 8.
15 Schalenberg, 'Humboldt in Großbritannien'.
16 Fisher, *Unfinished Autobiography*, p. 79.
17 Diehl, *Americans and German Scholarship 1770–1870*. Rothblatt records that 'examples of Englishmen benefiting from exposure to the lectures of German professors can be cited from all fields except physics and mathematics, where English achievements continued to be brilliant and the admiration of Europe' (*Tradition and Change in English Liberal Education*, pp. 166–7).
18 McClelland, *State, Society, and University in Germany 1700–1914*, pp. 35–7.
19 Seeley, *Life and Times of Stein*, vol. 2, p. 430.
20 Wilamowitz-Moellendorff, *History of Classical Scholarship*, p. 115.
21 Seeley, *op. cit.* p. 430
22 Russell, *Tour in Germany*, vol. 2, p. 85.
23 Arnold, *Culture and Anarchy*, p. 126.
24 Schalenberg, 'Humboldt in Grossbritannien', p. 233.
25 Ibid.
26 Ibid., pp. 241–2. The quotation is from Acton's essay 'German Schools of History' (1886). Mark Pattison had written scornfully of 'the muddled German plodder who has waded through every sheet of printing or manuscript to be found in all the libraries of all the universities of Europe, with a view to his new edition of Dictys Cretensis' (cited in Jones, *Intellect and Character*, p. 43.)
27 Vizetelly, *Berlin*, vol. II, p. 90.
28 Cited in Armytage, *The German Influence on English Education*, p. 18. For an account of Hermann's importance as a classicist see Grafton, *The Footnote*, pp. 87–92.
29 Litton, *University Reform*, p. 43. An early text which helped to disseminate information on the German universities was Walter Copland Perry's study, *German University Education, or, The Professors and Students of Germany*, which was published in 1845. Perry had studied for the doctorate in Göttingen (Jones, *Intellect and Character*, p. 45.)
30 Ibid., p. 44.
30 Pattison, *Suggestions on Academical Organisation*, pp. 161–2.
32 Marx had written 'Elf Thesen über Feuerbach' in 1845. Engels included the texts in an appendix to his *Ludwig Feuerbach und der Anfang der deutschen Philosophie*, in 1888.
33 Anderson, *European Universities from the Enlightenment to 1914*, p. 162.
34 Burnet, *Higher Education and the War*, pp. 13–14.
35 Wilamowitz-Moellendorff, *My Recollections*, p. 383. 61 of the 93 signatories were professors.
36 On the nazification of a German university, see Remy, *The Heidelberg Myth*; on Heidegger, see *inter alia* Leske, *Philosophen im 'Dritten Reich'* pp. 99–106 and Lang, *Heidegger's Silence*.
37 The ancient historian Ulrich Kahrstedt (1888–1962), quoted in Alice Gallin, *Midwives to Nazism*, p. 96. Kahrstedt was dismissed in 1946 but quickly reinstated.
38 Phillips, *Pragmatismus und Idealismus*, pp. 10–11.

[39] Birley, 'British Policy in Retrospect', p. 55.

[40] Dodds, *Missing Persons*, p. 166.

[41] Phillips, 'The *Wissenschaftsrat* and the Investigation of Teacher Education in the Former German Democratic Republic, 1991: A Personal Account', p. 114.

[42] *Higher Education: Appendix Five*, p. 79.

[43] *Higher Education: Report*, pp. 40–1.

[44] *Higher Education in the Learning Society: Appendix 5*, p. 35.

[45] Ibid., p. 47.

[46] See the papers in Part One of *German Universities Past and Future*, ed. Ash.

[47] See Führ, 'The German University: Basically Healthy or Rotten?'

[48] Renate Simpson traces German influence on the scholarship of British universities from the 19th century onwards in her study *How the PhD came to Britain*.

Notes to Chapter 6: Developments in England and Germany, 1918–39

[1] Flexner, *Universities: American, English, German*, p. 361.

[2] Erika Mann, *School for Barbarians*, p. 37.

[3] Röhrs, *Die Schulen der Reformpädagogik Heute*, pp. 13–14.

[4] The fullest study in English of education in the Weimar Republic from the time is that of Alexander & Parker, *The New Education in the German Republic* (1930). For comprehensive coverage in German, see Führ's *Zur Schulpolitik der Weimarer Republik* (1970).

[5] Richter's *Monumenta Geographica Germaniae* of 1896 lists half a dozen publications on the question of the overloaded curriculum (the *Überbürdungsfrage*) that had appeared in Germany since 1878 (pp. 775–6).

[6] Hearnden, *Education in the Two Germanies*, p. 22.

[7] Burnet, *Higher Education and the War*, p. 17.

[8] Sadler, 'The Ferment of Education on the Continent and in America', p. 7.

[9] Ibid. This type of criticism is commonplace, and writers have sometimes taken such unhappiness in school life to be an inevitability: cf., for example, Heinrich Spoerl's Professor Crey, talking of his understanding of the principles of 'classic pedagogy' in a comic novel of 1933: *Met der Schole est es wie met einer Medizin – sa moß better schmecken, sonst nötzt sä nechts* ('School is like medicine – it has to taste bitter, otherwise it's of no use', Spoerl, *Die Feuerzangenbowle*, p. 13). Karl Heinz Gruber wrote in 1977 of happiness not being an educational concept on the Continent (Gruber, 'Backwards to Europe'); in 1976 a British HMI report on aspects of education in Germany recognised problems with stress and anxiety (DES, *Education in the Federal Republic of Germany*, p. 38). There have been many publications in German on *Schulstress* and *Schulangst.*

[10] Hearnden, *Education in the Two Germanies*, pp. 22–3.

[11] Führ, *Zur Schulpolitik der Weimarer Republik*, p. 11.

[12] One source estimates that there were 37 different types of secondary school in Germany before the First World War (Alexander & Parker, *The New Education in the German Republic*, p. 272).

[13] Designated *humanistisch, neusprachlich* (modern languages) and *mathematisch-naturwissenschaftlich* (mathematical-scientific).

[14] *Education in the Two Germanies*, p. 26.

[15] Lawson, *Reform of the West German School System, 1945–1962*, pp. 22–3.

[16] Samuel & Thomas, *Education and Society in Modern Germany*, p. 32.

[17] Ibid., p. 33.

[18] Ibid., p. 32.

[19] Hearnden, *Education in the Two Germanies*, p. 23.

[20] The inspectorial authority of the clergy was removed, for example. In November 1918 the Prussian government had declared its policy to be 'Expansion of all educational establishments, in particular of the elementary school, creation of the integrated school [*Einheitsschule*], liberation of education from any kind of church control, separation of State and Church' (Hahn, *Education and Society in Germany*, p. 55.)

21 Wilson, 'Education and Politics', passim.
22 Theodore Huebener: *The Schools of West Germany*, p. 17.
23 National Archives: PRO: Ed 121/192; Welshman, 'Physical Education and the School Medical Service in England and Wales, 1903–1939', p. 40. Hjalmar Schacht (1877–1970) was President of the Reichsbank and though he spent time in prison after the war he was eventually acquitted. Richard-Walther Darré (1895–1953) survived the war but had held high-ranking posts under the Nazis in food and agriculture, as well as being head of the 'Central Office for Race and Resettlement'. Robert Ley (1890–1945) was head of the Deutsche Arbeitsfront; he was indicted by the International Military Tribunal and committed suicide in his cell in Nuremberg.
24 *Physical Education in Germany*, p. 65.
25 Ibid., p. 19.
26 Julius Streicher (1885–1946) was found guilty of crimes against humanity and executed at Nuremberg. Baldur von Schirach (1907–74) was sentenced to twenty years' imprisonment and served the full term.
27 *Physical Education in Germany*, pp. 77–8.
28 http://www.steinerwaldorf.org/whatissteinereducation.html
29 *Schools and School Systems of Germany and Holland*, pp. 4–5.
30 Ibid., p. 27.
31 *Schools of Austria and Germany*, p. 7.
32 Hadow Report, *The Education of the Adolescent*, p. xix.
33 Ibid., p. 14.
34 See Kandel, *History of Secondary Education*.
35 Spens Report, *Secondary Education*, pp. 427–8.

Notes to Chapter 7: From the Second World War to Post-War Reconstruction, Radical Reform, and Beyond in England: Lessons from Germany Since 1939

1 DES, *Education in the Federal Republic of Germany*, p. vi.
2 *Norwood Report*, p. 15.
3 *Rahmenplan für das deutsche Bildungswesen*, p. 9.
4 *Norwood Report*, p. 17.
5 'Parity of esteem in our view cannot be conferred by administrative decree nor by equality of cost per pupil; it can only be won by the school itself' (*Norwood Report*, p. 14).
6 Education Act, 1944, section II 8 (1), pp. 4–5.
7 Ibid., section II 23 (1), p. 19.
8 Barnett, *The Verdict of Peace*, p. 460.
9 See McCulloch: *The Secondary Technical School* and Sanderson, *The Missing Stratum*.
10 Benn & Simon: *Half Way There*, p. 48.
11 Crowther Report, *15–18*, p. 183.
12 Ibid., p. 486.
13 Ibid., p. 487.
14 DES, Circular 10/65, 12 July 1965: The Organisation of Secondary Education, p. 1.
15 Lawton, *Education and Labour Party Ideologies*, p. 58.
16 Crosland, *Tony Crosland*, p. 148.
17 Maclure, Educational Documents, p. 301.
18 *Geographical Handbook Series: Germany, vol. II: History and Administration*, pp. 376–422.
19 Phillips, 'War-time Planning for the "re-education" of Germany: Professor E. R. Dodds and the German Universities'.
20 *Minds in the Making*, pp. 30–2.
21 Copies of the *Memorandum* survive in the Dodds Papers (in the present author's possession).
22 Balfour and Nair, *Four-Power Control in Germany and Austria*, p. 230.
23 *Protocol of the Proceedings of the Berlin Conference* [Potsdam Agreement], Section II A 8, p. 5.
24 TNA: PRO: FO 1050/1648, release date 24 August 1945.

25 Ibid.: PRO: FO 1051/69. Also in Ruhm von Oppen (ed.), *Documents on Germany Under Occupation 1945–1954*, pp. 233–4.
26 Phillips, 'British Educational Policy in Occupied Germany: Some Problems and Paradoxes in the Control of Schools and Universities', p. 75.
27 Hellmut Becker, 'Retrospective View from the German Side', p. 273.
28 OECD, *Review of National Policies for Education: Germany*, p. 103.
29 In the British Zone some 24.3 per cent of the teaching force had been suspended by June 1945. Pakschies, *Umerziehung in der Britischen Zone 1945–1949*, p. 165.
30 Birley, *British Educational Control and Influence in Germany after the 1939–45 War*, (typescript) p. 12.
31 AUT, *The Universities in the British Zone of Germany*, pp. 204–5. For a full discussion of the AUT report, see Phillips, *Zur Universitätsreform in der britischen Besatzungszone 1945–1948*.
32 Studienausschuß für Hochschulreform: *Gutachten zur Hochschulreform*, 1948; English version: *University Reform in Germany. Report by a German Commission*, 1949. For a full account see Phillips, *Pragmatismus und Idealismus. Das 'Blaue Gutachten und die britische Hochschulpolitik in Deutschland 1948*.
33 Robinsohn & Kuhlmann, 'Two Decades of Non-reform in West German Education', p. 316.
34 Ibid., pp. 312–13.
35 For a full account of the *Rahmenplan* see Hearnden, *Education, Culture and Politics in West Germany*, pp. 60–6.
36 NFER, *Procedures for the Allocation of Pupils in Secondary Education*, p. 6.
37 Benn & Chitty, *Thirty Years On*, p. 355.
38 *Review of National Policies for Education: Germany*, p. 55.
39 Callaghan, *Time and Chance*, p. 410.
40 'What the PM Said', *Times Educational Supplement*, 22.10.76, p. 72.
41 Discussion Paper No. 60, June 1983.
42 The title changed to 'Schooling Standards in England and Germany: Some Summary Comparisons Bearing on Economic Performance' and this version was published in the *National Institute Economic Review*, no. 112, May 1985, pp. 53–73, in *Compare*, vol. 16, no. 1, 1986, pp. 5–35, and in Phillips, *Education in Germany*, pp. 95–134.
43 *Compare*, vol. 16, no. 1, 1986, p. 22.
44 Produced by the European Parliamentary Labour Party and Socialist Group, European Parliament.
45 DES, *Education in the Federal Republic of Germany*, p. v.
46 Ibid., p. vi.
47 Ibid., p. vi.
48 Ibid., p. 34.
49 Pearce et al., *Assessment in West German Schools*, p. 8.
50 Glowka, 'Anglo-German Perceptions of Education', p. 321.
51 *Times Educational Supplement*, letters of 15 and 29 July 1977 from Howard Corbishley and Irene Gill.
52 'German Secondary Schools in Context', typescript, November 1986, pp. 24–5. The text was later published in *BJES* as 'Lessons from Germany? – The Case of German Secondary Schools' (vol. XXXV, no. 3, 1987) and is reprinted in Phillips, *Education in Germany*, pp. 60–79. The quotation is from Michael Sadler, *The Ferment in Education on the Continent and in America*, p. 7.
53 Ibid. (typescript), p. 4.
54 As Arthur Hearnden put it in 1976, 'the *Gymnasium* is the *Gymnasium* is the *Gymnasium*' (*Education, Culture and Politics in West Germany*, p. 148.)
55 Transcript of a television interview with Matthew Parris, London Weekend Television, 7.12.86.
56 Baker, *The Turbulent Years*, p. 165.
57 Ibid., p. 479.
58 Maclure, 'Parents and Schools: Opting In and Out', pp. 5–6.
59 *The Next Moves Forward*, 1987 Conservative Party General Election Manifesto.
60 *The Downing Street Years*, p. 593.

[61] The GDR published material in English describing its education system, among them *Polytechnical Education in the GDR* and *Education for Today and Tomorrow*. A good introduction is provided in *Education in East Germany* (1973) by Moore-Rinvolucri. The chapter on 'East Germany' in Nigel Grant's *Society, Schools and Progress in Eastern Europe* is also useful.

[62] Hurd, *Memoirs*, p. 385. Thatcher makes a point in her memoirs of mentioning that Chancellor Kohl had given her 'pig's stomach' (*Saumagen*) for lunch at a meeting in Deidesheim, Rheinland-Pfalz, in 1989, a dish he at least 'clearly enjoyed' . . . (*The Downing Street Years*, p. 748.)

[63] The memorandum was written by Charles Powell. The full text was published in *The Independent*, 15.7.90, p. 19 ('What the PM Learnt About the Germans').

[64] Führ, *On the Education System of the Five New Laender of the Federal Republic of Germany*, pp. 35–7. It was argued that to have only one type of school, the *Gesamtschule*, would be unconstitutional, since it would not allow the essential principle of parental choice. For accounts of developments since Unification, see: Rust & Rust, *The Unification of German Education*; Pritchard, *Reconstructing Education*; Weiler et al., *Educational Change and Social Transformation*; and Rodden, *Repainting the Little Red Schoolhouse*.

[65] Lawson, *The View from No. 11*, p. 439. Lawson's role in the thinking behind the reform has not been widely recognised: see ibid., pp. 606–11.

[66] Rose & Wignanek: *Training Without Trainers? pp.* 2–3.

[67] *Aspects of Vocational Education and Training in the Federal Republic of Germany*, pp. 1–2.

[68] Ibid., pp. 2–3.

[69] *Education and Training for the 21st Century*, 1991.

[70] Wrongly titled 'Aspects of *Higher* Education in Germany' on its cover.

[71] In addition there were reports on the German *Fachhochschulen* (DFE, 1992) and on the initial training of teachers in Hessen and Rheinland-Pfalz (Ofsted, 1993).

[72] *Aspects of Education in Germany: Design, Technology and Engineering 14–19*, p. viii.

[73] *Aspects of Full-time Vocational Education in the Federal Republic of Germany*, p. vi.

[74] *The Development of Double Qualification Courses in Secondary Schools in North Rhine Westphalia*, p. 2.

[75] *Post-16 Vocational Education and Training in Germany*, p. 10.

[76] DfEE, Statistical First Release 06/2001, 22 February 2001: 'The Level of Highest Qualification Held by Young People and Adults: England 2000'. The 2010 Labour Party manifesto, 'A Future Fair for All', reiterated the policy: 'to ensure a new wave of social mobility, we are committed to an historic change: raising the education and training leaving age to 18. All young people will stay on in learning until 18, Education Maintenance Allowances will be retained and there will be an entitlement to an apprenticeship place in 2013 for all suitably qualified 16–18 year olds', p. 3:6.

[77] The aim was that all young people would remain in education or training up to age 17 by 2013 and to age 18 by 2015.

[78] *The Educational System in Germany: Case Study Findings*, p. 2.

[79] Interviewed by Susan Crosland in the *Sunday Telegraph*, 18 December; cited in Rawnsley: *The End of the Party*, p. 354.

[80] Ibid., p. 350.

[81] *Invitation to Join the Government of Britain*, p. 50, p. 53.

[82] Department for Education, Press Notice, 26 May 2010.

[83] Rawnsley, op. cit., p. 354.

[84] *A Future for All*, p. 3:2.

[85] Karl Heinz Gruber, 'The German PISA-Schock', p. 202. For the relevant tables see *Knowledge and Skills for Life: First Results from PISA 2000*, p. 45, p. 79, p. 88.

Notes to Chapter 8: Evaluating the German Example

[1] Quoted in Adamson, *English Education, 1789–1902*, p. 492.

[2] Bell & Grant, *Mythology of British Education*, p. 88.

[3] Armytage, *The German Influence on English Education*, p. 59.

⁴ Broadfoot & Osborn, *Perceptions of Teaching.*
⁵ Sadler, in Higginson, *Selections from Michael Sadler,* pp. 49–50.

Note to Appendices: Towards a National System of Education in England, 1870–1918

¹ This early mention of the rationale for the school starting age of six in Germany resonates with much current discussion of the relatively early age at which English children begin school. The preference generally in Europe is for the school starting age to be six, which is still the case in Germany.

Bibliography

[Note: Royal Commissions and other significant reports are listed under the name of the chairperson, since they are habitually referred to as 'the Newcastle Report', 'the Norwood Report', etc.]

Adams, Francis (1972) [1882]: *History of the Elementary School Contest in England*, London (Harvester Press), ed. Asa Briggs.

Adams, John Quincy (1804): *Letters on Silesia, Written During a Tour Through that Country in the Years 1800, 1801*, London (J. Budd).

Adamson, John William (1930): *English Education, 1789–1902*, Cambridge (Cambridge University Press).

Albisetti, James C. (1983): *Secondary School Reform in Imperial Germany*, Princeton (Princeton University Press).

Alexander, Thomas (1919): *The Prussian Elementary Schools*, New York (Macmillan).

Alexander, Thomas, & Beryl Parker (1930): *The New Education in the German Republic*, London (Williams & Norgate Ltd).

Allsobrook, David Ian (1986): *Schools for the Shires. The Reform of Middle-Class Education in Mid-Victorian England*, Manchester (Manchester University Press).

Alter, Peter (1987): *The Reluctant Patron. Science and the State in Britain, 1850–1920*, Oxford, Hamburg, New York (Berg).

Anderson, Robert David (2004): *European Universities from the Enlightenment to 1914*, Oxford (Oxford University Press).

Andrews, Lawrence (1976): *The Education Act, 1918*, London (Routledge & Kegan Paul).

Archer, R.L. (1921): *Secondary Education in the Nineteenth Century*, Cambridge (Cambridge University Press)

Argles, Michael (1964): *South Kensington to Robbins. An Account of English Technical and Scientific Education Since 1851*, London (Longmans).

Armytage, W. H. G. (1969): *The German Influence on English Education*, London (Routledge & Kegan Paul).

Arnold, Matthew (1861): *The Popular Education of France, with Notices of that of Holland and Switzerland*, London (Longman, Green, Longman, and Roberts).

Arnold, Matthew (1868): *Schools and Universities on the Continent*, London (Macmillan).

Arnold, Matthew (1886): *Special Report on Certain Points Connected with Elementary Education in Germany, Switzerland, and France*, London (HMSO).

Arnold, Matthew (1910) [1889]: *Reports on Elementary Schools, 1852–1882*, London (HMSO/Eyre and Spottiswoode).

Arnold, Matthew (1966) [1869]: *Culture and Anarchy*, Cambridge (Cambridge University Press).

Ash, Mitchell G. (ed.) (1997): *German Universities Past and Future. Crisis or Renewal?* Providence/Oxford (Berghahn).

Ashby, Eric & Mary Anderson (1974): *Portrait of Haldane at Work on Education*, London (Macmillan)

Ashton, Rosemary (1980): *The German Idea. Four English Writers and the Reception of German Thought, 1800–1860*, Cambridge (Cambridge University Press).

Ashton, Rosemary (1986): *Little Germany. Exile and Asylum in Victorian England*, Oxford (Oxford University Press).

Ashton, Rosemary (2009): 'A Machine for Progress. Henry Brougham and Radical Reform in Nineteenth-Century London', *Times Literary Supplement*, 23 January.

[Austin, Sarah] (1833): 'Cousin's Report on the Prussian System of Education: Necessity and Practicability of a National System of Education', *The Foreign Quarterly Review*, vol. 12, no. 24, pp. 273–301.

Austin, Mrs [Sarah] (1854): *Germany, from 1760 to 1814, or Sketches of German Life from the Decay of the Empire to the Expulsion of the French*, London (Longman, Brown, Green, and Longmans).

AUT (1947): 'The Universities in the British Zone of Germany. [Report of the Delegation of the Association of University Teachers]', *The Universities Review*, vol. 19, no. 3, pp. 203–22.

Bache, Alexander Dallas (1839): *Report on Education in Europe, to the Trustees of the Girard College for Orphans*, Philadelphia (Lydia R. Bailey).

Bairoch, Paul: (1976): 'Europe's Gross National Product: 1800–1975', *Journal of European Economic History*, vol. 5, pp. 273–340.

Baker, Kenneth (1993): *The Turbulent Years. My Life in Politics*, London (Faber and Faber).

Balfour, Michael & John Mair (1956): *Four-Power Control in Germany and Austria, 1945-1946*, London (oxford University Press)

Ball, Nancy (1983): *Educating the People. A Documentary History of Elementary Schooling in England, 1840–1870*, London (Maurice Temple Smith).

Banks, Olive (1955): *Parity and Prestige in English Secondary Education. A Study in Educational Sociology*, London (Routledge and Kegan Paul).

Baring-Gould, S. (1879): *Germany Present and Past*, London (C. Kegan Paul & Co.).

Barker, J. Ellis (1907): *Modern Germany*, London (Smith, Elder, & Co.).

Barnard, Henry (1854): *National Education in Europe*, Hartford (Frederick B. Perkins).

Barnard, Henry (1876): *German Pedagogy: Education, the School, and the Teacher in German Literature*, Hartford, Conn. (Brown & Gross) (second edition).

Barnett, Corelli (2001): *The Verdict of Peace: Britain Between Her Yesterday and the Future*, London (Macmillan).

Barron, Henry Wenston (=Winston) (1840): *A Few Notes on the Public Schools and Universities of Holland and Germany, Taken during a Tour in the Summer of 1839*, London (James Ridgway).

Bashford, John L. (1881): *Elementary Education in Saxony*, London (Sampson Low, Marston, Searle, & Rivington).

Beale, Dorothea, Lucy H. M. Soulsby, & Jane Frances Dove (1898) *Work and Play in Girls' Schools*, London (Longmans, Green, and Co.) .

Beales, Derek (1969): *From Castlereagh to Gladstone, 1815–1885*, London (Nelson).

Becker, Hellmut (1978): 'Retrospective View from the German Side', in: Arthur Hearnden (ed.): *The British in Germany: Educational Reconstruction After 1945*, London (Hamish Hamilton), pp. 268–282.

Beckmann, Emmy (1936): *Die Entwicklung der höheren Mädchenbildung in Deutschland von 1870–1914, dargestellt in Dokumenten*, Berlin (F. H. Herbig Verlagsbuchhandlung).

Bell, Robert, & Nigel Grant (1974): *A Mythology of British Education*, Frogmore (Panther).

Benn, Caroline & Brian Simon (1972): *Half Way There*, Harmondsworth (Penguin).

Benn, Caroline and Clyde Chitty (1996): *Thirty Years On: Is Comprehensive Education Alive and Well or Struggling to Survive?* London (David Fulton).

Benner, Dietrich (1995): *Wilhelm von Humboldts Bildungstheorie. Eine problemgeschichtliche Studie zum Begründungszusammenhang neuzeitlicher Bildungsreform*, Weinheim and Munich (Juventa).

Bennett, J. A. (1983): *Science at the Great Exhibition*, Cambridge (Whipple Museum of the History of Science).

Berg, Christa (1991) (ed.): *Handbuch der deutschen Bildungsgeschichte, vol. IV, 1870–1918: Von der Reichsgründung bis zum Ende des Ersten Weltkriegs*, Munich (C. H. Beck).

Berry, Robert M. (1910): *Germany of the Germans*, London (Sir Isaac Pitman & Sons).

Bertram, H. (1902) 'The Continuation Schools in Berlin', in: Board of Education, Special Reports on Educational Subjects, Vol.9, *Education in Germany*, London (HMSO), pp.451-464

Biber, Eduard (1827): *Beitrag zur Biographie Heinrich Pestalozzi's und zur Beleuchtung seiner neuesten Schrift* [etc.], St Gallen (Huber und Compagnie).

Biber, Eduard (1831): *Henry Pestalozzi, and his Plan of Education; Being an Account of his Life and Writings* [etc.], London (John Souter).

Birch, Dinah (2008): *Our Victorian Education*, Oxford (Blackwell).

Birchenough, C. (1914): *History of Elementary Education in England and Wales*, London (University Tutorial Press).

Bird, Charles (1884): *Higher Education in Germany and England, Being a Brief Practical Account of the Organization and Curriculum of the German Higher Schools With Critical Remarks and Suggestions With Reference to Those of England*, London (Kegan Paul, Trench & Co.).

Birkbeck College Centenary Lectures (1924), London (University of London Press).

Birley, Robert (1963): *British Educational Control and Influence in Germany after the 1939–45 War*, Irvine Memorial Lecture, St Andrews, 24 April (typescript).

Birley, Robert (1978): 'British Policy in Retrospect', in Arthur Hearnden (ed.): *The British in Germany. Educational Reconstruction After 1945*, London (Hamish Hamilton), pp. 46–63.

Blackie, W. G. (1932): *A Scottish Student in Leipzig. Being Letters of W.G. Blackie, his Father and his Brothers in the Years 1839–40*, London & Glasgow (Blackie).

Bode, Mabel (1905): *German Universities. A Review of Prof. Paulson's Work on the German University System*, London (P. S. King & Son).

Bolton, Frederick E. (1900): *The Secondary School System of Germany*, London (Edward Arnold).

Boyle, David (2001): *The Tyranny of Numbers*, London (Harper Collins).

Brebner, Mary (1898): 'The Teaching of Modern Languages in Germany', in Education Department: *Special Reports on Educational Subjects*, London (HMSO), vol 3, pp. 481–98.

Brereton, Cloudesley (1913): *Studies in Foreign Education, with Special Reference to English Problems*, London (Harrap).

Brewer, Walter Vance (1971): *Victor Cousin as a Comparative Educator*, New York (Teachers College Press).

Broadfoot, Patricia & Marilyn Osborn (1993): *Perceptions of Teaching. Primary School Teachers in England and France*, London (Cassell).

Brock, M. G. (1997): 'The Oxford of Peel and Gladstone', in: M. G. Brock & M. C. Curthoys (eds): *The History of the University of Oxford*, vol. VI: *Nineteenth-Century Oxford*, Part 1, Oxford (Clarendon Press), pp. 7–71.

Brockliss, L. W. B. (1997): 'The European University in the Age of Revolution', in: M. G. Brock & M. C. Curthoys (eds): *The History of the University of Oxford*, vol. VI: *Nineteenth-Century Oxford*, Part 1, pp. 77–133.

Brougham, Henry Lord (1841): *Speeches of Henry Lord Brougham Upon Questions Relating to Public Rights, Duties, and Interests*, Philadelphia (Lea and Blanchard).

Brown, C. K. Francis (1942): *The Church's Part in Education, 1833–1941*, London (National Society/Society for Promoting Christian Knowledge).

Bryce Report (1895). *Royal Commission on Secondary Education. Report of the Commissioners*, London (Eyre & Spottiswoode for HMSO).

Buller, E. Amy (1943): *Darkness Over Germany*, London (Longmans, Green and Co.).

Bulwer-Lytton, Edward (1833): *England and the English*, London (Richard Bentley), 2 vols, 2nd ed.

Burnet, John: (1918): *Higher Education and the War*, London (Macmillan).

Buzard, James (1998): *The Beaten Track. European Tourism, Literature, and the Ways to 'Culture', 1800–1918*, Oxford (Clarendon Press).

Callaghan, James (1987): *Time and Chance*, London (Collins).

Carnoy, Martin & Diana Rhoten (2002): 'What Does Globalization Mean for Educational Change? A Comparative Approach', *Comparative Education Review*, vol. 46, no. 1, pp. 1–9.

Caruso, Marcelo (2004): 'Locating Educational Authority: Teaching Monitors, Educational Meanings and the Import of Pedagogical Models. Spain and the

German States in the 19th Century', in: David Phillips & Kimberly Ochs (eds):
   Educational Policy Borrowing: Historical Perspectives, Wallingford (Symposium Books).
Casson, William A. & G. Cecil Whiteley (1903): *The Education Act, 1902*, London
   (Knight & Co.).
Central Society of Education (1837): *First Publication*, London (Taylor and Walton).
Central Society of Education (1838): *Second Publication*, London (Taylor and Walton).
Central Society of Education (1839): *Third Publication*, London (Taylor and Walton).
Chadwick, Owen (1997): *Prince Albert and the University*, Cambridge (Cambridge
   University Press).
Clarendon Report (1864). *Report of Her Majesty's Commissioners appointed to inquire into
   the Revenues and Management of certain Colleges and Schools, and the studies pursued and
   instruction given therein*, London (Eyre & Spottiswoode for HMSO).
Clay, H. A. (1910): *Compulsory Continuation Schools in Germany*, London (HMSO).
Cogan, T. (1794): *The Rhine, or, A Journey from Utrecht to Francfort, Chiefly by the Borders of
   the Rhine, from Mentz to Bonn*, London (G. Woodfall), 2 vols.
Cole, G. D. H. & Raymond Postgate (1968) [1938]: *The Common People, 1746–1946*,
   London (Methuen).
Collins, Bruce & Keith Robbins (eds) (1990): *British Culture and Economic Decline*, New
   York (St Martin's Press).
Conrad, J. (1885): *The German Universities for the Last Fifty Years*, Glasgow (David Bryce &
   Son).
Connell, W.F. (1950): *Educational Thought and Influence of Matthew Arnold*, London
   (Routledge & Kegan Paul)
Cousin, Victor (1834): *Report on the State of Public Instruction in Prussia*, London
   (Effingham Wilson). Translated by Sarah Austin.
Cousin, Victor (1838): *On the State of Education in Holland, as Regards Schools for the Working
   Classes and for the Poor*, London (John Murray). Translated by Leonard Horner.
Crosland, Susan (1983): *Tony Crosland*, London (Coronet).
Cross Report (1888). *Report of the Royal Commission on the Elementary Education Acts*,
   London (Eyre & Spottiswoode for HMSO).
Crowther Report (1959). *15 to 18. A Report of the Central Advisory Council for Education
   (England)*, London (HMSO).
Cruickshank, Marjorie (1963): *Church and State in English Education*, London (Macmillan).
Cubberley, Ellwood P. (1919): *Public Education in the United States*, Boston etc.
   (Houghton Mifflin).
Cubberley, Ellwood P. (1920): *Readings in the History of Education*, Boston etc.
   (Houghton Mifflin).
Cubberley, Ellwood P. (1948) [1920]: *The History of Education*, Cambridge, Mass.
   (Houghton Mifflin).
Curtin, D. Thomas (1917): *The Land of the Deepening Shadow*, London (Hodder and
   Stoughton).
Davis, George B. (1897): *Report on Schools in Germany and Switzerland*, Birmingham
   (Houghton & Hammond).
Davis, John R. (1999): *The Great Exhibition*, Thrupp (Sutton Publishing).
Dearing Report (1997). *Higher Education in the Learning Society*, London (HMSO).
Department of Education and Science (DES) (1986) *Education in the Federal Republic of
   Germany. Aspects of Curriculum and Assessment*, London (HMSO)
Department of Education and Science (DES) (1991): *Education and Training for the 21st
   Century*, Cm 1536, London (HMSO), 2 vols.
Deutscher Ausschuß für das Erziehungs- und Bildungswesen (1959): *Rahmenplan
   zur Umgestaltung und Vereinheitlichung des allgemeinbildenden öffentlichen Schulwesens*,
   Stuttgart (Klett).
Deutsche Schulkonferenzen, vol. 1: *Verhandlungen über Fragen des höheren Unterrichts*, Berlin,
   4. bis 17. Dezember 1890 (1972): Glashütten im Taunus (Verlag Detlev Auvermann)
   1972.
Diebolt, Claude (1995): *Education et Croissance Economique. Le Cas de l'Allemagne aux XIXᵉ
   et XXᵉ Siècles*, Paris (L'Harmattan).
Diebolt, Claude, Vivien Guiraud & Marielle Monteils (2003): *Education, Knowledge, and*

Economic Growth. France and Germany in the 19ᵗʰ and 20ᵗʰ Centuries, Frankfurt am Main, etc. (Peter Lang).

Diehl. Carl (1978): *Americans and German Scholarship, 1770-1870*, New Haven and London (Yale University Press)

[Dodd, Charles Edward] (1818): *An Autumn Near the Rhine; or, Sketches of Courts, Society, Scenery, &c. in Some of the German States Bordering on the Rhine*, London (Longman, Hurst, Rees, Orme, and Brown).

Dodds, E.R. (1941) *Minds in the Making*, London (Macmillan)

Dodds, E. R. (1977): *Missing Persons. An Autobiography*. Oxford (Clarendon Press).

Doherty, Bernard (1966): 'Compulsory Day Continuation Education: An Examination of the 1918 Experiment', *The Vocational Aspect of Secondary and Further Education*, vol. XVIII, no. 39, pp. 41–56.

Donaldson, [Sir] James (1874): *Lectures on the History of Education in Prussia & England and on Kindred Topics*, Edinburgh, A. & C. Black.

Dunford, John E. (1998): *Her Majesty's Inspectorate of Schools Since 1944. Standard Bearers or Turbulent Priests?* London (Woburn Press).

Dyce, William (1840): *Schools of Design*, London (House of Commons), 3 March.

Dyson, A. E. & Julian Lovelock (eds) (1975): *Education and Democracy*, London (Routledge & Kegan Paul).

Eastwood, David S. (1994): 'Thomas Hodgskin', in: *The Dictionary of National Biography: Missing Persons*, ed. C. S. Nicholls, Oxford & New York (Oxford University Press), pp. 318–19.

Education for Today and Tomorrow (1973), Dresden (Verlag Zeit im Bild).

Education in Nazi Germany (1938): 'By Two English Investigators', London (Kulturkampf Association)

Ellsworth, Edward W. (1979): *Liberators of the Female Mind. The Shirreff Sisters, Educational Reform, and the Women's Movement*, Westport & London (Greenwood Press).

Engels, Friedrich (1926) [1892]: *The Condition of the Working-Class in England in 1844*, London (George Allen & Unwin).

Ertl, Hubert (ed.) (2006): *Cross-National Attraction in Education: Accounts from England and Germany*, Didcot (Symposium) .

Fahrholz, Bernd, Gabriel Sigmar & Peter Müller (eds) (2002) *Nach dem PISA-Schock. Plädoyer für eine Bildungsreform*, Hamburg (Hoffmann und Campe).

Fallon, Daniel (1980): *The German University: A Heroic Ideal in Conflict with the Modern World*, Boulder, Colorado (Colorado Associated University Press).

Farrington, Frederic Ernest (1914): *Commercial Education in Germany*, New York (Macmillan).

Fichte, Johann Gottlieb (1973) [1808]: *Reden an die deutsche Nation*, Osnabrück (Editio Simile).

Finegold, David, Laurel McFarland & William Richardson (eds) (1992, 1993): *Something Borrowed, Something Blue? A Study of the Thatcher Government's Appropriation of American Education and Training Policy*, Wallingford (Triangle), 2 vols.

Fisher, H. A. L. (1918): *Educational Reform: Speeches*, Oxford (Clarendon Press).

Fisher, H. A. L. (1940): *An Unfinished Autobiography*, London, etc. (Oxford University Press).

Fitch, Sir Joshua (1904): *Thomas and Matthew Arnold and their Influence on English Education*, London (William Heinemann).

Flexner, Abraham (1930): *Universities: American, English, German*, New York, London, Toronto (Oxford University Press).

Fränzl, Moritz (1838–41): *Statistik*, Vienna (J. G. Heubner), 3 vols.

Fraser, Stewart (1964) *Jullien's Plan for Comparative Education, 1816–17*, New York (Teachers College).

Fraser, Stewart E. & William W. Brickman (1968): *A History of International and Comparative Education. Nineteenth-Century Documents*, Glenview, Illinois (Scott, Foresman and Company).

Freese, Rudolf (ed.) (n.d.): *Wilhelm von Humboldt. Sein Leben und Werk dargestellt in Briefen, Tagebüchern und Dokumenten seiner Zeit*, Berlin (Verlag der Nation).

Friedel, V. H. (1918): *The German School as a War Nursery*, London (Andrew Melrose Ltd.).

Friederich, Gerd (1987): 'Das niedere Schulwesen', in Karl-Ernst Jeismann & Peter
    Lundgreen (eds): *Handbuch der deutschen Bildungsgeschichte*, vol. III, *1800–1870: Von
    der Neuordnung Deutschlands bis zur Gründung des Deutschen Reiches*, Munich (C. H.
    Beck), pp. 121–52.
Frith, Sir Charles (1929): *Modern Languages at Oxford, 1724-1929*, London (Oxford
    University Press)
Froude, James Anthony (1882): *Thomas Carlyle. A History of the First Forty Years of his Life,
    1795–1835*, London (Logmans, Green, and Co.), 2 vols.
Führ, Christoph (1970): *Zur Schulpolitik der Weimarer Republik: Darstellung und Quellen*,
    Weinheim, Berlin, Basel (Beltz).
Führ, Christoph (1992): *On the Education System of the Five New Laender of the Federal
    Republic of Germany*, Bonn (inter Nationes).
Führ, Christoph (1995): 'The German University: Basically Healthy or Rotten?' in:
    David Phillips (ed.): *Education in Germany: Tradition and Reform in Historical Context*,
    London & New York (Routledge), pp. 80–91.
Gallin, Alice (1986): *Midwives to Nazism. University Professors in Weimar Germany, 1925–
    1933*, Macon, Georgia (Mercer University Press).
Gardner, Phil (1984): *The Lost Elementary Schools of Victorian England*, London (Croom
    Helm).
Gautrey, Thomas (n.d.): *'Lux Mihi Laus'. School Board Memories*, London (Link House
    Publications Ltd.).
Geitz, Henry, Jürgen Heideking & Jurgen Herbst: *German Influences on Education in the
    United States to 1917*, Cambridge (German Historical Institute, Washington DC &
    Cambridge University Press)
Geographical Handbook Series: Germany (1944). London (Naval Intelligence Division), 4 vols.
Giese, Gerhardt (1961): *Quellen zur deutschen Schulgeschichte seit 1800*, Göttingen
    (Musterschmidt-Verlag).
Glowka, Detlef (1989): 'Anglo-German Perceptions of Education', *Comparative
    Education*, Vol.25 No.3, pp.319-332
Goldstrom, J. M. (1972): *Education: Elementary Education, 1780–1900*, Newton Abbot
    (David & Charles).
Gonon, Philipp (1998): *Das Internationale Argument in der Bildungsreform*, Bern, etc.
    (Peter Lang).
Goodman, Joyce (2002): 'A Historiography of Founding Fathers? Sarah Austin
    (1793–1867) and English Comparative Education', *History of Education*, vol. 31,
    no. 5, pp. 425–35.
Goodrich, Charles A. (1836): *The Universal Traveller*, Hartford (Canfield and Robins).
Gordon, Peter & John White (1979): *Philosophers as Educational Reformers. The Influence
    of Idealism on British Educational Thought and Practice*, London (Routledge & Kegan
    Paul).
Gosden, P. H. J. H. (1966): *The Development of Educational Administration in England and
    Wales*, Oxford (Basil Blackwell).
Gosden, P. H. J. H. (1969): *How They Were Taught. An Anthology of Contemporary Accounts
    of Learning and Teaching in England, 1800–1950*, Oxford (Basil Blackwell).
Gougher, Ronald L. (1969): 'Comparison of English and American Views of the
    German University, 1840–1865: A Bibliography', *History of Education Quarterly*, vol.9,
    no.4, pp. 477–91.
Grafton, Anthony (2003): *The Footnote. A Curious History* (London (Faber and Faber).
Grant, Nigel (1969): *Society, Schools and Progress in Eastern Europe*, Oxford, etc.
    (Pergamon Press).
Grasby, W. Catton (1891) *Teaching in Three Continents: Personal Notes on the Educational
    Systems of the World*, London (Cassell).
Green, Abigail (2001): *Fatherlands. State-Building and Nationhood in Nineteenth-Century
    Germany*, Cambridge (Cambridge University Press).
Green, Andy (1990): *Education and State Formation. The Rise of Education Systems in
    England, France and the USA*, Basingstoke and London (Macmillan).
Green, V. H. H. (1957): *Oxford Common Room. A Study of Lincoln College and Mark Pattison*,
    London (Edward Arnold).

Gruber, Karl Heinz (1977): 'Backwards to Europe', *Times Educational Supplement*, 24 June.
Gruber, Karl Heinz (2006): 'The German "PISA-Schock": Some Aspects of the Extraordinary Impact of the OECD's PISA Study on the German Education System', in: Hubert Ertl, ed.: *Cross-National Attraction in Education: Accounts from England and Germany*, Didcot (Symposium).
Hackl, Bernd & Hans Pechar (eds) (2007): *Bildungspolitische Aufklärung: Um- und Irrwege der österreichischen Schulreform*, Innsbruck, Vienna, Bozen (Studien Verlag).
Hadow Report (1927): *The Education of the Adolescent*, London (HMSO).
Hahn, H.-J. (1998): *Education and Society in Germany*, Oxford & New York (Berg).
Haines, George (1957): *German Influence Upon English Education and Science, 1800–1866*, New London, Conn. (Connecticut College).
Haines, George (1958): 'German Influence upon Scientific Instruction in England, 1867–1887', *Victorian Studies*, March, pp. 215–44.
Haldane, Richard Burdon (1929): *An Autobiography*, Garden City, New York (Doubleday, Doran)
Halévy, Elie (1956): *Thomas Hodgskin*, London (Ernest Benn).
Halévy, Elie (1961) [1923]: *A History of the English People in the Nineteenth Century*, vol. 2, *The Liberal Awakening, 1815–1830*, London (Ernest Benn).
Halsall, Elizabeth (1990): *A Comparative-Historical Reference List of School Education in 13 Countries*, British Comparative and International Education Society.
Halsalle, Henry de (1915): *Degenerate Germany*, London (T. Werner Laurie).
Hamburger, Lotte & Joseph Hamburger (1985): *Troubled Lives: John and Sarah Austin*, Toronto (University of Toronto Press).
Hart, Ernest (1884): *The International Health Exhibition: Its Influence and Possible Sequels*, London (Smith, Elder and Co.).
Harte, Negley (1986): *The University of London, 1836–1986*, London (The Athlone Press).
Hartshorne, Edward Yarnall (1937): *The German Universities and National Socialism*, London (George Allen & Unwin).
Hawkins, Bisset (1838): *Germany*, London (John W. Parker).
Hawkins, Eric (1981): *Modern Languages in the Curriculum*, Cambridge (Cambridge University Press).
Hayward, F. H. (1903): *The Critics of Herbatianism and Other Matter Contributory to the Herbartian Question*, London (Swan Sonnenschein).
Heafford, Michael (1967): *Pestalozzi. His Thought and its Relevance Today*, London (Methuen).
Hearnden, Arthur (1974): *Education in the Two Germanies*, Oxford (Basil Blackwell).
Hearnden, Arthur (1976): *Education, Culture and Politics in West Germany*, Oxford (Pergamon).
Hearnden, Arthur (ed.) (1978): *The British in Germany. Educational Reconstruction After 1945*, London (Hamish Hamilton).
Helmreich, Ernst Christian (1959): *Religious Education in German Schools. An Historical Approach*, Cambridge, Mass. (Harvard University Press).
Herold, J. Christopher (1959): *Mistress to an Age. A life of Madame de Staël*, London (Hamish Hamilton).
Herrlitz, Hans-Georg, Wulf Hopf & Hartmut Titze (1993): *Deutsche Schulgeschichte von 1800 bis zur Gegenwart*, Weinheim & Munich (Juventa).
Hibbert, Christopher (1998): *George III. A Personal History*, London (Viking).
Hickson, W. E. (1840): *An Account of the Present State of Education in Holland, Belgium, and the German States, with a View to the Practical Steps which should be taken for Improving and Extending the Means of Popular Instruction in Great Britain and Ireland*, London (Taylor and Walton).
Higginson, J. H. (n.d.): 'The European Groundwork of Sir Michael Sadler', paper delivered at a colloquium on 'Secondary and Higher Education', Rugby School.
Higginson, J. H. (1958): 'Sadler's German Studies', *British Journal of Educational Studies*, vol.VI, no.2, pp. 119–27.
Higginson, J. H. (ed.) (1979): *Selections from Michael Sadler*, Liverpool (Dejall & Meyorre).
Higginson, J. H. (1997): 'Ein englischer Pionier der Studien ausländischer Schulsysteme und sein Einfluss auf Reformen und Entwicklung des englischen

Schulwesens', in: Elmar Lechner (ed.): *Pädagogische Grenzgänger in Europa*, Frankfurt a. M., etc. (Peter Lang).

Hill, Frederic (1836): *National Education. Its Present State and Prospects*, London (Charles Knight), 2 vols.

Hilton, Boyd (2006) *A Mad, Bad, and Dangerous People? England 1783–1846*, Oxford (Clarendon Press).

Hinde, Wendy (1987): *Richard Cobden. A Victorian Outsider*, New Haven and London (Yale University Press).

Hines, E. C. (1838): *Hints on a System of Popular Education*, Philadelphia (Hogan and Thompson).

Hinsdale, B. A. (1913): *Horace Mann and the Common School Revival in the United States*, New York (Charles Scribner's Sons).

Hinton, John Howard (1972) [1852]: *A Review of the Evidence Taken Before a Committee of the House of Commons in Relation to the State of Education in Manchester and Salford*, Manchester (E. J. Morten).

Hinton, John Howard (1972) [1854]: *A Review of the Evidence Taken Before a Committee of the House of Commons in Relation to a Scheme of Secular Education*, Manchester (E. J. Morten).

Hobsbawm, Eric (1999): *Industry and Empire: From 1750 to the Present Day*, revised ed., London (Penguin).

Hodgskin, Thomas (1820): *Travels in the North of Germany*, Edinburgh (Archibald Constable and Co.), 2 vols.

Holland, Arthur William (1910), 'Germany', *Encyclopaedia Brittanica*, 11th edition, vol. XI, pp. 804–901.

Holman, H. (1898): *English National Education. A Sketch of the Rise of Public Elementary Schools in England*, London (Blackie & Son).

Holmes, Richard (1989): *Coleridge: Early Visions*, London (Hodder & Stoughton).

Honey, J. R. de S. (1977): *Tom Brown's Universe. The Development of the Victorian Public School*, London (Millington).

House of Commons (1834): *Report from Select Committee on the State of Education*, 7 August.

Howitt, Margaret (ed.) (1889): *Mary Howitt: An Autobiography*, London (Wm Isbister Limited), 2 vols.

Howitt, William (1842): *Life in Germany; Or, Scenes, Impressions, and Every-day Life of the Germans, Including the Popular Songs, Sports, and Habits of the Students of the Universities*, London (George Routledge and Co.).

Howitt, William (1844): *German Experiences: Addressed to the English; Both Stayers at Home and Goers Abroad*, London (Longman, Brown, Green, and Longmans).

Howitt, William (1849): *Life in Germany*, London (George Routledge and Co.).

Huebener, Theodore (1962): *The Schools of West Germany. A Study of German Elementary and Secondary Schools*, New York (New York University Press).

Hughes, James L. & L. R. Klemm (1907): *Progress of Education in the Century*, Toronto & Philadelphia (Linscott)/London (W. & R. Chambers).

Hughes, R. E. (1901): *Schools at Home and Abroad*, London (Swan Sonnenschein & Co.).

Humboldt, Wilhelm von (1969): *Werke*, vol. IV, *Schriften zur Politik und zum Bildungswesen*, ed. Andreas Flitner & Klaus Giel, Stuttgart (Cotta).

Hurd, Douglas (2003): *Memoirs*, London (Little, Brown).

Hurt, John (1971): *Education in Evolution. Church, State, Society and Popular Education, 1800–1870*, London (Rupert Hart-Davis).

Hurt, J. S. (1979): *Elementary Schooling and the Working Classes, 1860–1918*, London (Routledge & Kegan Paul).

James, Harold (1990): 'The German Experience and the Myth of British Cultural Exceptionalism', in: Bruce Collins & Keith Robbins (eds): *British Culture and Economic Decline*, New York (St Martin's Press), pp. 91–128.

Jarausch, Konrad H. (1982): *Students, Society, and Politics in Imperial Germany. The Rise of Academic Illiberalism*, Princeton (Princeton University Press).

Jarman, T. L. (1970): *Landmarks in the History of Education. English Education as Part of the European Tradition*, London (John Murray).

Johnson, Fanny (1922): *The German Mind*, London and Sydney (Chapman & Dodd).

Jones, H. S. (2007): *Intellect and Character in Victorian England. Mark Pattison and the Invention of the Don*, Cambridge (Cambridge University Press).

Kamm, Josephine (1965): *Hope Deferred. Girls' Education in English History*, London (Methuen).

Kandel, I. L. (1910): *The Training of Elementary School Teachers in Germany*, New York (Teachers College, Columbia University).

Kandel, I. L. (1930): *History of Secondary Education. A Study in the Development of Liberal Education*, Boston, etc. (Houghton Mifflin Company).

Kandel, I. L. (n.d.) (1933): *Studies in Comparative Education*, London, etc. (George G. Harrap).

Kay, Joseph (1850): *The Social Condition and Education of the People*, London (Longman, Brown, Green, and Longmans), 2 vols.

Kay-Shuttleworth, Sir James (1973) [1873]: *Thoughts and Suggestions on Certain Social Problems*, Manchester (E. J. Morten).

Kazamias, Andreas M. (1966): *Politics, Society and Secondary Education in England*, Philadelphia (University of Philadelphia Press).

Kekewich, Sir G. W. (1920): *The Education Department and After*, London (Constable).

Kleinau, Elke & Claudia Opitz (eds) (1996): *Geschichte der Mädchen- und Frauenbildung*. vol 1: *Vom Mittelalter bis zur Aufklärung*; vol. 2: *Vom Vormärz bis zur Gegenwart*, Frankfurt & New York (Campus Verlag).

Knoll, Joachim & Horst Siebert (1967): *Wilhelm von Humboldt: Politician and Educationist*, Bad Godesberg (Inter Nationes).

Kolb, G. Fr. (n.d.) [1880]: *The Condition of Nations, Social and Political. With Complete Comparative Tables of Universal Statistics*, London (George Bell & Sons).

Kretschmer, Winfried (1999): *Geschichte der Weltausstellungen*, Frankfurt & New York (Campus Verlag).

Küpper, Erika (1987): 'Die höheren Mädchenschulen', in: Karl-Ernst Jeismann & Peter Lundgreen (eds): *Handbuch der deutschen Bildungsgeschichte*, vol.III, *1800–1870: Von der Neuordnung Deutschlands bis zur Gründung des Deutschen Reiches*, Munich (C. H. Beck).

Laing, Samuel (1842): *Notes of a Traveller, or the Social and Political State of France, Prussia, Switzerland, Italy, and Other Parts of Europe During the Present Century*, London (Longman, Brown, Green, and Longmans).

Laing, Samuel (1850): *Observations on the Social and Political State of the European People in 1848 and 1849*, London (Longman, Brown, Green, and Longmans).

Laishley, R. (1886): *Report Upon State Education in Great Britain, France, Switzerland, Italy, Germany, Belgium, and the United States of America; Including a Special Report Upon Deaf-Mute Instruction*, Auckland, New Zealand (New Zealand General Assembly).

Lamberti, Marjorie (1989): *State, Society, and the Elementary School in Imperial Germany*, New York & Oxford (Oxford University Press).

Lamberti, Marjorie (2004): *The Politics of Education. Teachers and School Reform in Weimar Germany*, Oxford (Berghahn).

Lancaster, Joseph (1979) [1803]: *Improvements in Education*, Clifton, New Jersey (Augustus M. Kelley), reprint of 3rd edition (1805).

Landes, David S. (1977): *The Unbound Prometheus. Technological Change and Industrial Development in Western Europe from 1750 to the Present*, Cambridge (Cambridge University Press).

Lang, Berel (1996): *Heidegger's Silence*, Ithaca & London (Cornell University Press).

Lange, Helene (1901): *Higher Education of Women in Europe*, New York (D. Appleton and Company).

Laqueur, Thomas Walter (1976): *Religion and Respectability. Sunday Schools and Working Class Culture, 1780–1850*, New Haven & London (Yale University Press).

La Vopa, Anthony J. (1980): *Prussian Schoolteachers. Profession and Office, 1763–1848*, Chapel Hill (University of North Carolina Press).

Lawn, Martin (ed.) (2009): *Modelling the Future. Exhibitions and the Materiality of Education*, Didcot (Symposium).

Lawrence, Evelyn (ed.) (1969): *Friedrich Froebel and English Education*, London (Routledge & Kegan Paul).

Lawson, Nigel (1992): *The View from no. 11. Memoirs of a Tory Radical*, London (Bantam Press).

Lawton, Denis & Peter Gordon (1987): *HMI*, London (Routledge & Kegan Paul).

Lawton, Denis (ed.) (1989): *The Education Reform Act: Choice and Control*, London (Hodder & Stoughton).

Lawton, Denis (2005): *Education and Labour Party Ideologies 1900–2001 and Beyond*, London (Routledge Falmer).

Learned, William Setchel (1914): *The Oberlehrer. A Study of the Social and Professional Evolution of the German Schoolmaster*, Cambridge, Mass. (Harvard University Press).

Leathes, Sir Stanley (1934): 'Great Britain', in *The Cambridge Modern History*, vol. XII, *The Latest Age*, ed. Sir A.W. Ward, Sir G.W. Prothero & Sir Stanley Leathes, Cambridge (Cambridge University Press), pp. 23–64.

Lee, Amice (1955): *Laurels & Rosemary. The Life of William and Mary Howitt*, London (Oxford University Press).

Leschinsky, Achim & Peter Martin Roeder (1976): *Schule im historischen Prozeß*, Stuttgart (Klett).

Leske, Monika (1990): *Philosophen im 'Dritten Reich'*, Berlin (Dietz).

Lexis, W. (1904): *A General View of the History and Organisation of Public Education in the German Empire*, Berlin (A. Asher & Co.).

Litton, Edward Arthur (1850): *University Reform. A Letter to the Right Hon Lord Russell*, London (Thomas Hatchard).

Liverpool Education Committee (1928): *Schools and School Systems of Germany and Holland*, Liverpool (Education Committee).

Liverpool Education Committee (1929): *Schools of Austria and Germany*, Liverpool (Education Committee).

Lowndes, G. A. N. (1969): *The Silent Social Revolution. An Account of the Expansion of Public Education in England and Wales, 1895–1965*, Oxford (Oxford University Press), 2nd edn.

Lyster, Mary A. (1902): 'Higher Schools for Girls in Germany. An Introductory Sketch', in: Board of Education, Special Reports on Educational Subjects, Vol.9, Education in Germany, London (HMSO), pp.207-285

McCann, Phillip (ed.) (1977): *Popular Education and Socialization in the Nineteenth Century*, London (Methuen).

McClelland, Charles E. (1980): *State, Society, and University in Germany 1700–1914*, Cambridge (Cambridge University Press).

McCrum, Michael (1989): *Thomas Arnold Headmaster. A Reassessment*, Oxford (Oxford University Press)

McCulloch, Gary (1989): *The Secondary Technical School. A Usable Past?* London (Falmer Press).

MacDonagh, Oliver (1977): *Early Victorian Government, 1830–1870*, London (Weidenfeld and Nicolson).

Maclure. J. Stuart (1986): *Educational Documents: England and Wales, 1816 to the Present Day*, London (Methuen).

Maclure, Stuart (1989): 'Parents and Schools: Opting In and Out, in: Denis Lawton (ed.): *The Education Reform Act: Choice and Control*, London (Hodder & Stoughton).

Maczak, Antoni & Jürgen Teuteberg (eds) (1982): *Reiseberichte als Quellen europäischer Kulturgeschichte. Aufgaben und Möglichkeiten der historischen Reiseforschung*, Wolfenbüttel (Herzog August Bibliothek).

Mann, Erika (1939): *School for Barbarians. Education Under the Nazis*, London (Lindsay Drummond)

Mann, Heinrich (1965) [1905]: *Professor Unrat*, Reinbek (Rowohlt).

Mann, Horace (1846): *Report of an Educational Tour in Germany, and Parts of Great Britain and Ireland*, London (Simpkin, Marshall, and Company).

Marriott, Stuart (1995): *English-German Relations in Adult Education, 1875–1955*, Leeds (Leeds Studies in Continuing Education).

Matthew, H. C. G. (1999): *Gladstone, 1809–1898*, Oxford (Oxford University Press).

Mayhew, Henry (1860): *The Upper Rhine: The Scenery of its Banks and the Manners of its People*, London (Routledge, Warne, & Routledge).

Mayhew, Henry (1864): *German Life and Manners, as Seen in Saxony at the Present Day*, London (Wm H. Allen & Co.), 2 vols.

Maynes, Mary Jo (1985): *Schooling for the People: Comparative Local Studies of Schooling History in France and Germany, 1750–1850*, New York & London (Holmes & Meier).

Max Planck Institute for Human Development and Education (1983): *Between Elite and Mass Education. Education in the Federal Republic of Germany*, Albany (State University of New York Press).

Melton, James Van Horn (1988): *Absolutism and the Eighteenth-Century Origins of Compulsory Schooling in Prussia and Austria*, Cambridge (Cambridge University Press).

Mitchell, James (1819): *A Tour Through Belgium, Holland, Along the Rhine; And Through the North of France, in the Summer of 1816*, etc., London (T. and J. Allman).

Montmorency, J. E. G. de (1902): *State Intervention in English Education. A Short History from the Earliest Times down to 1833*, Cambridge (Cambridge University Press).

Montmorency, J. E. G. de (1904): *The Progress of Education in England: A Sketch of the Development of English Organization from Early Times to the Year 1904*, London (Knight & Co.).

Moore-Rinvolucri, Mina J. (1973): *Education in East Germany*, Newton Abbott (David & Charles).

Morgan, B. Q. (1965): *Critical Bibliography of German Literature in English Translation, 1481–1927*, New York & London (The Scarecrow Press), 2nd edn.

Morley, Edith J. (ed.) (1929): *Henry Crabb Robinson in Germany, 1800–1805*, London (OUP).

Morley, John (1972) [1873]: *The Struggle for National Education*, London (Harvester Press), ed. Asa Briggs.

Morley, John (1903): *The Life of William Ewart Gladstone*, Macmillan (London), 3 vols.

Morrish, Ivor (1970): *Education Since 1800*, London (George Allen and Unwin).

Morrison, Michael A. (1918): *Sidelights on Germany. Studies of German Life and Character During the Great War, Based on the Enemy Press*, London (Hodder and Stoughton).

Mullen, Richard & James Munson (2009): *'The Smell of the Continent': The British Discover Europe, 1814–1914*, London (Macmillan).

Müller, Detlef K., Fritz Ringer & Brian Simon (eds) (1987): *The Rise of the Modern Educational System. Structural Change and Social Reproduction, 1870–1920*, Cambridge (Cambridge University Press/Éditions de la Maison des Sciences de l'Homme).

Murphy, James (1971): *Church, State and Schools in Britain, 1800–1970*, London (Routledge & Kegan Paul).

Murphy, James (1972): *The Education Act 1870: Text and Commentary*, Newton Abbot (David & Charles).

Murray, Nicholas (1996): *A Life of Matthew Arnold*, London (Sceptre).

Musgrave, P. W. (1976): *Society and Education in England Since 1800*, London (Methuen).

Myers, George E. (1915): *Problems of Vocational Education in Germany, With Special Application to Conditions in the United States*, Washington (Government Printing Office).

Nash, Paul (1966): *Culture and the State. Matthew Arnold and Continental Education*, New York (Teachers College).

'National Education' (1833): *The Mirror of Literature, Amusement, and Instruction*, no. 636, 7 December, pp. 380–3.

'National Education in England and France' (1833), *Edinburgh Review*, vol. 58, no. 117, July, pp. 1–30

Newcastle Report (1861). *Report of the Commissioners appointed to inquire into the State of Popular Education in England*, London (Eyre & Spottiswoode for HMSO).

Newsome, David (1961): *Godliness and Good Learning. Four Studies on a Victorian Ideal*, London (John Murray).

NFER (1963): *Procedures for the Allocation of Pupils in Secondary Education*, London (NFER).

Nipperdey, Thomas (1976): 'Mass Education and Modernization – The Case of Germany, 1780–1850', *Transactions of the Royal Historical Society*, pp. 155–72.

Nipperdey, Thomas (1998): *Deutsche Geschichte, 1800–1866: Bürgerwelt und starker Staat*, Munich (C.H. Beck).

Noah, Harold J. & Max A. Eckstein (1969): *Toward a Science of Comparative Education*, London (Macmillan).

Norwood Report (1941. *Curriculum and Examinations in Secondary Schools*, London (HMSO).

Ochs, Kimberly & David Phillips (2002a): *Towards a Structural Typology of Cross-national Attraction in Education*, Lisbon (Educa,).

Ochs, Kimberly, & David Phillips (2002b): 'Comparative Studies and "Cross-national Attraction" in Education: A Typology for the Analysis of English Interest in Educational Policy and Provision in Germany' *Educational Studies*, vol. 28, no. 4, pp. 325–39.

OECD (1972): *Reviews of National Policies for Education: Germany*, Paris (OECD).

OECD (2001): *Knowledge and Skills for Life: First Results from PISA 2000*, Paris (OECD).

Pakschies, Günter (1979): *Umerziehung in der Britischen Zone 1945–1949: Untersuchungen zur britischen Re-education-Politik*, Weinheim/Basel (Beltz).

Paterson, W. P. (ed.) (1915): *German Culture. The Contribution of the Germans to Knowledge, Literature, Art, and Life*, London (T. C. & E. C. Jack).

Pattison, Mark (1868): *Suggestions on Academical Organisation*, Edinburgh (Edmonston and Douglas).

Paulin, Roger (1991): *Goethe, the Brothers Grimm, and Academic Freedom*, Cambridge (Cambridge University Press).

Paulsen, Friedrich (1895): *The German Universities. Their Character and Historical Development*, New York and London (Macmillan and Co.).

Paulsen, Friedrich (1902): *Die Deutschen Universitäten und das Universitätsstudium*, Berlin (A. Asher & Co.).

Paulsen, Friedrich (1906a): *Das deutsche Bildungswesen in seiner geschichtlichen Entwicklung*, Leipzig (Teubner).

Paulsen, Friedrich (1906b): *The German Universities and University Study*, London (Longmans, Green, and Co.).

Paulsen, Friedrich (1908): *German Education Past and Present*, London (T. Fisher Unwin).

Paulsen, Friedrich (1921): *Geschichte des gelehrten Unterrichts*, Berlin & Leipzig (Walter de Gruyter), 3rd edn, 2 vols.

Payne, Joseph (1892): *Lectures on the History of Education, with a Visit to German Schools*, London (Longmans, Green, and Co.).

Paz, D. G. (1980): *The Politics of Working-Class Education in Britain, 1830–50*, Manchester (Manchester University Press).

Pearce, John, Bryan Goodman-Stephens & Colin Robinson (1985): *Assessment in West German Schools*, Huntingdon (Education Department).

Perry, Charles Copland (1887): *Reports on German Elementary Schools and Training Colleges*, London (Rivingtons).

Perry, Walter C. (1845): *German University Education, or, The Professors and Students of Germany*, London (Longman, Brown, Green, and Longmans).

Phillips, David (1983): *Zur Universitätsreform in der britischen Besatzungszone 1945–1948*, Cologne, Vienna (Böhlau Verlag).

Phillips, David (1986): 'War-time Planning for the "Re-education" of Germany: Professor E. R. Dodds and the German Universities', *Oxford Review of Education*, vol. 12, no. 2, pp. 195–208.

Phillips, David (1987): Lessons from Germany? – The Case of German Secondary Schools', *British Journal of Educational Studies*, vol. XXXV, no. 3, pp. 211–32.

Phillips, David (1988): 'British Educational Policy in Occupied Germany: Some Problems and Paradoxes in the Control of Schools and Universities', in: *International Currents in Educational Ideas and Practices*, ed. Peter Cunningham & Colin Brock, Leicester (History of Education Society), pp. 75–88.

Phillips, David (1989a): 'Neither a Borrower nor a Lender Be? The Problems of Cross-national Attraction in Education', in David Phillips (ed.): *Cross-National Attraction in Education*, special issue of *Comparative Education*, vol. 25, no. 3, pp. 267–74.

Phillips, David (1989b): 'Problems with an Alien Tongue: the Nineteenth-century Traveller in Germany', *Modern Languages*, vol. 70, no. 2, pp. 104–109.

Phillips, David (1993): 'Borrowing Educational Policy', in David Finegold,
L. McFarland, W. Richardson, (eds): *Something Borrowed? Something Learned?*
The Transatlantic Market in Education and Training Reform, Washington, DC (The
Brookings Institution), pp. 13–19.

Phillips, David (1994): 'Periodisation in Historical Approaches to Comparative
Education: Some considerations from the examples of Germany and England and
Wales', *British Journal of Educational Studies*, vol. 42, no. 3, pp. 261–72.

Phillips, David (1995a): *Pragmatismus und Idealismus. Das 'Blaue Gutachten' und die
britische Hochschulpolitik in Deutschland 1948*, Cologne, Weimar, Vienna (Böhlau).

Phillips, David (ed.) (1995b): *Education in Germany: Tradition and Reform in Historical
Context*, London (Routledge).

Phillips, David (1997): 'Prolegomena to a History of British Interest in Education in
Germany', in Christoph Kodron et al. (eds): *Vergleichende Erziehungswissenschaft,
Herausforderung – Vermittlung – Praxis. Festschrift für Wolfgang Mitter zum 70. Geburtstag*,
vol. 2, Cologne, etc. (Böhlau), pp. 673–87.

Phillips, David (2000): 'Beyond Travellers' Tales: Some Nineteenth-Century British
Commentators on Education in Germany', *Oxford Review of Education*, vol. 26, no. 1,
pp. 49–62.

Phillips, David (2000a): 'The *Wissenschaftsrat* and the Investigation of Teacher
Education in the Former German Democratic Republic, 1991: A Personal Account',
in: David Phillips (ed.): *Education in Germany Since Unification*, Wallingford
(Symposium, pp. 111–23.

Phillips, David (2000b): 'Learning from Elsewhere in Education: Some Perennial
Problems Revisited with Reference to British Interest in Germany', *Comparative
Education*, vol. 36, no. 3, pp. 297–307.

Phillips, David (2002a): 'Comparative Historical Studies in Education: Problems of
Periodisation Reconsidered', *British Journal of Educational Studies*, vol. 50, no. 3,
pp. 363–77.

Phillips, David: (2002b) *Reflections on British Interest in Education in Germany in the
Nineteenth Century: A Progress Report*, Lisbon (Educa).

Phillips, David (2004): 'A Typology of Cross-National Attraction in Education', in: Gita
Steiner-Khamsi (ed.): *Lessons from Elsewhere: The Politics of Educational Borrowing and
Lending*, New York (Teachers College Press).

Phillips, David (2006): 'Michael Sadler and Comparative Education', *Oxford Review of
Education*, vol. 32, no. 1, pp. 39–54.

Phillips, David (2007): 'Four Periods of Educational Reform in England: Some
Personalised Reflections on Developments in Secondary Education', in Bernd Hackl
& Hans Pechar (eds): *Bildungspolitische Aufklärung: Um- und Irrwege der österreichischen
Schulreform*, Innsbruck, Vienna, Bozen (Studien Verlag), pp. 120–33.

Phillips, David & Kimberly Ochs (2003): 'Processes of Policy Borrowing in Education:
Some Explanatory and Analytical Devices', *Comparative Education*, vol. 39, no. 4,
pp. 451–61.

Phillips, David & Kimberly Ochs (eds.) (2004a): *Educational Policy Borrowing: Historical
Perspectives*, Didcot (Symposium)

Phillips, David & Kimberly Ochs (2004b): 'Researching Policy Borrowing: Some
Methodological Problems in Comparative Education', *British Educational Research
Journal*, vol. 30, no. 6, pp. 773–84.

Physical Education in Germany (1937): Board of Education Pamphlets no. 109, London
(HMSO).

Pickering, O. S. (1982): *Sir Michael Sadler. A Bibliography of His Published Works*, Leeds
(Leeds Studies in Adult and Continuing Education).

Pile, [Sir] William (1979): *The Department of Education and Science*, London (George
Allen & Unwin).

Polytechnical Education in the GDR (1973), Berlin (Ministry of Education of the GDR).

Pope, Rex (ed.) (1989): *Atlas of British Social and Economic History Since c.1700*, London
(Macmillan).

Pritchard, Rosalind M. O. (1990): *The End of Elitism? The Democratisation of the West
German University System*, New York, Oxford, Munich (Berg).

Pritchard, Rosalind M. O. (1999): *Reconstructing Education. East German Schools and Universities After Unification*, New York & Oxford (Berghahn).

Radcliffe, Ann (1795): *A Journey Made in the Summer of 1794, Through Holland and the Western Frontier of Germany*, etc., Dublin (William Porter).

Rawnsley, Andrew (2010): *The End of the Party. The Rise and Fall of New Labour*, London (Viking).

Recent Measures for the Promotion of Education in England (1972) [1839], Manchester (E. J. Morten).

Reddie, Cecil (1900): *Abbotsholme*, London (George Allen).

Reid, T. Wemyss (1888): *Life of the Right Honourable William Edward Forster*, London (Chapman and Hall), 2 vols.

Remy, Steven P. (2002): *The Heidelberg Myth. The Nazification and Denazification of a German University*, Cambridge, Massachusetts & London (Harvard University Press).

Rhys, Isabel L. (1905): *The Education of Girls in Switzerland and Bavaria*, London (Blackie & Son, Limited).

Richter, Paul Emil (n.d.) [1896]: *Bibliotheca Geographica Germaniae. Litteratur der Landes- und Volkskunde des Deutschen Reiches*, New York (Burt Franklin).

Roach, John (1960): 'Education and the Press', in: J. P. T. Bury (ed.): *The New Cambridge Modern History, vol. X: The Zenith of European Power, 1830–1870*, Cambridge (Cambridge University Press).

Robbins Report: Committee on Higher Education (1963): *Report*, London (HMSO) Cmnd 2154.

Robbins Report: Committee on Higher Education (1964): *Higher Education, Appendix Five: Higher Education in Other Countries*, London (HMSO) Cmnd 2154-V.

Roberts, Andrew (1999): *Salisbury. Victorian Titan*, London (Weidenfeld & Niciolson)

Robertson, David Brian & Jerold L. Waltman (1992): 'The Politics of Policy Borrowing', in Finegold *et al.*, vol. I, 1992, pp. 25–48.

Roberts, R. D. (ed.) (1901): *Education in the Nineteenth Century*, Cambridge (Cambridge University Press).

Robinsohn, Saul & J. Caspar Kuhlmann (1967): 'Two Decades of Non-reform in West German Education', *Comparative Education Review*, vol. 11 no. 3, pp. 311–30.

Robinson. Henry Crabb (1869): *Diary, Reminiscences, and Correspondence*, ed. Thomas Sadler, London (Macmillan and Co.).

Robson, E. R. (1972) [1874]: *School Architecture*, Leicester (Leicester University Press).

Rodden, John (2002): *Repainting the Little Red Schoolhouse. A History of East German Education*, Oxford (Oxford University Press).

Roderick, Gordon W. & Michael D. Stephens (1972): *Scientific and Technical Education in Nineteenth-Century England*, Newton Abbot (David & Charles).

Roderick, Gordon W., and Michael D. Stephens (1978): *Education and Industry in the Nineteenth Century*, London and New York (Longman).

Röhrs, Hermann (1986): *Die Schulen der Reformpädagogik Heute*, Düsseldorf (Schwann).

Röhrs, Hermann (1995): *The Classical German Concept of the University and Its Influence on Higher Education in the United States*, Frankfurt am Main, etc. (Peter Lang).

Ronge, J. & B. Ronge (1855): *A practical guide to the English kinder garten (children's garden): for the use of mothers, nursery governesses, and infant teachers, etc.* London (Hodson & Son).

Rooper, T[homas] G[odolphin] (1896): *School and Home Life*, London (A. Brown & Sons, Limited).

Rose, Richard & Günter Wignanek (1990): *Training Without Trainers? How Germany Avoids Britain's Supply-side Bottleneck*, London (Anglo-German Foundation for the Study of Industrial Society).

Ross, George W. (1894): *The Schools of England and Germany*, Toronto (Warwick Bros. & Rutter).

Rothblatt, Sheldon (1976): *Tradition and Change in English Liberal Education. An Essay in History and Culture*, London (Faber and Faber).

Rowse, A. L. (1976): *Matthew Arnold: Poet and Prophet*, London (Thames and Hudson).

Ruhm von Oppen, Beate (ed.) (1955) *Documents on Germany Under Occupation 1945–1954*, London (Oxford University Press).

Russell, James E. (1899): *German Higher Schools. The History, Organization and Methods of Secondary Education in Germany*, New York (Longmans, Green, and Co.).

Russell, John (1825): *A Tour in Germany, and Some of the Southern Provinces of the Austrian Empire, in the Years 1820, 1821, 1822*, Edinburgh (Archibald Constable and Co.).

Rust, Val D. & Diane Rust (1995): *The Unification of German Education*, New York & London (Garland).

Sadler, Michael (1900): 'How Far Can We Learn Anything of Practical Value from the Study of Foreign Systems of Education?' Address of 20 October, in: J. H. Higginson (ed.) *Selections from Michael Sadler*, Liverpool (Dejall & Meyorre), 1979, pp. 48–51.

Sadler, Michael (1903): *The Ferment in Education on the Continent and in America*, London (*Proceedings of the British Academy*).

Sadler, Michael (1907) (ed.): *Continuation Schools in England & Elsewhere: Their Place in the Educational System of an Industrial and Commercial State*, Manchester (Manchester University Press).

Sadler, Michael (1912): 'The History of Education', in: *Germany in the Nineteenth Century. Five Lectures*, Manchester (Manchester University Press), pp. 103-127

Sadler, Michael (1915): 'The Strength and Weakness of German Education', in: W. P. Paterson (ed.): *German Culture: The Contribution of the Germans to Knowledge, Literature, Art and Life*, London (T. C. & E. C. Jack), pp. 301–14.

Sadler, Michael (1916): 'Need We Imitate German Education?', *The Times*, 14 January.

Sadler, Michael (1924): 'Progress of Education in England, 1823–1923', in: *Birkbeck College Centenary Lectures*, London (University of London Press), pp. 65–83.

Sagarra, Eda (1980): *An Introduction to Nineteenth Century Germany*, London (Longman).

Samoff, Joel (1999): 'Institutionalizing International Influence', in: Robert F. Arnove & Carlos Alberto Torres: *Comparative Education. The Dialectic of the Global and the Local*, Lanham, etc. (Rowman & Littlefield), pp. 51–89.

Samuel, R.H. & R. Hinton Thomas (1949): *Education and Society in Modern Germany*, London (Routledge & Kegan Paul)

Sanderson, Michael (1972): *The Universities and British Industry, 1850–1970*, London (Routledge & Kegan Paul).

Sanderson, Michael (1994): *The Missing Stratum. Technical School Education in England, 1900–1990s*, London & Atlantic Highlands (Athlone Press).

Sanderson, Michael (1995): *Education, Economic Change and Society in England, 1780–1870*, Cambridge (Cambridge University Press), 2nd edn.

Sanderson, Michael (1999): *Education and Economic Decline in Britain, 1870 to the 1990s*, Cambridge (Cambridge University Press).

Schalenberg, Marc (2001) 'Humboldt in Großbritannien, oder: Was ein preußischer Gesandter an englischen Universitäten ausrichten kann', in: Rainer Christoph Schwinges (ed.), *Humboldt International*, Basel (Schwabe), pp. 231–45.

Schleunes, Karl A. (1989): *Schooling and Society. The Politics of Education in Prussia and Bavaria, 1750–1900*, Oxford etc. (Berg).

Schneider, Friedrich (1943) *Geltung und Einfluss der deutschen Pädagogik im Ausland*, Munich and Berlin (R. Oldenbourg).

'School Education of Prussia, The' (1838), *New Monthly Magazine* (June), pp. 205–16.

Schubert, Friedrich Wilhelm (1838): *A Memoir of Bernard Overberg [. . .] with a Short Account of National Education in Prussia . . .*, from the German of Professor Schubert, London (L. and G. Seeley).

Schubert-Weller, Christoph (1991):'Vormilitärische Jugenderziehung', in: Christa Berg (ed.): *Handbuch der deutschen Bildungsgeschichte, vol. IV, 1870–1918: Von der Reichsgründung bis zum Ende des Ersten Weltkriegs*, Munich (C. H. Beck), pp. 503–15.

Schütte, Friedhelm (2007): 'Jahrzehnt der Neuordnung 1890–1901. Die Reform des technischen und allgemeinen Bildungssystems in Deutschland', *Zeitschrift für Pädagogik*, vol. 53, no. 4, pp. 544–61.

Schweizer, Karl W. & John W. Osborne (1990): *Cobbett in His Times*, Leicester & London (Leicester University Press).

Schwinges, Rainer Christoph (2001): *Humboldt International: Der Export des deutschen Universitätsmodells im 19. Und 20.Jahrhundert*, Basel (Schwabe).

Seaborne, Malcolm (1966): *Education*, London (Studio Vista).
Seeley, J. R. (1878): *Life and Times of Stein*, Cambridge (Cambridge University Press), 3 vols.
Seeley, Levi (1896): *The Common-School System of Germany and its Lessons to America*, New York & Chicago (E. L. Kellogg & Co.).
Selby-Bigge, Sir Lewis Amherst (1927): *The Board of Education*, London & New York (Putnam's).
Selleck, R. J. W. (1968): *The New Education, 1870–1914*, London (Pitman).
Selleck, R. J. W. (1994): *James Kay-Shuttleworth. Journey of an Outsider*, Ilford (The Woburn Press).
Sherer, Moyle (1826): *Notes and Reflections During a Ramble in Germany*, London (Longman, Rees, Orme, Brown, and Green).
Sherrington, Geoffrey (1981): *English Education, Social Change and War, 1911–20*, Manchester (Manchester University Press).
Shrosbee, Colin (1988): *Public Schools and Private Education. The Clarendon Commission 1861–64 and the Public Schools Acts*, Manchester and New York (Manchester University Press).
Silver, Harold (1975): *English Education and the Radicals, 1780–1850*, London (Routledge & Kegan Paul).
Silver, Pamela, & Harold Silver (1974): *The Education of the Poor. The History of a National School, 1824–1974*, London (Routledge & Kegan Paul).
Simon, Brian (1974): *The Two Nations and the Educational Structure, 1780–1870*, London (Lawrence & Wishart).
Simond, Louis (1968) [1815]: *An American in Regency England*, ed. Christopher Hibbert, Oxford (Pergamon Press).
Simpson, Renate (1983): *How the PhD Came to Britain. A Century of Struggle for Postgraduate Education*, Guildford (Society for Research into Higher Education).
Sislian, Jack (2002): *Sir Michael Sadler 1861–1943: England's Interpreter and America's Admirer*, New York (Nova Science Publishers).
Sislian, Jack (2004): *Representative Sadleriana: Sir Michael Sadler 1861–1943 on English, French, German and American Schools and Society: A Perennial Reader for Academics and the General Public*, New York (Nova Science Publishers).
Sislian, Jack (2005): *State and Education in England and Germany: A Sadlerian Perspective*, New York (Nova Science Publishers).
Smith, Frank (1923): *The Life and Work of Sir James Kay-Shuttleworth*, London (John Murray).
Smith, Frank (1931): *A History of English Elementary Education, 1760–1902*, London (University of London Press).
Smith, R. (1827): *Notes Made During a Tour in Denmark, Holstein, Mecklenburg-Schwerin [etc.] Interspersed with some Observations on the Foreign Corn Trade*, London (C. & J. Rivington).
[Smith, Sydney] (1806): 'Mrs Trimmer on Lancaster's Plan of Education', *Edinburgh Review*, vol. IX, no. 17, pp. 177–84.
Smith, Thomas F. A. (1916): *The Soul of Germany. A Twelve Years Study of the People from Within, 1902–14*, London (Hutchinson).
Spens Report (1938). *Secondary Education, With Special Reference to Grammar Schools and Technical High Schools*, London (HMSO).
Spoerl, Heinrich (1976 [1033]): *Die Feuerzangenbowle*, Munich (dtv).
Sprigade, Almut (2005): *Where There is Reform There is Comparison: English Interest in Education Abroad, 1800–1839*, unpublished D.Phil. thesis, University of Oxford.
Staël Holstein, Baroness [Anne Louise Germaine Necker, Baronne de Staël-Holstein] (1814) [1813]: *Germany*, London (John Murray), 3 vols.
Steiner-Khamsi, Gita (2002): 'Reterritorializing Educational Import: Explorations into the Politics of Educational Borrowing', in António Nóvoa & Martin Lawn (eds): *Fabricating Europe. The Formation of an Education Space*, Dordrecht (Kluwer), pp. 69–86.
Stephens, W. B. (1987): *Education, Literacy and Society, 1830–70. The Geography of Diversity in Provincial England*, Manchester (Manchester University Press).

Stephens. W. B. (1998): *Education in Britain, 1750–1914*, London (Macmillan).

Stone, Lawrence (1969): 'Literacy and Education in England, 1640–1900', *Past and Present*, 42 (February), pp. 69–139.

Stowe, Calvin E. (1837): *Report on Elementary Public Instruction*, Columbus (Samuel Medary).

Strang, John (1836): *Germany in MDCCCXXXI*, London (John Macrone), 2 vols.

Studienausschuß für Hochschulreform (1948): *Gutachten zur Hochschulreform*, Hamburg.

Sutherland, Gillian (1971): *Elementary Education in the Nineteenth Century*, London (Historical Association).

Sutherland, Gillian (1973): *Policy-Making in Elementary Education, 1870–1895*, London (Oxford University Press).

Sweet, Paul R. (1978, 1980): *Wilhelm von Humboldt. A Biography*, Columbus (Ohio State University Press), 2 vols.

Sylvester, D. W. (1970): *Educational Documents, 800–1816*, London (Methuen).

Taunton Report (1868): *Schools Inquiry Commission*, London (Eyure & Spottiswoode for HMSO).

Tawney, R. H. (1922): *Secondary Education for All: A Policy for Labour*, London (The Labour Party & George Allen & Unwin Ltd.).

Taylor, J. Orville (1836): *A Digest of M. Victor Cousin's Report on the State of Public Instruction in Prussia*, Albany (Packard and Van Benthuysen).

Tenorth, Heinz-Elmar (1988): *Geschichte der Erziehung*, Weinheim & Munich (Juventa).

Tews, J. (1914): *Ein Jahrhundert preußischer Schulgeschichte*, Leipzig (Quelle & Meyer).

Thatcher, Margaret (1993): *The Downing Street Years*, London (Harper Collins).

Tholfsen, Trygve R. (1974): *Sir James Kay-Shuttleworth on Popular Education*, New York (Teachers College Press).

Thomas, Keith (2009): *The Ends of Life. Roads to Fulfilment in Early Modern England*, Oxford (Oxford University Press).

Thomson, David (1950): *England in the Nineteenth Century, 1815–1914*, Harmondsworth (Penguin).

Thwing, Charles Franklin (1928): *The American and the German University. One Hundred Years of History*, New York (Macmillan).

Tower, Charles (n.d.) (1913): *Germany of To-Day*, London (Williams & Norgate).

Trimmer, Mrs [Sarah] (1805): *A Comparative View of the New Plan of Education promulgated by Mr Joseph Lancaster*, London.

Trollope, Mrs [Frances] (1834): *Belgium and Western Germany in 1833*, London (John Murray), 2 vols.

Truscott, Bruce (1943): *Red Brick University*, London (Faber and Faber).

Turnbull, G. H. (1926): *The Educational Theory of J. G. Fichte*, Liverpool & London (University of Liverpool Press/Hodder and Stoughton).

Ulich, Robert (1935): *A Sequence of Educational Influences: Traced Through Unpublished Writings of Pestalozzi, Fröbel, Diesterweg, Horace Mann, and Henry Barnard*, Cambridge, Mass.(Harvard University Press).

University Reform in Germany. Report by a German Commission (1949), London (HMSO).

US Department of Education (1999): *The Educational System in Germany: Case Study Findings*, Washington DC (US Government Printing Office).

Vaughan, Robert (1843): *The Age of Great Cities: Or, Modern Society Viewed in its Relation to Intelligence, Morals, and Religion*, London (Jackson and Walford).

Viëtor, Wilhelm ['Quousque Tandem'] (1905): *Der Sprachunterricht muss umkehren! Ein Beitrag zur Überbürdungsfrage*, Leipzig (O. R. Reisland), 3rd edn.

Vizetelly, Henry (1879): *Berlin Under the New Empire*, London (Tinsley Brothers), 2 vols.

Wagner, Ernst (1864): *Das Volksschulwesen in England und seine Neueste Entwicklung*, Stuttgart (J. B. Metzler).

Wallace, Stuart (1988): *War and the Image of Germany. British Academics 1914–1918*, Edinburgh (John Donald).

Walpole, Spencer (1889): *Life of Lord John Russell*, London (Longmans, Green, and Co.), 2 vols.

Walz, John A. (1936): *German Influence in American Education and Culture*, Philadelphia (Carl Schulz Memorial Foundation).

Ware, Fabian (1898): 'The Teacher of Modern Languages in Prussian Secondary Schools. His Education and Professional Trainoing', in Education Department: *Special Reports on Educational Subjects*, London (HMSO), vol. 3, pp. 521–53.

Ware, Fabian (1901): *Educational Foundations of Trade and Industry*, London & New York (Harper & Brothers).

Waterfall, Edith Anna (1923): *The Day Continuation School in England: Its Function and Future*, London (George Allen & Unwin).

Watson, Foster (1968) [1916]: *The Old Grammar Schools*, London (Frank Cass).

Watson, Peter (2010): *The German Genius: Europe's Third Renaissance, the Second Scientific Revolution, and the Twentieth Century*, London (Simon & Schuster).

Weber, Thomas (2008): *Our Friend 'The Enemy'. Elite Education in Britain and Germany Before World War I*, Stanford (Stanford University Press).

Weiler, Hans N., Heinrich A. Mintrop & Elisabeth Fuhrmann (1996): *Educational Change and Social Transformation: Teachers, Schools and Universities in Eastern Germany*, London & Washington DC (Falmer Press).

Weinstock, Heinrich (ed.) (1957): *Wilhelm von Humboldt*, Frankfurt am Main (Fischer).

Wellesley Index (1966–1989): *The Wellesley Index to Victorian Periodicals, 1824–1900*, Toronto & Buffalo/London (University of Toronto Press/Routledge & Kegan Paul).

Welshman, John (1996): 'Physical Education and the School Medical Service in England and Wales, 1907–1939', *Social History of Medicine*, vol. 9, pp. 31–48.

Welton, John (1910): 'Education', *Encyclopaedia Britannica*, 11th edn, Cambridge (Cambridge University Press).

West, E. G. (1975): *Education and the Industrial Revolution*, London (Batsford).

Wiener, Martin J. (1982): *English Culture and the Decline of the Industrial Spirit, 1850–1980*, Cambridge (Cambridge University Press).

Wilamowitz-Moellendorff, Ulrich von (1930): *My Recollections, 1848–1914*, London (Chatto & Windus).

Wilamowitz-Moellendorff, Ulrich von (1959) [1921]: *History of Classical Scholarship*, London (Duckworth).

Williams, E. E. (1896): *"Made in Germany"*, London (William Heinemann).

Wilson, Ian C. (1877): 'Education and Politics. The Education Policy of the German Social Democratic Party, 1906–1922', *Oxford Review of Education*, vol. 3 no. 1, pp. 37–56.

Wilson, Percy (1961): *Views and Prospects from Curzon Street*, Oxford (Basil Blackwell).

Wiener, Peter F. (1942): *German With Tears*, London (The Cresset Press)

Wines, E. C. (1838): *Hints on a System of Popular Education*, Philadelphia (Hogan and Thompson).

Wolf, A. (1944): *Higher Education in Nazi Germany, or Education for World-Conquest*, London (Methuen)

Woodward, Sir Llewellyn (1987): *The Age of Reform, 1815–1870*, Oxford (Clarendon Press).

Wyatt, Horace (1914): *Malice in Kulturland*, London (The Car Illustrated).

Wyse, Thomas (1968 [1839]: 'On the Present State of Prussian Education', in: *Central Society of Education, Third Publication of 1839*, London (The Woburn Press), pp. 375–433.

Young, J. W.A. (1900): *The Teaching of Mathematics in the Higher Schools of Prussia*, New York (Longmans, Green, and Co.).

Young, Kenneth (1963); *Arthur James Balfour*, London (G. Bell and Sons, Ltd).

Ziemer, Gregor (1942): *Education for Death. The Making of the Nazi*, London (Constable)

Zymek, Bernd (1975): *Das Ausland als Argument in der Pädagogischen Reformdiskussion*, Ratingen (Aloys Henn Verlag).

Index